AUGUSTINE

His Thought in Context

T. KERMIT SCOTT

PAULIST PRESS
New York/Mahwah, NJ

Acknowledgements: The Publisher gratefuly acknowledges use of the following material: excerpts from *A Manichean Psalm-Book,* edited by R.C. Alberry, copyright (c) 1938, W. Kohlhammer, Stuttgart; excerpts from *The Enneads* by Plotinus, Stephen MacKenna, trans., copyright (c) 1969, Faber and Faber, Ltd., London; excerpts from *Augustine: Earlier Writings* by St. Augustine, J.H.S. Burleigh, trans. (Library of Christian Classics), copyright (c) 1953, SCM Press, London; excerpts reproduced from *Augustine: Earlier Works* edited by John H.S. Burleigh (Library of Christian Classics), used by permission of Westminster John Knox Press; excerpts from *City of God* by Saint Augustine, translated by Henry Bettenson (Penguin Classics, 1972) copyright (c) Henry Bettenson, 1972; excerpts from *Augustine of Hippo: A Biography* by Peter Brown, copyright (c) 1967, University of California Press, Berkeley; excerpts from *Augustine on Romans* by P.F. Landes, copyright (c) 1982, Scholars Press; excerpts from *The Advantage of Believing* by Saint Augustine, L. Meagher, trans. (The Fathers of the Church, vol. 4), copyright (c) 1947, The Catholic University of America Press, Washington, D.C.; excerpts from *Answer to Skeptics* by Saint Augustine, D.J. Kavanaugh, trans. (The Fathers of the Church, vol. 5), copyright (c) 1948, The Catholic University of America Press, Washington, D.C.: excerpts from *The Basic Writings of St. Augustine,* translated by P. Holmes, copyright (c) 1948 by Random House, Inc. Reprinted by permission of Modern Library, Inc., a division of Random House, Inc. and by permission of T&T Clark, Ltd.; excerpts from *The Confessions of St. Augustine* by John K. Ryan. Copyright (c) 1960 by Doubleday, a division of Bantam Doubleday Dell Publishing Group, Inc. Used by permission of Doubleday, a division of Bantam Doubleday Dell Publishing Group Inc.; excerpts from Benjamin/Hackstaff, *Augustine: On the Free Choice of the Will,* (c) 1964. Reprinted by permission of Prentice-Hall, Upper Saddle River, New Jersey.

Cover design by Christine Taylor, Wilsted & Taylor Publishing Services, Inc.

Copyright © 1995 by T. Kermit Scott

Library of Congress Cataloging–in–Publication Data

Scott, Kermit T., 1936-
 Augustine : his thought in context / T. Kermit Scott.
  p. cm.
 Includes bibliographical references and index.
 ISBN 0-8091-3566-3
 1. Augustine, Saint, Bishop of Hippo. I. Title.
BR1720.A9S36 1995
270.2′092—dc20

95-5573
CIP

Published by Paulist Press
997 Macarthur Boulevard
Mahwah, NJ 07430

Printed and bound in the
United States of America

Contents

for Aadron

Preface

Augustine remains a figure of enduring fascination for many in the modern world. I am always somewhat surprised that students find him still utterly absorbing, despite the chasm that separates his world from theirs. And theologians, philosophers, historians, psychologists and students of great literature are still drawn to him as they have been for over fifteen hundred years.

In this book, I have tried to introduce readers to Augustine by placing his life and central teachings in the context of his place and time. The focus is only on those core doctrines that I regard as most distinctive of Augustinianism, so that the book omits enormously more than it discusses. Still it is hoped that by placing a general overview of those key doctrines in the context of Augustine's life and world, the reader will be helped to a more balanced view of Augustine's thought and to a better understanding of his enormous influence.

While those already familiar with Augustine will hopefully find here something of interest, this is assuredly not a book for specialists. There is no attempt to survey or utilize the great sweep of Augustinian scholarship, nor is there an attempt to carry through a complete or careful analysis of all his philosophical ideas. The attempt is rather to make Augustine more accessible and intelligible to the non-specialist and to invite the reader to further study. If the "picture" here offered stirs some thought and encourages some further exploration, it will have served its purpose.

In line with this aim, I have tried to draw primarily on sources available in English translation, and all quotations are offered in translation. We are fortunate that so much of Augustine's primary writing has been translated, so that it is possible to construct an accurate portrayal of his thought from such sources. In only a few places was it necessary to

1

make reference to untranslated material, and none of those references is crucial to the interpretation offered.

On the other hand, I have tried to support and illustrate the interpretation by use of rather extensive quotations from Augustine's work. This is important because so little of Augustine's philosophical theology is developed in formal treatises and so much of it emerges out of letters, sermons, scriptural commentaries, autobiographical accounts and epic history. But it is also important because only in that way can the reader gain some sense of the combination of careful analysis and intense eloquence that gives Augustine's writing its timeless appeal.

Augustine belongs to every one of us today. He is our spiritual and intellectual father in more ways than many of us care to admit. A stern and demanding father he may be, and most of us are no doubt grateful that we no longer have to live in his house. But even as we distance ourselves from him, we are apt to find that he remains a part of what we are, embedded in our historical consciousness and still shaping the ways we think and feel. Hopefully, what follows will be a further small contribution to our ongoing attempt to come to terms with his legacy.

In committing these ideas to paper, I am grateful to the many students who, through the years, have studied Augustine with me and whose enthusiasm and curiosity have deepened my own. Especially I want to thank my friend and former student, Jeffrey Bulington, whose keen insight and passion for making sense of Augustine have helped me so often to improve my own understanding.

My colleague, Larry May, offered a number of valuable comments on a portion of the manuscript. And it was my old friend, Fae Spurlock, who first encouraged me to undertake the project.

My deepest gratitude is reserved for my life partner, Aadron Scott. She has patiently listened to my musings about Augustine and mused with me, and she played a major role in preparation of the manuscript. But immeasurably beyond that, her love and support have sustained me for nearly forty years.

Citations of Augustine's Works

For ease of reference, I have cited Augustine's works by abbreviated titles in the body of the text, rather than using footnote citations. Following is a listing of those abbreviations, together with the Latin title of the work and a reference to the translation used. All the Latin works can be found in J. P. Migne (ed.), *Patrologiae cursus completus.* 221 vols. Paris, 1844–1864. In those few cases where no translation is available, the citation of the Migne edition is offered.

Adv. of Bel. (*De utilitate credendi*). *The Advantage of Believing*, tr. by L. Meagher (included in a volume with *The Immortality of the Soul, The Magnitude of the Soul, On Music* and *On Faith in Things Unseen*) New York, 1947.

Ag. Ep. Fund. (*Contra epistolam quam vocant fundamenti*). *Against the Epistle of Manichaeus Called Fundamental*, tr. by E. R. Dods in *The Works of Aurelius Augustinus.* Edinburgh, 1871–1876.

Ans. to Skep. (*Contra Academicos*). *Answer to Skeptics*, tr. by D. J. Kavanaugh (included in a volume with *The Happy Life, Divine Providence and the Problem of Evil*, and *Soliloquies*). New York, 1948.

Cath. and Man. (*De moribus ecclesiae Catholicae et de moribus Manichaeorum*). *The Catholic and Manichaean Ways of Life*, tr. by D. A. Gallagher and I. J. Gallagher. Washington, 1966.

City. (*Civitas Dei*). *Concerning the City of God against the Pagans*, tr. by H. Bettenson, with an introduction by J. J. O'Meara. London/ New York, 1984.

Conf. (*Confessiones*). *The Confessions of St. Augustine*, ed. and tr. by J. K. Ryan. Garden City, NY, 1960.

3

Contra Fortunatum. (*Acta seu disputatio contra Fortunatum Manichaeum*) in Migne, Vol. 42, 112–130.

De Duabus Animabus. (*De duabus animabus contra Manichaeos*) in Migne, Vol. 42, 93–112.

Div. Prov. (*De ordine*). *Divine Providence and the Problem of Evil*, tr. by R. P. Russell (included in a volume with *The Happy Life, Answer to Skeptics* and *Soliloquies*). New York, 1948.

Free Choice. (*De libero arbitrio*). *On Free Choice of the Will*, tr. by A.S. Benjamin and L. H. Hackstaff. New York, 1964.

Gift of Persev. (*De dono perseverantiae*). *The De Dono Perseverantiae of Saint Augustine*, tr. by M. A. Lesousky. Washington, 1956.

Happy Life. (*De beata vita*). *The Happy Life*, tr. by L. Schopp (included in a volume with *Answer to Skeptics, Divine Providence and the Problem of Evil* and *Soliloquies*). New York, 1948.

Harm. of Evan. (*De consensu evangelistarum*). *The Harmony of the Evangelists*, tr. by E. R. Dods in *The Works of Aurelius Augustinus*. Edinburgh, 1871–1876.

Letters. (*Epistolae*). *Letters, Vol. I (1–82)*, tr. by W. Parsons. Washington, 1951. *Letters, Vol. II (83–130)*, tr. by W. Parsons. Washington, 1953. *Letters, Vol. III (131–164)*, tr. by W. Parsons. Washington, 1953. *Letters, Vol. IV (165–203)*, tr. by W. Parsons. Washington, 1955. *Letters, Vol. V (204–270)*, tr. by W. Parsons. Washington, 1956.

Lit. Gen. (*De Genesi ad litteram*). *The Literal Meaning of Genesis*, tr. by J. H. Taylor. 2 vols. New York, 1982.

Lord's Serm. (*De sermone Domini in monte*). *The Lord's Sermon on the Mount*, tr. by J. J. Jepson. Westminster, MD, 1956.

Prop. on Rom. (*Expositio 84 propositionum Epistolae ad Romanos*). *Augustine on Romans*, tr. by P. F. Landes (includes also a translation of *Epistolae ad Romanos inchoata expositio*). Chico, CA, 1982.

Rep. to Faustus. (*Contra Faustum Manichaeum libri triginta tres*). *Reply to Faustus the Manichaean*, tr. by E. R. Dods, in *The Works of Aurelius Augustinus*. Edinburgh, 1871–1876.

Retrac. (*Retractiones*). *The Retractions*, tr. by M. I. Bogan. Washington, 1968.

Serm. (*Sermones*) in Migne, Vols. 38–39.

Sol. (Soliloquia). Soliloquies, tr. by T. F. Gilligan (included in a volume with *The Happy Life, Answer to Skeptics* and *Divine Providence and the Problem of Evil*). New York, 1948.

Spirit and Letter. (De spiritu et littera). On the Spirit and the Letter, tr. by P. Holmes in *Basic Writings of St. Augustine*, ed. by W. J. Oates. New York, 1948.

Teacher. (De magistro). The Teacher. The Free Choice of the Will. Grace and Free Will, tr. by R. P. Russell. Washington, 1968.

To Simpl. (Ad Simplicianum de diversis quaestionibus). To Simplician—On Various Questions, Book I, tr. by J. H. S. Burleigh in *Augustine: Earlier Writings*. Philadelphia, 1953.

True Rel. (De vera religione). Of True Religion, tr. by J. H. S. Burleigh in *Augustine: Earlier Writings*. Philadelphia, 1953.

Introduction

As a teacher, I have worked with Augustine for nearly thirty years. Almost every year, his work has been included, to a greater or lesser extent, in at least one course. There have been dozens of graduate and undergraduate seminars and annual surveys of medieval philosophy. He has played his part in studies of social and political philosophy, the philosophy of religion and ethics. Hundreds of students and fellow teachers have shared him with me and helped me examine and re-examine the almost overpowering complexity of the evolution of what seems to me clearly the most titanic intellect in western history. And hundreds of publications from the seemingly bottomless well of Augustinian scholarship have shaped and directed my understanding. Today, as I near the end of my teaching career and of our formal relationship, Augustine occupies a unique place in my life not only as a mentor, but as an old and comfortable friend. He is, to be sure, a friend with whom I disagree about almost everything most fundamental to him, but also one whose honesty, strength of commitment, spiritual depth and psychological insight have enriched me enormously.

In working with students to explore Augustine's thought and place in history, I have tried to avoid closure in interpretation, to leave questions open and to encourage each class to explore them with a fresh eye. So I am somewhat surprised to find that at this point I have, willy-nilly, evolved a fairly complete interpretation of Augustine. And because his thought and personality seem to remain of such fascination to so many, it occurred to me that there might be some interest in what my experience with him has taught me. This book is an effort to share that experience.

Understanding is always a communal endeavor, and that is especially true of a world-historical figure such as Augustine. I have no sense that any aspect of my interpretation is mine alone or is entirely original. Furthermore, I am certainly aware that any interpretation is in some way partial, falls short of the "whole truth" and reflects the values, priorities and interests of the interpreter. This interpretation is no exception, and the reader will certainly profit from comparing it to others. But it is also true that this interpretation has emerged almost solely out of prolonged and repeated wrestling with Augustine's own texts, and the influence of other interpreters, both as challenging and as confirming my reading of the texts, has been indirect and often impossible to specify. As a non-historian, my interpretation of the social and political context of Augustine's thought is of necessity based on what I take to be the most reliable and established original scholarship, and I have tried to cite those sources to which I am most indebted. But for the most part, the interpretation of Augustine's thought itself I have tried to ground in the texts out of which it arose for me, without thereby diminishing in the least my gratitude to all those who have gone before and helped to teach me. So far as I know, the interpretation presented here has not been offered in its entirety elsewhere, and my aim is just to make this "picture" of Augustine available. Those who wish to explore alternative interpretations will find that there are resources aplenty easily accessible.

Augustine has been seen as a champion of freedom and as a crude and unbending determinist; as a Neoplatonic mystic, as a strict biblical literalist and as the most consistent and rational of Christian theologians; as the doctor of hope and grace and as a brooding pessimist; as a celebrant of the depth and beauty of the human soul and as implacable censor of the damned and putrid mass of fallen humanity; as giving unqualified priority to the relationship of each soul to God and as demanding unquestioning obedience to an authoritarian church; as a profound and sensitive student of the inscrutable depths of individual motives and as a relentless persecutor of those whose consciences carried them away from Catholic orthdoxy. Part of the task of interpreting Augustine at this late date is to make plausible how able and informed students have come to such divergent views. The explanation, it seems to me, is that there is a very large measure of truth in each of these perceptions. And I hope that by looking at the context of Augustine's life and thought, the fundamental priorities that were molded by that context and the development of the core of his theological system on the basis of those priorities, we can better understand how he has been so many things to so many people.

Let me now sketch the "picture" of Augustine that will be developed in what follows, setting aside the many qualifications and details that will be necessary later. To begin with, he was, it seems to me, very much a man of his time, rooted in the culture and class structure of African and western Roman society, and his most fundamental ideas were absorbed uncritically and almost unconsciously from that culture. Augustinianism was able to triumph and survive as the dominant ideology of the western empire precisely because it was grounded in beliefs that were accepted as simple "common sense" by most members of society or, in some cases, at least by the ideological vanguard of the dominant classes. In particular, he never doubted or questioned the almost universal perception that the world is an arena in which a host of "gods," spirits and demons are constantly at work. But he also thought it would be utterly absurd for anyone living after the conversion of Constantine and the Christianization of the empire to doubt that the Christian god was the supreme ruler of the universe who was establishing his church throughout the world. That great imperial god had put to rout all the demonic pretenders to deity so long worshiped by the Romans and had established once for all both the immeasurable rewards that attended unquestioning devotion to him and the unspeakable punishment that awaited those who failed to surrender entirely to him.

At the same time, Augustine always identified completely with the ruling class of Roman society, sought to associate himself with that class and adopted without question the outlook and philosophical ideas of the leisured elite that constituted the intellectual vanguard of that class. As an ambitious young student and teacher from a marginal small-town family, he had little trouble abandoning the primitive Catholicism of his devout mother for the fashionable Manichaeism of the provincial Carthaginian elite. And when he arrived in Rome and then in Milan and began to move in the company of the intellectuals of the senatorial aristocracy, he shifted easily to the Platonism fashionable among those men and then (not so easily, since it involved eschewing some pleasures and ambitions) to the Catholic Christianity championed by such leading lights as the senator-turned-bishop, Ambrose of Milan.

From a theological and philosophical point of view, his pilgrimage from the Catholicism of his mother to the Catholicism of Ambrose was in no way a journey through unbelief to renewed faith. Even his brief flirtation with academic skepticism involved not a loss of certainty about the existence of God, but despair and disgust at the arrogance of those who pretended to have all the answers and yet could not answer his questions. What he needed was not a reason to believe in God, but rather a conception of God, a way of understanding God, a unifying myth that would satisfy his needs and intuitions.

On the one hand, he never completely lost the god of his mother and his childhood, that awesome conquerer of the pagan deities who promised triumph and blessedness to those who bowed before him unquestioningly, but who also visited the most terrible wrath on those whose allegiance wavered. This was the sort of god familiar to Romans of all classes (and, for that matter, to the Berber peasantry of Augustine's native Africa), a god demanding that cult be paid, a god to be appeased and petitioned. But more particularly, this was the god of Constantine and the Christianized military and administrative stratum that actually ruled the empire, the god who had entered into partnership with the emperors to unify the empire, tear down the pagan temples and establish his church universal.

On the other hand, Augustine's god needed to be something very much more and different. The road he followed in his struggle to join the ruling class of Roman society did not involve pursuing military, political or administrative advancement. He became an intellectual and sought acceptance into those circles whose aristocratic patrons saw themselves as the keepers of ancient culture and wisdom. While in Carthage, he made himself a leader among young scholars, many of whom were themselves from provincial senatorial families, who gloried in pursuit of "wisdom," were contemptuous of the "primitive" religion of their African home towns and sometimes returned home to flaunt before their horrified elders the Manichaeism they had adopted as a higher truth. Augustine himself was without the means to sustain himself as part of this rarified culture, but he had no difficulty finding provincial aristocrats happy to act as patrons and so gain at least indirect recognition as "lovers of wisdom." When he moved on to Rome and then to Milan, Augustine found himself in the far more heady company of gentlemen of the oldest aristocratic families, some of whom devoted their time to leisured contemplation, while others directed the spiritual life of the empire as Christian leaders of the new imperial church. And in this new context, Augustine had no trouble at all abandoning Manichaeism with the same disdain that he had rejected his childhood religion and identifying competely with the Platonism of his new mentors.

This intellectual elite, whether in the provinces or in the metropolitan centers, shared an outlook quite different not only from that of the masses, but from that of the men of action who administered the state—an outlook that Augustine quickly absorbed and made his own. These men (and, with the possible exception of Augustine's mother, Monica, they were all males) saw their noble souls as lost from a realm of perfect being, with which they were essentially identified. In periods of leisured meditation, they enjoyed moments of spiritual insight, in which they caught a glimpse of that eternal reality from which they were lost and to which they yearned to return. They saw their souls as trapped in this physical world and in the prison of the fleshly body. While they often continued with cultic practice or Christian worship, their real aim was a spiritual transformation that would lift them from the degradation of this realm of suffering and ceaseless change back to that eternal source which was their true home. The provincial intellectuals of Carthage found at least some of what they were seeking in a Manichaean dualism that allowed them to identify their true selves with a cosmic principle of light which was forever at war with the principle of darkness that constituted the fleshly world of suffering and death. The old aristocracy of Rome and Milan, on the other hand, scorned that Persian import and clung to the ancient Platonist wisdom which identified their souls with an ideal world of unitary being in which this phenomenal world participates and finds its meaning.

Augustine moved from his original Catholicism to Manichaeism and then to Platonism gradually but with relative ease, always searching for a cosmic myth that would allow him to combine his intuition of the omnipotent imperial deity with that of the enveloping source of being for which he had come to yearn. Among the Christian Platonists of Milan, he thought he had found what he sought. He converted again to Catholicism, and for a short time he seems to have believed that there was an unbroken truth that found its first expression in Plato and its ultimate realization in Christ. However, once he returned to

Africa and enlisted as a soldier of the church, it soon became apparent to him that while God might indeed be that immutable oneness of the Platonists, he was, far more importantly, the utterly omnipotent person who created and directed the whole world by his inscrutable and irresistible will. Platonism had indeed enabled him to shake free of the limitations placed on God by Manichaeism and by the anthropomorphism of his childhood religion. And Platonism had pointed him in a direction that enabled him to see God not only as immaterial, but as *both* utterly omnipotent and abolutely good. In fact, as the dominant world-view of elite culture, Platonism always seemed to Augustine superior to all other philosophies and closer to Christianity than any other.

But although Platonism helped him purge his idea of God of its cruder anthropomorphic aspects, the God at which he arrived once he returned to Africa and joined the priesthood was far closer to the conquering deity of Constantine than to the mystical one of Plotinus. His god was indeed an immaterial being, perfect in goodness, the source of all other being and that to which all rational creatures yearn to return. But this god was, far more importantly, that great personal imperial deity who creates and rules the world by his *will*, who directs and controls every event in his universe and who brooks no deviation from his divine plan and purpose.

Once he arrived, finally, at the myth that would dominate his thought and action, Augustine moved very quickly to develop the theological implications of that myth. He returned to Africa in 388 and was ordained a priest at Hippo in 391. By 395, when he was consecrated bishop of Hippo, his theology was already well developed, and by 396, when he wrote a letter to his old mentor, Simplician, the central doctrines of his theology had taken their final form. The doctrines of divine foreknowledge, human freedom, grace, predestination, original sin and the fall were all developed in a way that remained unchanged until his death. More than a decade before he had even heard of the Pelagians, the theological weapons with which he would battle that heresy were already forged and sharpened.

The theology he developed in those few years and elaborated throughout his life is what we know as Augustinianism, the ideology and theology that would dominate western culture for centuries and that remains a potent force today. It is a theology that has as its driving force an effort to develop a rationally consistent and coherent system which reconciles the power of an omnipotent god with both the goodness and justice of that god and the freedom and responsibility of creatures for their choices and their actions. It presents us with a magnificent cosmic drama in which God directs all things and calls back to himself those fallen souls whose misdirected wills have cast them into a corruption so deep that only the grace of God can give them hope of returning to beatitude.

But while Augustine makes a titanic effort to preserve both human freedom and the goodness of God, it is clear that his god is, above all, the imperial ruler of the universe, and what cannot be sacrificed at any price is the absolute *power* of that god. This is the guiding thread of Augustine's thought, that which gives shape to those doctrines most associated with his name and that which, in my view, is finally the rock on which his system is broken.

In what follows, I want to develop this "picture" of Augustine and Augustinianism in three stages. In Part One, I shall discuss, in a summary way, some of the social, political and economic conditions of the western Roman empire in the fourth and fifth centuries, the various forms of religious consciousness that found a home in those conditions and the location of Augustine's religious institutions among those forms. Part Two will survey Augustine's life and development up to the time of his ordination and will attempt to understand to some extent how and why he came to hold those beliefs, especially beliefs about the nature of God, that were to be the foundation of his system. Part Three will sketch the development of the core ideas of his systematic theology from those basic beliefs and will attempt to display, on the one hand, the coherence and consistency of that system and, on the other hand, the reasons that it ultimately falters. Hopefully, by displaying the development of Augustinianism in a way that is at once chronological, biographical and philosophical, the reader will emerge with a better sense of Augustine as a person and a thinker and a better understanding of the way in which a seminal ideology was absorbed and elaborated into a philosophical and theological system that could exercise such power for so many centuries.

Part One

AUGUSTINE'S WORLD

To begin a study of Augustine is to begin with God. The basic concept of his thought is the concept of God, and his most basic belief is in the existence of God. But to approach an understanding of Augustine, it must really be put in much stronger terms than that. The fact is that no one can read even a single page of Augustine's writing and not see that his God utterly pervades his thought and his life. Virtually all of his philosophical and theological system grows directly from his concept of the being that he knew simply by the name "God." By his own account, his early life was dominated by an obsessive longing to "find" his God. And once God was "found" during his stay in Milan, the rest of his life consisted of a constant personal effort (always falling short) to "cleave to" God, together with an almost superhuman drive to bring the world to God and establish the dominance of God's church. Even on his deathbed, he lay in solitary fear and longing, weeping and searching his heart to be sure that he had "repented worthily and adequately" of any forgotten sin that might yet keep his soul from his God for eternity.[1]

Augustine is at almost endless pains to depict his God as the center both of the universe and of every human life, a being of such consummate greatness as to reduce human pretensions to dust. It is God who created the world entirely, not even requiring a material with which to work. He is the unchallenged ruler of reality, unlimited in power and knowledge. This same God is also perfectly good (including perfectly just), loving and providential. Wholly immanent in every mind, personally dwelling in every believing heart, spiritually present in all times and places, God is also utterly transcendent, unchanging and fixed in timeless eternity. God completely and perfectly orders all real-

15

ity and is the source of human understanding of that order. He created human beings for himself, and their fulfillment is found only in relationship with God. Though humans may disobey the commands of God, they can never thwart his will. And though they have turned from God, he reveals his power by using their sinfulness to fulfill his purpose, even as he shows his love in sending the Christ as his very incarnation to redeem them. His mercy and inscrutable wisdom lead him to grant special aid to some in their struggle toward his presence, even as his unswerving justice insures the richly deserved eternal damnation of those who willfully refuse to heed his call. Intimately present within the soul of every person, God is more known to us than we are to ourselves. And yet, lost to him, we are as profoundly ignorant of his nature as we are of the reasons for his always perfect plan. The following passage may convey something of the intensity and seeming paradox of his thought and feeling about God.

> What, then, is my God? What, I ask, unless the Lord God? Who is Lord but the Lord? Or who is God but our God? Most high, most good, most mighty, most almighty; most merciful and most just; most hidden and most present; most beautiful and most strong; stable and incomprehensible; unchangeable, yet changing all things; never new, and never old, yet renewing all things; leading proud men into senility, although they know it not; ever active, and ever at rest; gathering in, yet needing nothing; supporting, fulfilling and protecting things; creating, nourishing, and perfecting them; searching them out, although nothing is lacking in you. You love, but are not inflamed with passion; you are jealous, yet free from care; you repent, but do not sorrow; you grow angry, but remain tranquil. You change your works, but do not change your plan; you take back what you find, although you never lost it; you are never in want, but you rejoice in gain; you are never covetous, yet you exact usury. Excessive payments are made to you, so that you may be our debtor—yet who has anything that is not yours? You pay debts, although you owe no man anything; you cancel debts, and lose nothing. What have we said, my God, my life, my holy delight? Or what does any man say when he speaks of you? Yet woe to those who keep silent concerning you, since even those who speak much are as the dumb. (*Conf.* I. 4)

Now Augustine himself was very much aware that his conception of God was not without its problems, and he made a concerted and prolonged effort both to carry out an analysis of the concept of God and to develop the implications of that concept with rigor and honesty. Many studies of his thought have begun by taking for granted this most fundamental of his beliefs and proceeding with an analysis of his idea of God and an investigation of the implications of this concept. But for the purposes of this study, it is important to spend a little more time with this fundamental idea, before going on to look at its development.

As the quotation above shows, the existence of God was not, for Augustine, anything like a postulate or assumption. He certainly takes it to be a statement of the most fundamental *fact* about reality, without the knowledge of which any attempt to understand the nature and workings of the world can have no more relation to reality than the wildest fantasies. And the influence of Augustine's thought makes sense only because the existence of God was taken by most people of the age to be as obvious as it was to Augustine himself. Our first step must then be an attempt to understand Augustine's certainty that the awesome being on which he rests his life and thought exists in the first place and, beyond that, to understand how that belief found such a receptive audience.

A philosopher approaching this issue will begin by looking to see what *arguments* Augustine develops for the claim that God exists and by investigating the *evidence* he is able to marshall in support of this claim. Or, the philosopher might ask, was Augustine's belief based not in evidence and argument, but in some sort of direct *experience* that made God's existence indubitable? Or perhaps some reasons can be given for supposing that some "sense" or innate awareness of God is implanted in all persons, such that no one whose "instincts" are in good order can possibly doubt the existence of God. All of this the philosopher might lump together in the form of the question "Did Augustine have any good *reasons* to think that God exists?" or "Was Augustine's belief in the existence of God *rational*?"

These are legitimate questions, and in Part Two I shall say something about them. But in Part One, I want first to look at other factors that I think bore on Augustine's belief. In particular, I want to look at him as a person of his age, an age in which the existence and activity of gods was so obvious as to make doubts seem to most people silly or insane. This is important not only for understanding Augustine's own convictions, but also for understanding why at least some of his ideas found easy acceptance.

Augustine himself certainly never thought of his belief as *depending* on any proofs. For him, expressions of doubt about the existence of God were at best philosophical quibbles and at worst sinful perversity. Far from seeing belief as a matter of "blind faith" or "superstition," he sees the existence of God as simply obvious. As he puts it at one point,

> This truth most above all was to be believed, for no hostile and slander-ous questions, so many of which I had read in philosophers who contra-dict one another, could extort from me the answer that I would at any time believe that you do not exist, whatsoever might be your nature (for this I did not know), or that the governance of human affairs did not belong to you. Sometimes I believed this more strongly and at other times in a more feeble way. But always I believed both that you are and that you have care for us, although I did not know either what must be thought concerning your substantial being or what way led up to you or back to you. (*Conf.* VI. 5)

So now as a first step, I want to look briefly at some conditions in which that sort of comfortable certainty was possible even for a mind as demanding as Augustine's.

Knowledge of conditions of life and of religious practice in the later Roman empire is, as is most historical study, still very much incom-plete. But while much remains to be done, a good deal of splendid work has been done, and it is now possible to form a fairly complete picture of at least the main features of life and religious attitudes dur-ing the period at which Augustinianism developed. While there are certainly important disagreements, it does seem to me that, at least among a number of leading scholars, there is a fairly broad consensus regarding some of the most basic conditions obtaining at the time. Based on my reading of some of those scholars, I want to begin by pre-senting a "layman's" interpretation of some aspects of late Roman society, in order to place Augustine's thought and beliefs in context.

Part One will consist of three sections. In the first, I attempt to con-vey something of the pervasive religious consciousness that marked Augustine's time. Next, I want to say something about the material conditions of the day which may have helped sustain that conscious-ness. And in the third section, I shall try to indicate, in a general way, something of the various forms taken by religious consciousness among persons of different social classes.

I. The Prevalence of Belief

As Robin Lane Fox shows so well in his *Pagans and Christians*, the presence and activity of the gods were constant realities for almost everyone in the ancient world, so that, in this sense, Augustine was simply typical. Each city (and many smaller towns) had its own special protecting goddess or god, while also recognizing the reality and activity of other deities as well. Indeed, along with the gods, the world was full of demons, sprites, nymphs and a host of other beings seldom seen but never questioned.[2]

Nor was there any doubt (excepting an occasional Epicurean) of the gods' interaction with human beings. The gods drew near their devotees in time of crisis, and ill fortune was readily attributed to the unpredictable anger of an offended deity who felt neglected or poorly served. Though the performance of the gods was a bit unreliable, it was a very stupid person indeed who did not perform the obligatory sacrifices and so seek to propitiate and enlist the aid of the gods in any important undertaking. To their worshipers, the gods were likely to bring victory in battle, a bountiful corn harvest, a miraculous cure, a fair voyage and a safe return home. On the other hand, the wrath of an offended or neglected deity was often the best available explanation of plague, drought, famine, miscarriage and defeat in battle.[3]

In fact, although it is impossible to trace the exact causes of most of the sporadic and localized persecutions of Christians before the middle of the third century, many scholars agree that the Christian refusal to perform obligatory sacrifices often played a prominent role.[4] If suffering or ill fortune befell a city, it was believed that it must be due to divine anger, and it was only natural for attention to be focused on those "atheists" who clung to their exclusive faith and rejected the modest cult demands of the local gods. As Lane Fox remarks, "'No rain, because of the Christians,' had become proverbial by the mid-fourth century."[5]

The historical record, too, or what served as such, contained a wealth of testimony to the existence and activity of the gods. From the Greek Homer to the Hebrew Moses, from the pagan Thucydides to the Christian Eusebius, the greatest and most ancient authorities constantly reminded everyone that however obvious the presence of the gods might still be, there had been a time long ago when it was yet more obvious. There was an age in which the gods had lived among humans, consorted with them, sired progeny, sat in the door of Abraham's tent, spoken to Moses from a burning bush and to John the Baptist in the form of a dove.

Not that the gods had, even at so late a date, ceased to put in an appearance from time to time. Christians and Jews report many fewer direct manifestations than do pagans, and it appears that one reason for that may have been a long-time ban on paintings and statues of their god. Since Jews and Christians did not know what their god looked like, the unseen god was more apt to be manifested through visible objects. And for that matter, pagans also often detected a god under the disguise of an animal or an old man. But pagans also encountered their gods in the most direct way. There were statues everywhere to let them know just how the gods looked, so that they were easy to recognize when they appeared. And such appearances were by no means rare.[6]

The most likely context for a divine manifestation was a moment of extreme crisis. It is true that Pan might be heard piping or a nymph might be glimpsed by a special cave on a perfect spring day. But the more common case was the appearance of a god or goddess in a situation of extreme danger or stress. Lane Fox reports that soldiers attacking Aquileia in the third century were dismayed to see Apollo standing above the city and joining its defense. Even as late as the fifth century, Alaric and his invaders are reported to have encountered a protecting Athena Promachos striding atop the walls of her beloved Athens.[7]

But even if the face of the god remained hidden, the manifestation was no less obvious. The gods had their favorite places, and it was there that they were most apt to present themselves, though often only by voice or perhaps disguised as ordinary men. Yearly pilgrimages to the great shrines of Claros, Didyma and Delphi brought at least the ruling classes into close contact with the great god and provided typically enigmatic responses to the pressing questions of supplicants.[8]

Nor were Christians and Jews excluded from these more indirect manifestations. Yahweh appears in a cloud or ball of fire above the ark of the covenant and holds back the sun in its course for Joshua and his troops. Christ speaks to Saul of Tarsus on the road to Damascus and displays his cross to Constantine in the sky above the Milvian Bridge. And of course, Jesus himself is the invisible Christ made visible in human form.

Augustine seems never to have experienced personally divine manifestations of this sort, and in fact he believed that God seldom revealed himself so directly in more recent days, a time that he thought of as "the old age of the world" (*Serm.* 81). But he had no doubt that God had so revealed himself in the past, and he accepted without question the manifestations of other gods, though these he regarded as demons who merely posed as gods. The first six books of the *City of God* are filled with loathing and contempt for those demons who had tricked the Romans into worshiping them and relying on them. He makes fun of people so foolish as to trust their whole empire to impotent demons who cannot even deliver on their specialties:

> Many worshipers of Juventas have been far from flourishing in their early years; while many non-worshipers enjoy robust health in youth, many suppliants of Bearded Fortune have no beard at all, or have achieved only an unprepossessing growth and expose themselves to the ridicule of her bearded detractors for having venerated her in the hope of hirsute adornment. (*City* VI. 1)

And he is full of loathing for those filthy demons posing as gods who have corrupted public morals by inducing their devotees to stage obscene plays and festivals in their honor and who are still worshiped secretly even after being outlawed by Christian emperors.

> I was therefore bound to prove that the false gods whom they used to worship openly and still worship secretly, are really unclean spirits; they are demons so malignant and deceitful that they delight in the wickedness imputed to them, whether truly or falsely, and have wished their crimes to be publicly represented at their festivals, so that it may be impossible for human weakness to be recalled from the perpetration of such enormities, because a supposedly divine authority is given for their imitation. (*City* IV. 1)

Augustine was, however, prepared to testify directly to another sort of divine manifestation that was also common to most people of his time—the witnessing of miracles and wonders.

Among pagans, there was always a great love of wonders, and despite its illegality during the earlier period of the empire, the effecting of wonders through magic was always popular. For a long time, Christians were suspicious of miracle claims and were hostile to the practice of magic, since they saw these things as associated with the pagan gods. But as the Christians developed cults of their own martyrs, their miracle claims increased. And by the time of Augustine, Christians were eager to compete with pagans in both numbers and impressiveness of miracles.[9] In fact, MacMullen goes so far as to claim that miracles were the greatest persuader convincing pagans to convert to Christianity.[10] Given the pagan tradition of miracles and magic, that may be an excessive statement.[11] But there is no doubt that by Augustine's time, Christians not only accepted the contemporary occurrence of miracles, but used them freely in support of the superiority of their religion.

While he was still under the influence of the Milanese intelligentsia, Augustine doubted whether miracles such as those in the age of the apostles still occurred (*True Rel.* XXV. 47). But once he had his feet back on the ground in Africa and was actively engaged in establishing the supremacy of the church, he came to see the world as fairly alive with miracles, portents, marvels and wonders of many sorts. He had absolutely no doubt that such wonders occurred and that they were effected both by his own god and by the demons whom the pagans took as their gods. Of course, he regarded the pagan miracles as "not worthy of comparison" with Christian ones and as due to the arrogant pride of malicious demons, rather than to the providence of God (*City* XXII. 10). But he thought it self-evident that miracles from a variety of sources occurred frequently, and he took their occurrence as the plainest manifestation of divine and demonic beings of all sorts, including his own god.

As is to be expected, many of the miracles Augustine cites are reported in scripture or in Roman historical sources. And he acknowledges that miracles are not so common in his own day as they were earlier. He thinks this relative decrease is due to the fact that the primary purpose of miracles is to induce wonder and so encourage belief and that there is no longer so great a need for such motivation when "all the world believes" (*City* XXII. 8), that is, since the empire is now Christian. But he insists that miracles still occur, and he is aware of many examples.

In Chapter 8 of Book XXII of the *City of God*, he compiles quite a lengthy catalogue of such wonders that had occurred in his own time. Apparently, only one of these was actually witnessed by Augustine himself. This was the case of one Innocentius, an advocate in the office of the deputy prefect of Carthage, whose rectal fistula was healed in response to his desperate prayer when he was faced with the horrible pain of surgery. But many other cases are so clearly attested by reliable witnesses that Augustine has no doubt of them. For example, he reports that while he was still in Milan, many people had witnessed the restoration of sight to a blind man in the presence of the bodies of the martyrs Protasius and Gervasius. And he knew of many other miracles at the shrines of martyrs, some in the area of his own home of Hippo.

He cites an impressive number of miracles performed at shrines of St. Stephen near Hippo and comments that if he were to enumerate all the miracles associated with those shrines alone, "the record would fill many books." One example may convey the flavor and confidence of his account: he tells of two children of a widow who had mistreated their mother and had been cursed by her, so that they were afflicted with constant violent trembling. After praying at the shrine of St. Stephen, first the brother and later the sister were cured. Augustine himself saw the brother just after the cure and saw the sister both immediately before and immediately after the cure. He remarks that this miracle was "so widely famed that I should imagine no one from Hippo failed to witness it or at least to hear about it, and no one could have forgotten it."

What I would like to emphasize here is that there is no air of wonder or even naiveté or credulity surrounding Augustine's discussion of these events. Not only did he accept miracles matter of factly as an obvious feature of experience, but he took for granted that his readers would have the same attitude toward them. His purpose is merely to collect and display samples, not to convince skeptics. There may have been doubts in the minds of some as to whether Christian miracles were more spectacular than pagan miracles, and it is certainly useful to keep a record to remind everyone of the power of one's own god (rather in the manner of comparing records of baseball stars to determine who is "the greatest"). But that many happenings are due to the work of invisible beings is a part of a conceptual background that is not so much actively believed as merely taken for granted both by Augustine and by his readers.

One or two additional examples may help reinforce this tone of unquestioning acceptance. Take first the case of Hesperius, a landowner and former tribune near Hippo, whose livestock and slaves were being infested with evil demons. One of the elders of Augustine's church went to Hesperius' estate and managed to exorcise the demons. In gratitude, Hesperius gave Augustine some holy earth he had brought from a pilgrimage to Jerusalem, and Augustine had a shrine established to house the earth. A young "rustic" who was paralyzed prayed at this shrine and regained the use of his legs.

A final example is centered at a house near Hippo which contained a relic of those same Milanese martyrs, Protasius and Gervasius. A boy was brought there having been possessed by a demon while washing his horse at a river. Hymns were sung while the boy clutched the altar of the martyrs' shrine. Finally, the demon announced that it was prepared to leave the boy's body but that it would not do so without inflicting some damage on the way out. When the demon departed, it left one of the boy's eyes dangling from its socket by a single vein. Fortunately, a relative was of sufficient faith to replace the eye in its socket and to enter into prayer for a solid week, after which the eye was fully restored to health.

So miracles were perfectly evident to Augustine, as they were to most of his contemporaries. But as evident as they were, they were not the most common form of divine manifestation. It was in *dreams* that most people encountered the gods, and while many might know of miracles only second-hand, almost everyone had first-hand experience of the divine in dream life.

As mentioned above, pagans had no trouble recognizing their gods, and their appearance in dreams was a regular feature of life doubted by no one. Lane Fox rejects the hypothesis suggested by some that pagans may have been drawn to Christianity because they longed for the sort of direct vision of God that was offered by the incarnation.

> Pagans kept nightly company with their gods and those who sported in dreams with Aphrodite needed no new route to heaven. Among pagans, these "visits" were freely enjoyed, and there was no restraining orthodoxy, no priestly authority which restricted the plain man's access to nightly contact with the gods.[12]

There were even special shrines that attracted sleepers hoping for a clear dream of the god, and there were formal techniques to bring about conditions most propitious for a divine visit.

For Christians, God himself seldom put in a dream appearance, since his face was unknown. To be sure, the emperor Constantine was

treated to a rare dream visitation from Christ himself and was instructed as to the symbol to be inscribed on the shields of his army. But this
was unusual, and it was much more common for the dreams of
Christians to be peopled with angels and martyrs (and, unhappily, with
demons as well) than with the person of their god. What was clear to
everyone was that the divine and demonic beings of the dream world
were as real as any solid object of the waking world.

As in the case of miracles, Augustine shared in this common acceptance of dream manifestations. He reports matter of factly that Bishop
Ambrose of Milan had been instructed in a dream where to find the
remains of Protasius and Gervasius. And in the same place, he tells of
a noblewoman of Carthage named Innocentia who was instructed in a
dream of the procedure to be followed in obtaining a miracle cure of
her cancer (*City* XXII. 8). In the *Confessions*, he tells of a dream of his
mother Monica, which assured her of his eventual conversion, and
while he at first doubted her interpretation of the dream, he raises no
questions about the reality of the shining young man who brought the
message to her in sleep (*Conf.* III. 11). And at least one of Augustine's
letters is a reply to a query from his friend Nebridius as to just what
method is used by supernatural beings to set things before us in dreams
(*Letter* 9, replying to *Letter* 8 from Nebridius).

What all this tells us is that in his unquestioning acceptance of the
existence of gods, Augustine reveals himself as no more than a perfectly normal person of his time. In Part Two, I shall look briefly at the
question of whether he was able to provide rational support for his
belief. But however that turns out, it seems fair to conclude at this
point that Augustine's belief in God should not be characterized as
"mere superstition" and that it appears just the sort of belief that the
most rational person of his day would be expected to hold. Given the
fact that almost no one doubted the existence and activity of divine
beings, given the unbroken testimony of the historical record, given
the "commonsense" explanation of both physical events and dream life
in terms of the activity of the gods, and given the lack of any serious
competing mode of explanation, it would have been a very odd and
perverse duck indeed who refused to believe. It is no wonder that
Augustine regards doubts of that sort as either insane or merely con-
tentious. He did for a time think there were serious questions as to how
God could be the absolutely supreme, omnipotent, omniscient and per-

fectly good being that the Christians claimed. But that the gods (and even beings that passed for gods) were real was not a matter for serious discussion, and the activity and presence of the Christian god were as obvious and undeniable as any.

In Augustine's world, there was, to be sure, a great deal of cynical manipulation of belief and cultic practice to serve political and economic interests. But even among those who had most to gain from perpetuation of religious traditions, it is hard to separate conscious manipulation from genuine personal feeling. For one thing, the higher classes shared with the poor the natural dependency of an agricultural society, the uncertainties of commerce and the insecurities of war and pillage. And after all, where life is so uncertain, good fortune as well as ill must be responded to with reverential care, so that those at the top had as much reason to propitiate the gods as did those at the bottom. The rise and persistent domination of the "great families" of Rome not only called forth their gratitude, but led them to be very solicitous of maintaining the conditions that had served them so well. Most aristocrats were undoubtedly quite sincere in seeing their dominant position as evidence that they had been favored by the gods, and most of them willingly accepted the responsibilities to the gods that their station demanded. But at the same time, those aristocrats were also often explicitly conscious that the rituals honoring the local gods helped to cement and legitimize a social order in which they were the dominant figures. And since the aristocracy also provided the priesthood of the cults, they could not fail to recognize that this gave them even greater control over a passive population.

Also there was, especially among the more educated, a tendency to view the traditional gods in mythic or symbolic ways (in this respect, Augustine was probably more literal-minded than many of his educated contemporaries). But even the philosophers who saw the gods as symbols of or "emanations" from the true God or Absolute Being were only redefining spiritual reality, not rejecting it. In other words, what there was *not*, to any significant extent, is what is today thought of as "atheism." As mentioned above, an atheist was one who refused to pay cult to the established gods, not a complete unbeliever. And for almost everyone, both fear of the gods and an interest in a healthy relationship with them were lively concerns. When philosophers disagreed or practices varied, the issue was almost always the proper interpretation of and relation to divine reality, not the existence of that reality.

The struggle of the Epicureans against oracular superstition and for a grounding of life in concrete reality was, despite its persistence and the commitment of some of its adherents, an exception that proves the rule. Lane Fox has given us the striking example of the city of Oenanda to illustrate that even where Epicureanism found the most explicit patronage and support, it did not win mass support. Though a massive pulpit extolling Epicureanism and attacking the oracles occupied the center of the city about the year 200 A.D., by the middle of the century the shrine had disappeared and the Most High God was the focus of worship.[13] In fact, even the Epicureans did not deny the existence of the gods, assigning to them rather a blissful life indifferent to the world and concentrating on what they saw as pernicious superstition about their activity and influence.[14]

Hopefully, these remarks are enough to suggest the prevalence of religious consciousness in Augustine's world. As a next step in providing some background for a discussion of Augustinianism, I want to review some of the material conditions described by leading historians, conditions that provided part of the context of that religious consciousness, focusing especially on conditions in the western empire where Augustinianism took root and flourished.

II. The Material Conditions of Belief

In discussing some of the material conditions in which Augustinianism was developed and adopted, I do not at all mean to suggest that there is a simple causal relation between material conditions and the acceptance of certain ideas. The question of what causes beliefs to be accepted is far too complex to be answered here, and I am not certain that it could be answered in any case. Nor do I mean to suggest that the material conditions in which beliefs are accepted have any bearing whatever on their truth or falsity. Given a set of material conditions, a belief may meet the needs or serve the interests of virtually everyone in a society and yet be false. And by the same token, a belief may meet no needs and serve no interests and yet be true.

Still it does seem that there are at least two reasons for looking briefly at some of the conditions within which Augustinianism developed. First, there is the fact that whether or not a belief is true, an overview of those conditions may help explain why the belief is accepted. A belief which meets the needs or serves the interests either of virtually all members of a society or of some particular groups or classes may be either true or false, but the fact that it does meet those needs or serve those interests may still help explain why the belief is accepted by those who accept it. And if we are trying to understand why Augustinianism became a dominant ideology, that will be an important consideration.

Second, it is worth looking at material conditions because it may be a help in making a judgment about the *justification* of beliefs. If a belief is widely held and if it also meets basic needs or serves basic interests, it often seems to people so obvious as to be in no need of justification. So, for example, in our society today, the belief that all persons have certain inalienable rights may be accepted by almost everyone, and it may be a belief that serves certain fundamental interests of many or even most persons and groups. And under these circumstances, it may seem silly or perverse to ask whether there is any justification for such a belief. However, it is worth noting that the mere fact that a belief serves certain interests never establishes its truth and that if the belief is to be justified, one must point to something other than its serving those interests. So a look at the material conditions of belief calls our attention to the question of the needs and interests served, and by doing so it forces us to look at the question of what, if any, justification there is for the belief.

The cultural diversity of the vast Roman empire produced a great variety of religious beliefs and practices. But whatever may have been the origins, reasons and grounds of these various systems, it is not difficult, from our historical vantage point, to see that a general religious consciousness was supported and reinforced by the conditions that were its medium.

We may begin with the most obvious fact, that the lives of most were filled with difficulty and that most faced a combination of radical uncertainty and helplessness. Brown reminds us that "the classical Mediterranean had always been a world on the edge of starvation."[15] Economic and social life was based on the most direct oppression and compulsion, and most lived lives of abject dependency. So, as Brown further notes, for the vast majority who supported the society by their labor, the demands and compulsions that filled their days were immemorial—"In places, they were as old as civilization itself."[16]

Virtually no one in Roman society could fail to be aware of a total dependence on a variety of forces that were both immensely powerful and apparently capricious. To begin with, since land was the principal means of production and since the surplus produced by agricultural labor was marginal at best, all were at the mercy of natural forces, though townspeople may have felt this somewhat less directly than the actual producers. In light of this, it is no surprise to find that many of the early gods were closely associated with natural forces of all kinds. The level of technology was and remained very low throughout the period, so that there was never any method of controlling conditions of production that offered any more hope than did the propitiation of local and cosmic deities. In the face of such harsh conditions, the main attitude toward the gods was fear, and most religious practice was aimed at avoiding or tempering the *anger* of the gods.[17]

During the period when Rome was extending its sway over the world and up to at least the beginning of the third century A.D., plunder was a second significant source of wealth. But as a means of appropriation, plunder is itself filled with uncertainty and insecurity. It goes without saying that the victims of this activity—those being plundered—found their lives filled with insecurity. But even for the plunderers, existence was precarious. A life of plunder is a life of war, and the insecurities of a warrior's life led to a constant preoccupation with searching for signs of divine favor. There were no "atheists in the foxholes," and army life was filled with a round of sacrifice and cult that was only slowly displaced by Christian prayer and ritual.[18]

So life was, by any standard, difficult even in purely natural terms. Best estimates place life expectancy at birth at less than thirty years, with infant mortality above two hundred per one thousand live births and perhaps half the people dying by the age of eight years.[19] The depth of want often drove poor parents to infanticide, and the selling of children was extremely common.[20] Cold facts such as these help explain the preoccupation of Christians with the souls of infants who die prior to baptism and Augustine's attention to this issue throughout his life.

In addition to natural hardships, however, there were social conditions that added to the difficulty. The social order and the economic system imposed on virtually everyone a host of dependencies, compulsions and exactions. To be sure, these burdens were not distributed evenly, and the poor bore by far the heavier share. But even many of the well-to-do felt victimized by an onerous system that only grew more onerous as the centuries went by.

We begin by looking at those on the bottom of the social pyramid, those on whose backs the system directly rested. And here the fundamental fact is, in Marx's words, that "direct forced labor is the foundation of the ancient world."[21] And forced labor existed not only in the most obvious form of chattel slavery, but also in the unfree labor of peasants and others.

Ste. Croix argues persuasively that the society of the Roman empire is best defined as a "slave society," rather than as a "peasant society."[22] His reason for this is not that slaves formed an actual majority of laborers, because in fact they were outnumbered by peasant producers who were technically free persons. Rather, he points out that given the low level of productivity, peasants were often hard-pressed to meet their own needs, much less to produce a surplus that would support the military adventures and lavish lifestyles of the ruling classes. Therefore, the system depended heavily on slave labor to secure an adequate surplus to allow the system to function. Ste. Croix compares it to the south of the United States during the eighteenth and nineteenth centuries, where slaves made up less than a third of the population, where fewer than a quarter of families owned slaves, and where only about three percent of slaveholders (or about six-tenths of one percent of all families) owned fifty or more slaves. Yet most historians agree in calling the American south a "slave society," since only slavery permitted the production of a surplus that could support the system.[23]

The institution of slavery was accepted universally and unquestioningly throughout the period we are reviewing, although it was justified in a variety of ways. It is frequently pointed out not only that Christianity did not eliminate slavery, but that Christians were at one with pagans in endorsing the institution.[24] This is true, but I am not sure that much should be made of it. The only reason to take special note of the perpetuation of slavery by Christians would be that one views Christians as somehow "special," so that they could be expected to transcend their time and place in a way others could not. There seems to be no basis for any such view, and Lane Fox shows in some detail that there were no important differences between pagans and

Christians in their attitudes toward slavery or their treatment of slaves.[25] So I shall say no more about specifically Christian attitudes to slavery or treatment of slaves by Christians in particular. As for Augustine himself, he not only did not oppose slavery, but saw it as divinely ordained and even as potentially beneficial for the slave (*City* XIX. 15-16).

Slaves were used in agriculture, mining, crafts and virtually all other employments. And while some slaves received relatively "humane" treatment (occasionally an imperial slave might even rise to high position in the later empire), there is no question that the lot of almost all slaves was that of the most oppressed and brutalized victims of an economic system that was throughout founded on force and compulsion.[26] Each senator had an army of slaves to supply his wants, and the problem faced by the ruling class was always to find a supply of human bodies to meet their needs. The slave was a dispensable property who often paid with his or her life if the other property of the master should be disturbed or stolen.[27] And, if anything, slaves were treated with increasing brutality from the middle of the second century. There were few, if any, slave revolts during this period, so that the lot of slaves seems to have been one of helpless dependency and hopeless exploitation.[28]

Alongside slaves, there had always been the small freeholder and free peasantry, some of whom were themselves small slaveholders (often working alongside their slaves), while others were landless peasants on larger estates or occasional agricultural wage laborers. In getting a picture of life at this period, it is extremely important to remember that this agricultural laboring population constituted fully ninety percent of the total population. This was overwhelmingly a society of rural laborers.[29]

Corresponding to this rural working class, there were in the cities small artisans, traders, shopkeepers and, perhaps most despised of all, those who hired out their labor-power for wages.[30] The lot of most of these people, both the peasantry and the urban lower classes, deteriorated steadily through the three centuries leading up to Augustine's time.

The abstract ideal of the Roman republic had at its heart the free-holding citizen farmer, and indeed there was never a time when the "free" peasantry was not the vast majority of the population. But already during the last century of the republic (the end of which is conventionally dated with the establishment of the principate by Augustus Caesar in 27 B.C.) the reality of the freeholding "citizen" was far removed from the "democratic" republican ideal. Already by that time,

> the Roman ruling class had amassed private fortunes of staggering proportions, by means of exploitation and corruption at home (from their landed estates and urban slum tenements, usury, trading in property, government contracts, etc.) and even more spectacularly by the systematic plunder of their expanding Empire.[31]

In those circumstances, the almost incredible differential in wealth between the rich and the poor meant that the state was effectively an instrument of wealth. But throughout the period of the principate and the later empire, the position of the "free" peasantry and urban lower classes continued to decline until they were denuded of rights and reduced to serfdom.

In some ancient societies, a ruling class exercised power by establishing a strong centralized state which controlled the subject population. But the Roman oligarchs always opposed a strong state as a threat to their freedom of operation. During the period of the republic, wealthy members of the aristocratic senate took turns holding office for limited terms, and the institutional apparatus of the state remained relatively weak.

In these circumstances, personal power and position came to depend almost exclusively on personal wealth. In Roman society, the golden rule was very much that "he who has the gold rules." Rome had followed the example of Athens in realizing that the loyalty of the masses can be made more certain if people feel they are a part of the system. Consequently, they had imitated the exceptional Athenian move of extending citizenship to the free peasantry and the urban lower orders or plebeians. But largely because of the extreme concentration of wealth in the hands of a few, this broad citizenship did not, as in Athens, lead to democracy. The Roman republic remained always clearly oligarchic, and most "citizens" were no more than a passive potential constituency to be simultaneously exploited and courted by competing aristocrats. This arrangement, in turn, reinforced the emphasis on expanding personal wealth, especially in the form of landed property. So what we have at the end of the republic is the spectacle of a small class of aristocrats seeking to amass fortunes and to outpace their rivals in purchasing favor with the masses. To be sure, these oligarchs worked to hold together their fragile cohesion by a gentlemanly etiquette that emphasized personal collegiality. But as Rome's domination spread, so did competition among the aristocrats. Finally, even the form of republican government could not be sustained, and Julius Caesar "crossed the Rubicon" to establish the reality of an imperial state.

While Caesar's motives may have included a genuine sympathy for the common people and a desire to reform a corrupt system (along with a drive for personal power and wealth), the real effect of the development of the empire was to deepen the misery and impotence of the masses. From a political point of view, conditions had always made it very difficult for the lower orders to organize effectively or to work for reforms that would extend their rights and power. As a result, their focus had come to be on finding a "great man" who would be "on their side." This tendency was reinforced as individuals rose to assume imperial authority, and people were only too willing to leave their destinies in the hands of an Augustus, whom they saw as their champion and heir of their great hero, Julius Caesar.[32]

But more importantly, the concentration of wealth in so few hands and the development of a larger and larger stratum of unproductive mouths to feed led to a progressive deterioration of the economic position of the peasantry. And as their economic position declined, their legal and juridical status as citizens was progressively whittled away as well.

A number of factors conspired against the peasants. For one thing, the establishment of the Augustan principate in 27 B.C. brought with it a period of relative peace which, ironically, accelerated a weakening of the position of the peasantry. Peace meant also a decline in plunder and its spoils, and in particular it meant that fewer slaves were imported from outside the empire. This in turn meant that the ruling class had to turn to breeding to replenish their supply of slaves. But the breeding of slaves turned out to be a quite expensive business. It meant that female slaves were unavailable for work for extended periods, and it meant that many slave children had to be supported until they could be exploited. To this must be added the additional calculation that many women died in childbirth, and children often had the inconsideration to die in infancy before maturing to yield a return on investment.

Along with difficulties in maintaining a supply of slaves, there were also logistical problems associated with the sheer size of holdings. As land came to be concentrated in fewer and fewer hands and holdings became both hugely extensive and widely scattered (and the concentration of land was even greater in the western empire than in the east[33]), problems of management and overseeing became greater. But if slave labor is the whole basis of production, a great deal of oversight is necessary, since slaves must be watched and driven if they are to be exploited satisfactorily. On the other hand, if a system of leasehold tenancy (a sort of "sharecropping") can be developed, then even if the profits are not quite as great, poor "free" people can be used to work the land almost without outside supervision. And increasingly throughout the succeeding centuries, such a system was in fact put in place. Peasants rented or leased bits of land from absentee landlords, usually at wildly exorbitant rates. They then produced a crop, from which the landlord received his share.

> These are the voiceless toilers, the great majority—let us not forget it—
> of the population of the Greek and Roman world, upon whom was built
> a great civilisation which despised them and did all it could to forget
> them.[35]

And as the centuries progressed, the misery of this great majority only deepened.

Beginning in the first century A.D. and with explicit legal formulation in the second and third centuries, the legal rights of the poorer classes were gradually eliminated. By the time of the Severan emperors (193-235 A.D.), those rights had vanished altogether. When Caracalla, in the *Constitutio Antoniniana* of the early third century, extended citizenship to virtually all free inhabitants of the empire, his principal intent was probably to broaden the tax base. But he was, at the same time, tacitly acknowledging that citizenship had come to mean so little that the old distinction between citizens (*cives*) and foreigners (*peregrini*) was irrelevant. Both Greek and Roman aristocrats had always had their suspicions of democracy and "the mob," and those suspicions had found expression from Plato's *Republic* to Cicero's *De republica*.[36] But under the principate and later empire, the distinction between the "better" (*honestiores*) and the "humbler" (*humiliores*)—a distinction that coincided with that between the rich and the poor—became more and more explicit. To an increasing extent, there was one law for the propertied and another for the poor. By the early third century, legal rights were a function no longer of citizenship, but of membership in one of the senatorial, equestrian or curial families. While these rights had no doubt always been more theoretical than real, even the veneer of legality was stripped away. The lower classes lost their formal standing before the law, their testimony in court was accorded less weight, and it was they alone among free persons who could be flogged, tortured for evidence, shipped off to the mines or other forced labor, crucified, burned alive or thrown to the beasts.[37]

The problem of the "better" people was always to find a way to squeeze enough from the laboring population to support the growing number of idle mouths to be fed. First, there was the senate which, though numerically small, was immensely rich and absorbed a huge share of social wealth. Each senator had his sizeable household, his many slaves and other servants. And each senator also indirectly employed a large number of craftsmen and merchants who lived by supplying him with luxury goods. Then as the empire grew, the growth of a standing army and a large civil service added to the burden. From the fourth century, the growth of the now "official" Christian church was a special problem, with more bishops and clergy than there were civil servants and with thousands of monks and hermits to be fed. And finally, there was the dole of bread and pork to some 120,000 citizens of Rome and later to large numbers in Constantinople, Antioch, Alexandria and perhaps Carthage.[38]

For the rural poor, this meant increasing coercion and devastating usurpations. Brown quotes Galen from the second century, telling of how townspeople descended on the countryside at summer's end and took all the desirable food, leaving the "rustics" to survive on "unwholesome" chaff and insects, which led, Galen believed, to body ulcers, tumors, boils, scabs and leprosy.[39] The city-dwelling landlords were so effective in their exploitation of the peasantry that in times of famine, it was usually the countryside that starved because grain was stockpiled in the cities.[40]

Nor was there much recourse for the victims. Both economic and political life fostered direct personal dependence. The emperor was a remote and lofty figure, and despite the virtually absolute power of the emperor and his appointed governors, there was no efficient empire-wide system of justice or governance. So the local aristocracy, dominated by the great landowners, exercised almost total control over the working population. As taxes increased, especially as the land tax soared after 300 A.D., the burden was easily passed on to the peasantry, and legal remedies were ever less available. Military conscription tore the strongest young men from the land without warning. And all attempts to gain protection or redress of grievances had to pass through the *patronus*, the "great man" who was, as likely as not, the source of the most brutal oppression in the first place.[41]

The situation of the urban poor was only slightly better. To be sure, they were not so isolated as the peasantry and so were able to press collective demands through the threat of riot. But they were very poor, completely dependent on the aristocracy for both work and bread and so not in much position to do more than seek an illusory "champion" who might reward them.[42] As late as the second century, the few "leading families" of the towns vied with each other in providing temples, festivals and other amenities which brought some marginal benefits to the urban poor. But as the empire developed and huge scattered estates were acquired, local allegiances waned and even those few amenities became harder to come by.[43] As Lane Fox puts it in a scholarly understatement,

> Socially, such a model is bleak, with little to span the gap between the rich few and the dependent, or servicing, many: lower still lay the base of slave labour, in the household, the farms (here and there) and the humble trades. This bleakness, I believe, is true to life. The social pyramid tapered much more steeply than we might now imagine when first surveying the monuments and extent of the major surviving cities.[44]

This would seem the very least that could be said.

The fourth century saw the destruction of whatever could possibly remain of the "republican" illusions of the laboring classes and the beginning of an effort to set the "tapering pyramid" in stone. Beginning with the tax reform of Diocletian (284–305) and continuing through the fourth century, the entire agricultural working population was legally tied to the land on a hereditary basis, and there were efforts to bind similarly other types of workers as well.[45]

It is not clear to what extent the legal restrictions that were introduced constituted changes in the actual status of the laboring population. As Jones points out, Roman society had been largely static for several centuries, with sons generally following their fathers' way of life. The efforts of emperors beginning with Diocletian to tie certain classes to their hereditary functions may have been less a matter of imposing new limits than of trying to prevent the erosion of traditional ones. A labor shortage throughout the empire encouraged people to desert their old responsibilities and go in search of greener pastures elsewhere, and the ruling class was apparently more concerned to preserve a static system than to impose a new one.[46]

A number of factors seem to have interacted to bring about the situation. Perhaps the best place to begin is with the increasingly heavy burden of taxation that was imposed to maintain the empire, support the imperial bureaucracy and supply a large standing army. One consequence of the higher taxes was that it became impossible to make a profit on marginal land, and as soils were exhausted, more and more land was abandoned for this reason.[47] But the burden of taxation also directly increased the suffering of the agricultural population. Most taxes were passed on to the peasantry either directly or indirectly in the form of increasingly outrageous rents from the landowners. As a result, by the time peasants paid their rent and taxes, they did not have enough left to feed enough children to offset the increasingly high death rate. Large numbers of children were left to die of exposure or sold as slaves, and men married late, further reducing the number of children.[48]

In the cities, the condition of the urban poor who were needed in a variety of occupations was no better, and, in fact, the evidence seems to suggest that their mortality rate may have been even higher.[49] The resulting labor shortage, while perhaps not catastrophic by itself, did combine with other factors such as the breakdown of local traditions to encourage a good deal of mobility in search of better conditions. And it was this instability that the emperors seem to have been concerned to reduce through the imposition of legal bondage.

The binding of the poor was gradual and uneven, but the tendency was inexorably toward establishing an unfree laboring population. Diocletian initially tied all of the agricultural population to the land, but subsequent experience showed that many peasant proprietors had less incentive to move, so that the restriction came to be applied only to the descendants of tenants who were originally registered on a given estate. It was not until the end of the fifth century that deterioration reached the point of requiring that all free tenants be bound to their plots for thirty years. In the cities, the pace was slower—urban crafts-men were not bound to their trades until the end of the fourth century in the western empire and were never so bound in the east. Until early in the fifth century, serfs could escape bondage by joining the army. And throughout these centuries, the actual enforcement of the laws was uneven and sporadic.[50]

But even with these qualifications, it seems clear that the direction of Roman society, especially in the west, was toward the increasing bondage and immiseration of the vast majority who formed the labor-ing population. And it seems equally clear that despite occasional and scattered minor revolts, the condition of that majority was one of helpless dependency and accommodation to a system that appeared forever set in concrete.

When we turn to look at the other classes of Roman society at this period, the situation is more complex and fluid, so I shall attempt to sketch only its broad outlines and most basic tendencies.

For centuries, the unit of social and political life had been the city and its immediate environs. In each city, a hereditary ruling elite had enjoyed unquestioned control. In addition to sheer wealth, which was the real basis of their power, they largely controlled the scattered rural population as well as the urban poor. Only members of this class could conduct sacrifices or participate in public cult, while those of the lower classes, whether rural or urban, were reduced to the role of onlookers in dealings with the principal gods. The "leading families" of the towns (never more than five percent of the population) vied with each other in constructing temples and public buildings, erecting statues and funding festivals, games, human "hunts" in the arena and gladiatorial combats. Not only were the poor completely dependent upon them for charity, but their assured position in local life provided a structure of seemingly immemorial solidity.[51]

In the third and succeeding centuries, this picture changed markedly. The very small aristocracy comprising the senate (always less than six hundred families before the fourth century[52]) managed to corner a larger and larger share of social wealth, and they eventually formed a stratum of enormous wealth that set them quite apart from all others. The leading families of the cities continued to enjoy wealth and privilege, but the gap between them and the senatorial aristocracy grew ever greater, and, correspondingly, the large cities where senators lived grew in opulence, while smaller cities and towns shrank in importance. To give some idea of the disparity, Brown estimates that the income of a Roman senator could be one hundred and twenty times that of a courtier, six hundred times that of a merchant and twenty four thousand times that of a peasant.[53]

Above even the senate, there was the figure of the emperor who, despite retaining the old title of "leading citizen" (*princeps*), was in fact always an absolute monarch whose directives had the force of law.[54] And in the third and fourth centuries, the center of political life shifted more and more away from the cities and toward the imperial court. With its standing army to ward off barbarian incursions, its growing bureaucracy, its need for heavier and heavier taxes, the empire needed a leader of maximum prestige and authority. And while the centralization of power served the interests of the great senators with their huge scattered estates, it undermined even further the role of the local "leading families" in the many cities of the empire. With their relative share of wealth decreasing and their power and prestige undermined, the local aristocrats lost both the means and the incentive to continue their tradition of civic munificence.[55] Increasingly, they found themselves in a "no-win" situation. On the one hand, the senators who controlled most of the wealth were no longer tied to a "home town" and were able to avoid most of the responsibilities of local citizenship, such as provisioning the passing army, maintaining the corn supply, supporting the local cults, etc. On the other hand, the provincial governor appointed by the emperor had a firm grip on power and was in a position to gain most of the economic benefits that came with the exercise and corruption of power. In this situation, the local leading families were increasingly pressed by the central authorities to carry out services and to assume responsibility for everything from tax collection to the corn supply, while most of the prestige and power that had formerly accompanied those duties was siphoned away, along with the greatest share of wealth.[56] This situation in turn drove many of this local "curial" class to ruin and contributed to an even greater concentration of wealth in fewer hands.[57]

The crisis in the empire which led to strengthening the position of the emperor also had other effects that shifted the balance of forces once again. Already in the first quarter of the third century, the Persians consolidated an empire that posed a constant threat in the east. Barbarians probed along the Danube and the Rhine and launched raids from Britain to the Aegean. In 250 the emperor Decius was lost with his entire army. In 260 Antioch was captured and the emperor Valerian taken prisoner by the Persians. Ephesus, Miletus, Athens and Alexandria were all threatened. Of the great cities, only Rome and Carthage survived without attack, and by 271, Aurelian found it necessary to surround Rome itself with a wall.[58]

One consequence of this threat was that the old senatorial aristocracy, while it retained its wealth and a good deal of prestige, lost its hold on the political and military reins of the empire. During the period 235–284, there were twenty-five emperors, almost all created by the army, and when the dust had settled in 284, Diocletian, the son of a Dalmatian peasant, was emperor. About 260, the senatorial aristocracy was excluded from military commands, replaced usually by professional soldiers who had risen from the ranks. The army doubled in size to about 600,000 men, and a new bureaucracy grew to serve its needs. Emperors were usually strong military men, often from the lower or middle classes, and they appointed their own people to administer the empire and to direct affairs of state. Thus there developed, alongside the old senatorial aristocracy, a new "aristocracy of service," paid in both gold and land, at the top of Roman society. Some of these were appointed by the emperor to the senate, but many others joined what was still called the equestrian order (i.e. order of knights), but which was in fact a wealthy and privileged sector of the ruling class, still inferior to the senate in wealth, but not necessarily in power. As Brown puts it,

> The son of a pork butcher, of a small-town notary, of a cloakroom attendant in the public baths, became the praetorian prefects on whom the prosperity and stability of the eastern parts of the empire depended under Constantine and Constantius II.[59]

It is both important and difficult to keep a proper perspective on these changes. It is true that at the imperial court, this new aristocracy exercised power that displaced much of the influence of the senate. But at the same time, the great landowners went right on amassing ever larger estates and controlling the rural population.[60] Some imperial appointments, especially that of provincial governor, provided both considerable power and great opportunities to gain a fortune through both legal and corrupt means, and some of these offices came to be sold by the emperor at ever rising prices.[61] But as mentioned above, many of the new aristocrats were integrated into the senate, and senators, some of whom now never even visited Rome, still commanded the highest prestige.[62] In fact, by the time of Theodosius I (379–395), senators (along with Christian bishops) were replacing the army and regaining their position as the dominant influence at court.[63] And finally, it should be noted that this aristocracy of service was never a significant percentage of the total population and probably never numbered more than thirty thousand.[64]

Still, remembering that the senate numbered only about six hundred or so, the growth of a new sector of civil servants and professionals totaling thirty thousand was important. In many ways, members of this new elite were eager not to remake Rome in their image, but rather to integrate themselves among the gentlemen of "eternal Rome." So, for example, the ideals of classical education and culture were warmly embraced by the new administrative elite.[65] But at the same time, they were a dynamic sector, not attached to ancient home towns and not linked in the same way with the old religious cults that were controlled by the senate. They were more rootless than the old aristocrats, and the new order brought both real opportunities for advancement and a simultaneous loss of traditional "place" in a society founded on tradition.[66] It is against this background that we can understand Augustine as a more typical and less anomalous figure—son of a provincial family of modest means who was nonetheless a leading professor in Rome and Milan by the time he was thirty years old, already considering an aristocratic marriage and a provincial governorship as his next career move. And it may make it also less astonishing that he abandoned those plans in favor of joining what was, by his day, the most influential sector of the new aristocracy of service, the Christian priesthood.

This then is a sketch of later Roman society that seems to me to be supported by some of the best historical scholarship. It was, above all, a society sustained by the absolute dependency and economic exploitation of the vast majority by a very small minority. While nature, warfare and technological primitiveness imposed burdens on all, the almost incredible disparities of wealth and income meant that those burdens were distributed very unevenly. Almost no one conceived the possibility of alternative forms of social or economic life, so that it remained also an essentially static society in which ancient relations of production were taken for granted by most and enforced in the most direct way when even mildly challenged. But while it was, in these ways, a static society, it was also a society experiencing significant strains. The huge sprawling empire was increasingly and almost constantly threatened by barbarian incursions, a situation that reinforced the concentration of power in the hands of the emperor and the decline of local authority. The needs of this empire encouraged greater migration and mobility and opened up new possibilities for traders and professionals. The decline of local culture and a chronic labor shortage combined with new economic opportunities to encourage more mobility among even the lower classes, a threat to stability that had to be countered by intensified legal bondage. And finally, the imperial system created a new stratum of aristocrats whose status was tied more to office than to ancient title and who were clearly the most dynamic stratum of the society. And when, in the early fourth century, the emperor Constantine set in motion the process by which the small Christian sect was transformed into the "official" religion of the empire, Christian priests and bishops became at once key members of this dynamic stratum and also guardians of the stability of the social order.

It was in these conditions that the religious consciousness discussed in Section I above took its various forms. And there were, in fact, a great many religious forms. The empire incorporated many ancient cultures and was in contact with many more. Eastern religious forms were imported, adapted and often combined with traditional cult into a host of hybrids. Competing philosophical schools developed competing forms of spiritual life. And new cults developed as one or another of the traditional gods was elevated to the status of Supreme God.

Despite this great diversity, however, it does seem that there was one central struggle that was clearly pivotal in establishing the ideological direction of the society—the struggle between traditional pagan cult and Christianity. While there were many religious forms in parts of the empire, and while a great deal of experimentation took place among intellectuals, the fact remains that for the vast majority of both the ruling classes and the laboring masses, there was no serious competitor to pagan cult until the emergence of Christianity in the fourth century. In fact, almost all religious forms except Judaism and Christianity co-existed quite comfortably with traditional cultic practice. But once Christianity did gain imperial endorsement, it not only challenged pagan cult, but replaced it entirely over the next two centuries. Therefore, I want to close Part One by looking briefly at the alignment of forces in that struggle against the background of the composition of Roman society that I have just discussed.

III. The Ideological Landscape

Most would agree that the pivotal year in the ideological struggle of the later empire was 312 A.D. In that year, the emperor Constantine threw in his lot with Christianity and set in motion the process by which the new religion and its church would become the central ideology and institution of western civilization.

That Constantine's conversion was indeed a crucial factor in the triumph of Christianity seems about as clear as can be hoped for in such cases. The evidence is scanty for determining just how strong Christianity was prior to Constantine, and some scholars believe that it was already a powerful force, at least in some parts of the empire.[67] But others are convinced that the empire remained overwhelmingly pagan at the beginning of the fourth century. Lane Fox, estimates, for example, that as late as 250 A.D., Christians comprised no more than two percent of the population and that as late as 300 A.D., they were probably no more than five percent.[68] And Jones argues that while there were Christians in most cities and many smaller towns, it was only in Egypt and Africa that significant inroads had been made among the rural majority.[69] Furthermore, it seems clear that in the so-called great persecution under Diocletian at the turn of the fourth century, many, and perhaps most, Christians had lapsed and taken "loyalty oaths" to the pagan gods.[70] Nor does there seem to be much evidence of avid Christian missionary zeal.[71] Yet by 341, the emperor Constans had issued an initial decree abolishing pagan sacrifices.[72] By the late fourth century, Christianity was the majority religion, and Christian bishops had become dominant figures in most cities and many towns.[73] Symbolic of the change is certainly the fact that by 390, the bishop Ambrose was able to demand and obtain public penance from the emperor Theodosius after a massacre in Thessalonica.[74]

From the time of Constantine, imperial policy, which in the past had always more or less actively supported traditional pagan practice, now more or less actively supported Christianity. The only significant exception would be the brief reign of Julian (361–363), which might in fact have been crucial had it not been cut short. Not only did Constantine and his successors endorse and practice the new faith, but they acted to support it in the most concrete ways. Christians, often even from the lower classes, were given preference in imperial appointments, and it soon became obvious that one's ambitions were more apt to be realized if one were of the emperor's faith.[75] In the twenty-five years between his conversion and his death, Constantine built huge churches from Rome to the holy land, and many of his successors followed suit.[76] Also under Constantine, there began the granting of large subsidies to the Christian churches, a practice that continued at some level (except during Julian's tenure) until at least the end of the sixth century.[77] Both because of these subsidies and because of gifts and endowments of land from the faithful, the church became immensely wealthy, and bishops received incomes matching or even exceeding those of provincial governors.[78] Whereas pagan priesthoods had been part-time offices, usually handled on a voluntary rotating basis by notables, the salary bill of the Christian church was far heavier than that of the empire itself.[79] And, finally, it might be mentioned that from the time of Constantine, the emperors saw the need for a united Christian church and did all they could to promote and even enforce doctrinal unity and to punish heresy and schism.[80] The emperors took an active role early on in attacking the Arian heresy, and in the fifth century, imperial power was brought to bear in forcibly suppressing the Donatist schism in Africa and in driving Pelagianism out of Rome.[81]

At the same time, paganism fell on increasingly hard times. Constantine himself was tolerant of paganism and harmed it mainly by withdrawing support, which, however, did make it harder and harder for pagan cults to obtain needed resources.[82] Still there were some laws restricting paganism even under Constantine, and restrictions slowly increased until in 391, the emperor Theodosius issued laws banning all pagan sacrifice and ceremony.[83] By 407, non-Christians were clearly outlaws, and MacMullen quotes a decree of that year, stating that

> If any images stand even now in temples and shrines...they shall be torn from their foundations....The buildings themselves of the temples which

are situated in cities or towns shall be vindicated to public use. Altars shall be destroyed in all places.[84]

In the last years of the fourth century, there was a wave of violent persecution against both pagans and Jews, with destruction of temples and synagogues.[85] Augustine himself preached a sermon (*Serm.* 24) in the year 399 calling for the annihilation of everything pagan, a speech which likely provoked riots in at least one African city.[86] As Brown remarks,

> The Christian congregations of the 380s wanted a "Christian" empire, purged of the heavy legacy of the gods, and ruled by an emperor who shared their prejudices against Jews, heretics and pagans.[87]

However, while Christianity fairly quickly gained the upper hand, it would be a mistake to see the victory as complete or easy. For example, in the mid-sixth century, Justinian (527–565) enacted legislation prohibiting pagans from holding chairs as professors and denying them the capacity to make wills, receive inheritances or testify in court. And in 529, he found it necessary to order all pagans to accept baptism on pain of confiscation and exile.[88] Such activity would suggest that there must still have been pagans aplenty to be concerned about. And we know that among intellectuals in particular, Christianity was slow to convince, and many of them clung to their pagan philosophical-religious systems for a very long time.[89]

What this tells us is that while Christians did, in the fourth century, succeed, by "flattery and battery alike,"[90] in driving paganism underground and in Christianizing the empire, the course by no means ran smooth, and there were strong competing forces at work. I think it will be a help both in understanding those forces and in understanding the project of Augustinianism to take a brief look at the struggle of religious ideologies against the background of some of the conditions discussed in Section II. In particular, I would like to look at the appeal of paganism and of Christianity to the various sectors of the population that were identified above.

Let me begin by discussing those at the extremes of the class spectrum, the rural poor, on the one hand, and the senatorial aristocracy, on the other. In doing so, what we find is that among those groups, the oldest and most traditional forms of religious consciousness remained most powerful, though for different reasons.

The rural poor, both free and unfree, remained loyal to their old gods and were only weaned from them slowly and painfully over long centuries. And even when they came to Christianity, they brought many of their customs and practices with them, simply adapting them to a Christian framework and interpretation. As noted above, it seems that at the beginning of the fourth century, Christianity had made few inroads in the countryside, and the peasantry was always slow to shift its allegiance. Tied to the land, victimized by forces natural and human and seldom traveling more than thirty miles from home, that vast majority whose labor moved the imperial machine remained steadfastly with the tried and true protectors of hearth and home—the gods of wind, sun and rain, of fertility and renewal.[91] For all its ignorance and backwardness, the peasantry remained rooted in a kind of common-sense religious "realism" that saw the gods, in straightforward terms, as unpredictable and wrathful powers to be propitiated, implored or (if one could find others yet more powerful) defeated. As also noted above, Augustine's Africa would be the greatest exception to this rule. Yet even in Africa, as one moved south from the coast, non-Christian cult (especially the cult of Saturn) remained powerful, and where Christianity did prevail, it was more likely to be that of the Donatist schism, rather than of Catholicism.[92]

At the other end of the scale, the senatorial aristocracy of the west also remained firmly rooted in traditional religion. The Roman senate was the keeper of ancient values and held a monopoly of public cult in the metropolis. Its members filled the civic priesthoods, and they were always conscious of the role of cult and the maintenance of religious tradition in perpetuating existing relations and in cementing their own position.[93] It was they who built the altars and temples, commissioned the statues of gods, performed the public sacrifices and financed religious festivals. In their role as priests, they were also the interpreters of the oracles and the transmitters of divine communications.

For these old aristocrats, the Christians, with their uncouth and inelegant books and their God who had died the most ignominious death by crucifixion, represented barbarism at its worst. And yet, they thought, these Christians, unlike other cults, did not wish merely to move their God in among others. They demanded the complete abandonment of the gods and of the ancient rites that had protected Rome for centuries.

As Jones remarks, for a Roman senator, it was not easy to swallow the Christian view of Jupiter Optimus Maximus as a malignant demon.[94]

As the most conservative element of society, much of the senatorial aristocracy of the west clung to traditional religion long after Christianity had effectively won the day. In the eastern empire, where both the imperial court and the senate were centered in Constantinople and where the most influential senators were imperial appointees who had risen through the ranks of service, the senate was Christianized as soon as the empire became Christian. But in the west, the emperor moved from place to place and his court (*comitatus*) moved with him, while the senatorial aristocracy continued to control Rome and its cultural and religious traditions. As a result, the Roman senate remained largely pagan down to the end of the fourth century.[95] The staying power of ancient cult is clearly seen in the intensity of the emperor Julian's struggle to re-establish traditional cult in the mid-fourth century and in the warm reception his efforts received.

By the same token, the cultural leaders of the empire, the philosophers and other intellectuals who depended on senatorial patronage, were also slow to adopt Christianity. In Part Two we shall have more to say about Platonist and other philosophers. For the moment, suffice it to say that the philosophical systems which sought the ultimate good and contact with the "divine" had no difficulty at all in accommodating themselves to traditional cult and in viewing the gods in symbolic or representational terms. But the exclusive Christian sect, with its crude scriptures and its denigration of human wisdom, was abhorrent to many of them.[96]

As with all things, these generalizations must be qualified. There were a few Christian senators even as early as 250, and once the emperor was Christian, those senators who lived outside Rome itself were much more apt to be Christian.[97] In the fourth century, there were prominent aristocrats such as Augustine's mentor Ambrose, who not only joined the Christians, but became leading officers of the church. And in Part Two, we shall have a look at some intellectuals who were attempting to adapt the Platonist philosophy to Christianity and who formed Augustine's immediate circle of friends. But even with all these exceptions, it still seems fair to say that in the ideology of the western aristocracy, the gods were only slowly displaced by the

Christian god as the bulwark of Roman culture and the support of "eternal Rome."

But what can be said of the religious consciousness of other sectors of society? What of slaves, both urban and rural? What of the urban poor living on the dole (in those few cities where there was such), private charity and occasional wage labor? What of the craftsmen, shopkeepers and service providers of the cities? What of the traders in slaves and other merchandise? What of the old curial order of the cities, still well-to-do but dwarfed by the obscene wealth of the great landowners and increasingly imposed upon by a host of official duties and exactions? And, from the middle of the third century, what of that new aristocracy of service attached to the emperor? Here the picture is both more obscure and more complex.

To begin once more from the "bottom," it must be said that information on the beliefs and practices of the most oppressed members of society is extremely scanty. Certainly after 312, there was a great deal of pressure on both slaves and free tenants of landowners to convert to Christianity when their masters converted.[98] And no doubt most slaves, those most vulnerable to such pressure, did in fact follow, more or less passively, the religious practices of their masters. Where there are known exceptions, it is much more common to find Christian masters with pagan slaves than to find pagan masters with Christian slaves.[99] As a general rule, conversion to Christianity offered no advantages whatever to slaves. Christianity never challenged slavery or made any significant effort to free slaves. Christians seem usually to have assumed (and here Augustine is typical) that social status is irrelevant to spiritual worth, so that believers were urged to remain in the station in which they found themselves.

> Like the Stoics, these Christian leaders began from a principle of the equality of man, yet argued that worldly differences of status should continue undisturbed. The greater slavery was man's slavery to his passions.[100]

Christians, even bishops, continued to have slaves and usually to oppose emancipation. Often church rules forbade baptism to slaves unless they had their masters' permission, and slaves of pagans who sought Christian teaching were urged not to offend their masters. Monks were cautioned against giving refuge to runaway slaves. And while it is true that runaway slaves could sometimes gain sanctuary in a church, it is also true that in the pagan empire, a runaway could take refuge at any statue of the emperor or within certain temples.[101] So most slaves, to the extent that they participated in any religious practice at all, likely followed the practice of their masters.

The "humbler" free persons of the cities present a somewhat different picture. As with all sectors of the population, the vast majority of these people also remained loyal to the traditional gods until well into the fourth century. But here we do find a really significant Christian presence fairly early on.

When we speak of the "humble" urban population, we are including both those mired in the deepest poverty and others whose skills or occupation left them still dependent but of at least some modest means. And when it comes to religious practice, these groups, to some extent, shared a common situation. Most town dwellers had long since been reduced to mere spectators in relation to public cult. And as the meaning of citizenship was undermined and the autonomy of individual cities waned, attachment to the traditional gods of one's city was further loosened. Furthermore, the continual hardening of class lines made it increasingly obvious that traditional cult belonged to the well-to-do and served their interests.[102]

If we focus on the very poorest members of the urban population, there do seem to have been some factors that attracted some of their number to Christianity. There is, for example, the sheer physical fact that the urban poor lived crowded in on each other, a setting that provided many opportunities to hear about the new Christian sect and to interact with Christians in a more immediate way that helped undermine pre-conceptions about them as dangerous atheists.[103] Secondly, it cannot be unimportant that the poor were at least not excluded from the Christian community and that they were even received, at least in theory, as equal souls in need of salvation. And then also there must be added the fact that Christians did make a virtue of charity and frequently were a source of real charitable benefit to those of their members who were poor.[104]

On the other hand, the appeal of Christianity to the urban poor should be kept in perspective. For one thing, Christian churches, with their obligation to charity, were often rather closed and exclusive groups who were very leery of taking on too many empty bellies to be filled.[105] Secondly, while Christianity did emphasize the equality of all souls in the eyes of God, this was done in a way that left actual inequalities in this world quite untouched. While Christians often commented on the temptations and burdens of wealth, there were few Christian attacks on property rights as such, and in fact, extremes of wealth and poverty became even greater after the empire adopted Christianity. As Lane Fox remarks,

> Christianity had never preached an outright social revolution. There was no "liberation theology," no sanction for a direct assault on the forms of social dependence and slavery....Distinctions of rank and degree multiplied [in the Christian Empire] and the inequalities of property widened.[106]

So while Christianity did draw some early converts from the urban poor, it seems wrong to see it as based primarily in that sector.

It seems more likely that Christianity had its greatest appeal not among the very poorest Romans, but among those still "humble" people whose status was perhaps most ambivalent. Since traditional religion had been overwhelmingly centered in the various cities and was such a "hometown" affair, the increase in migration in the third and fourth centuries tore many people loose from their roots and left them essentially godless, even as it destroyed the enveloping support of traditional communities.[107] Brown finds in this situation an "anxiety" that may have been relieved by Christianity:

> It is precisely the men who were being uprooted and cast adrift from their old life who provided the background to the anxious thoughts of the religious leaders of the late second century. The successful business-man, the freedman administrator, the woman whose status and educa-tion had slowly improved, found themselves no longer citizens of their accustomed town, but "citizens of the world"; and many, it appears, were finding that the world was a lonely and impersonal place. It is among such people that we find the Christians. By 200 the Christian communities were not recruited from among the "humble and oppressed": they were groupings of the lower middle classes and of the respectable artisans of the cities. Far from being deprived, these people had found fresh opportunities and prosperity in the Roman empire: but they had also had to devise ways of dealing with the anxieties and uncertainties of their new position.[108]

The sort of psychological states here supposed are difficult to document and may be viewed with some skepticism. But even if we leave aside assumptions about mass anxiety, the fact remains that Christianity did have much to offer this sector of the society. It offered a tight, disciplined and often intensely loyal community to people who had lost community supports. It did foster an abstract ideology of equality and was open to persons of all classes. It offered an empire-wide community, with a rapidly developing institutional base in the church, to people who had lost the identity of the home town. And it would seem that, in fact, the core of church membership was drawn from these humbler free persons, ranging from shopkeepers and merchants down to cobblers and wool workers.[109] For many such persons, Brown's further assessment is likely correct:

> The appeal of Christianity still lay in its radical sense of community: it absorbed people because the individual could drop into a miniature community whose demands and relations were explicit.[110]

In other sectors of the population, the appeal of Christianity was limited. It seems to have made few inroads in either the army or the leading families of the towns and cities prior to the fourth century. Army life was filled with pagan rituals and was only slowly Christianized by Christian emperors. And among the well-born curial sector of the towns, there seem to have been only occasional converts, though there were, from time to time, local notables who attempted to escape some of the increasing burdens of civic responsibility by giving their goods to the church and pursuing the life of a hermit, priest or bishop.

An interesting sidelight that might be mentioned is that well-to-do women were drawn to Christianity in disproportionate numbers. Women were usually married early, often to older men, so widowhood was the norm for women of middle age. Both custom and Roman law put heavy pressure on such women to undertake second marriages. Christianity, on the other hand, gave both widowhood and virginity an honored status, and the church was always eager to welcome women, especially those bringing large bequests with them. In fact, Lane Fox estimates that by the third century, women constituted a clear majority of Christians.[111]

Finally, a word may be said about that new sector of the ruling class, the "aristocracy of service" whose members owed their status to imperial appointment and who directly managed the affairs of the empire. Even though this is a small percentage of the Roman population, it is clearly of first importance as the sector that led the Christianization of the empire.

On the one hand, it is not surprising that Christianity became dominant among these people in the fourth century. They were, after all, most directly linked to the emperor, and after Constantine, the emperor was Christian. But it seems likely that Constantine himself was influenced by members of his court in his turn toward Christianity, in which case Christianity must already have exercised some appeal among them. And so it is of interest to ask what there was about Christianity that may have appealed both to the emperor and to those who most directly served imperial interests.

In light of the discussion above, it is not difficult to speculate on a number of factors that may have made Christianity appealing to these people. For a group attempting to impose a single empire-wide order and overcome localism, Christianity was a welcome alternative to traditional religion. It had no ties to any particular cities, shrines or places. It not only adopted the ideal of a single world community of believers, but it had already progressed far beyond any other cult in giving institutional expression to this ideal in the form of the church. For a new elite "on the make," Christianity provided a religious alternative to the old cults that were under monopolistic control of the senate and leading families of the towns. For a group of people who were constantly on the move both consolidating the empire and defending against incursions, Christianity offered a "portable" religion that could be practiced everywhere and a community of believers scattered across the Roman world, with at least a small congregation in most towns and cities.

None of this is meant to suggest that the decision by either the emperor or his *comitatus* to accept Christianity was at all cynical or even consciously pragmatic. In line with what has been said above, I would suggest that genuineness or honesty of belief is not an issue here at all. Everyone knew of the existence and activity of the gods. The selection of a god to whom to pay cult was in fact often a matter of one's special needs or interests, but that did not mean that the profession of belief was in any way insincere. While the Christian god was more jealous than most in demanding exclusive devotion, that did not mean that his devotees doubted the existence of other gods. And while the Christians did indeed emphasize goals—such as remission of sin and blissful life after death—that were not so important in many other cults, many who turned to the Christian god did so for quite traditional reasons—to win good fortune and ward off ill fortune. And if the Christian god proved to be more powerful than others, why would one not consider paying him cult?

The blending of sincere devotion and calculation of interest seems to have been present in Constantine himself. When Constantine crossed the Alps in 311/312 to press his imperial claims, it certainly appears that part of the appeal of Christianity lay in a keenly felt need for divine protection. In his push to lay claim to the title of Augustus of the west, Constantine was opposed most immediately by Maxentius, son of Diocletian's fellow-Augustus, Maximian. Maxentius was at that time claiming the western empire from his headquarters in Rome itself. This rival of Constantine was appealing to the oracles and Sibylline prophecies, and there is some evidence that the oracles may have been less than optimistic regarding Constantine's chances of success, should he march on Italy.[112] Constantine was pretty clearly in need of his own protecting divinity, and for him the Christian god would be a not unlikely candidate. There were probably Christians in his family, and his father Constantius had displayed devotion to a supreme god, perhaps Apollo, the great solar divinity. Furthermore, the Spanish Christian bishop Ossius was already in Constantine's company at this time and may well have had some influence on him. It is against this background that we can view the later reports of Christian writers that Constantine saw his famous vision of a cross in the noonday sky inscribed with the words "By this, conquer," which was followed that same night by a dream in which Christ instructed him as to the symbol to be emblazoned on the shields of his soldiers.[113]

Having interpreted his vision and dream in Christian terms and acted in obedience to them, Constantine quickly received the strongest possible confirmation that his devotion was not misplaced. He not only defeated Maxentius at the Milvian Bridge, but he found his new God leading him to victory after victory. As Lane Fox remarks: "The proof of a god is best found in his protection, and before long, Constantine was amply rewarded."[114] By 324 he had defeated his last rival, Licinius, who was actually a persecutor of Christians, had established secure control of the empire and had managed to establish a period of peace and stability.

In April of 325, the triumphant Constantine delivered a speech to Christian bishops assembled in council at Antioch. Lane Fox has argued for the basic authenticity of available texts of this oration and has discussed it at length.[115] The overwhelming focus of the oration is on God's providence in leading Constantine to "liberate" the empire and God's vengeance in bringing horrible fates upon the persecutors of Christians. Amid a potpourri of odd theological opinions (many that would certainly have been heretical coming from lesser lips), signs and prophecies (including prophecies of Christianity that he found in the poet Virgil), it is clear that what most impressed Constantine was that his God was a "winner."

In summary, then, it seems to me that Christianity held a number of appeals for the emperor and those who served imperial interests, and there seems no reason not to think that a number of influences were at work. While there is certainly an element of fortuitousness in the fact that the emperor threw his support to this particular religion, it is also true that Christianity had strengths that recommended its adoption. It seems pointless to ask what would have happened had Constantine (or some subsequent emperor) not turned to Christianity. What one can say is that there were ambiguities at work that left open many possibilities. One of those ambiguities is that while the Christians were still a small minority with only a small foothold in the ruling class, they were yet the most dynamic cult of the empire, growing more rapidly than any other and with greater institutional unity than any other. And another of those ambiguities is that while some Christian theologians may have seen their sect as radically different from pagan cults, there is no reason to think that ordinary believers, including the emperor and his court, saw it in that way. Given the depth and pervasiveness of religious consciousness, the decision to pay cult to the Christian god may have involved a smoother transition than seems possible to us, looking back from the vantage of later Christian development. The sharp difference between the practice and aims of paganism and those of Christianity, which seems so clear today, may have been by no means so clear in the fourth century. In fact, it is the explicit aim of Augustine's *City of God* to establish that difference and drive it home to an audience which was still very unclear about it.

Leaving aside speculations about what *might* have happened, the fact is that Constantine did turn to Christianity, and once the religion established itself throughout the empire during his long reign, the pattern of religious allegiances began to shift fairly rapidly. While Constantine himself was more inclined to promote his own new god than to do battle with the old gods, persuasion and promotion were soon linked to persecution in Christianizing the empire. As Lane Fox remarks: "Force alone could not make converts, but it did weigh heavily with the undecided, and by the lack of divine reprisals it did show that the 'anger' of the gods was no match for Christ."[116] Paganism hung on in the senate, but even there the picture was mixed, and the handwriting was on the wall. It was at the urging of Ambrose, senatorial aristocrat turned bishop, that Theodosius disestablished the state cults, destroyed pagan statues and converted temples into churches. And while the senate did, in the later fourth century, manage to push the army aside and re-establish its influence at court, it found itself sharing that influence with Christian bishops, while in most towns of the empire the bishop clearly was the dominant figure.[117]

Summary

These then are some of the features that stand out for me as relevant when I look, through the eyes of leading historians, at the world in which Augustine came to maturity and developed his theology. While paganism still retained some real strength and while Christianity continued to compete with both paganism and other cults for the hearts and minds of the population, it was a competition whose outcome was already a foregone conclusion. In a world in which no one doubted the ubiquitous presence and activity of the gods, the Christian God and his church moved inexorably into a position of exclusive dominance.

The development of religious ideology in the fourth century mirrored these conditions. In particular, the tendency was for different sections of the ruling elite to move toward an accommodation in ideology. On the one hand, increasing numbers of aristocrats and the intellectuals who served them began to find ways of adapting their spiritual needs and religious philosophies to Christian belief and practice. And on the other hand, Christian thinkers assumed a new role as ideologists of the empire and so worked to develop a theology that could, at one and the same time, strike a responsive chord in the souls of gentlemen, win the allegiance of the masses and provide a unifying institutional prop for the existing social and economic order of the disintegrating empire.

I would not, for a moment, suggest that anyone consciously and intentionally set out to develop an ideology for these purposes. As already noted, it is very hard to explain how it is that thinkers who are working honestly to interpret their experience and to follow questions where they lead nonetheless end up with a system that seems almost consciously designed to serve certain purposes. Still it seems to me that this does happen, and I think that it happened with much of the philosophical and theological thought of the fourth century. More particularly, in what follows, I want to look at the extent to which Augustine's thought is itself an example of a pursuit of truth that ended as the dominant ideology of a social order.

Augustine's own belief, thought and practice were shaped first in the confusion of evolving tendencies in his provincial homeland, later in the rarified atmosphere of aristocratic soul-searching in Milan, and finally in the hard day-to-day struggle to consolidate the power and universal sway of the church. At every step, he was engaged in the most intense effort not to fabricate an ideology that would serve the interests of a ruling elite or to dupe the masses into subservience, but to probe the depths of his soul and to face truth as he saw it honestly and courageously. Yet the system he ended up with was certainly not the only possible Christian theology, and it was, in fact, a theology that was especially suited to serve some of those ends. The development of his basic ideas has been chronicled countless times, beginning with his own *Confessions*. But in Part Two, I want to take another look at that development as a sort of case study of the way in which dominant ideas are internalized and developed.

Part Two

THE SEARCH FOR GOD

In Part One, we saw that the idea of God is the absolutely fundamental one in Augustinian ideology, and we reviewed the general context within which religious ideology played its dominant role in the late ancient world. In Part Three, we shall see in more detail how the essentials of Augustinianism flow from the conception of God that he finally adopted. But first, in Part Two, I want to look at the evolution of that idea in Augustine's early life and at some of the forces that shaped that evolution.

It seems to me that there are three basic reasons for the triumph of Augustinian Christianity over competing ideologies in the late Roman world. One of those is certainly that it was an ideology uniquely suited to serve the needs of the dominant classes of Roman society. It provided a cosmic justification for the existing hierarchical order as rooted in human sinfulness and divine justice, and it encouraged every person to accept her or his place in that order. It fostered unquestioning acceptance of the will of God as conveyed by his church, which was now completely allied with the emperor and the ruling class. And it called on the oppressed to regard their present misery as of no account and to focus attention exclusively on the long-range welfare of their immortal souls.

A second reason for the success of Augustinianism was that it was, while not without its own problems, far more consistent, coherent and complete than any competing ideology. A question frequently asked about Augustinianism is: "Why were people willing to accept such bleak conclusions?" And in Part Three, I shall suggest that at least part of the answer to that question is that those conclusions followed from commonly accepted premises in a way that made them more compelling than any alternative system of ideas.

But of course, those conclusions would not have been accepted were it not for the fact that there were indeed commonly shared premises from which they followed. And I believe that one of the most important of Augustine's accomplishments was his success in establishing a conception of God that was compelling not only for most parties to theological discussion, but for most Christians of whatever rank and education. And this, I would suggest, established Augustinianism on a solid basis that made it extremely difficult to reject. Augustine's ability to capture what we might call the "core" ideas of the culture regarding the nature of God and of God's relation to mankind is what I would offer as the third basic reason for the victory of Augustinian ideology.

In Part One there was some discussion of the basic elements of religious consciousness during this period. It will be remembered, first of all, that there was no question whatever of the existence of gods and that divine activity was part of the commonsense obviousness of everyday life. We saw furthermore that the gods were, on the one hand, a source of fear, and, on the other, a source of protection and favor. Given this basic outlook, it becomes clear what features are most to be wished for in one's gods: they are power and reliability. If the gods are to be sources of favor and protection, they must have the power to deliver, and if they are to be propitiated, their demands must be consistent and their wrath must not be capricious. And of course, if one can believe that there is a single god of unlimited power who dispenses favor to all and only those who are faithful to him according to strict principles of justice (hopefully, tempered by mercy), the deepest needs of such a consciousness would seem to be met.

But while such a conception of a supreme god may have been necessary to serve as the basis for a general religious ideology, it was not sufficient for an ideology that could win the allegiance of the ruling classes. For centuries there had been developing, alongside and amalgamated with this basic religious outlook, another and more "sophisticated" outlook which had deeply permeated the educated strata. This more rarified world-view was utterly alien not only to the vast majority of the laboring classes, but even to many members of the upper classes (including many emperors) who had little time for speculation and were busy in the administration and defense of the empire. For this reason, it is going too far to paint the entire mental and spiritual life of the society with this brush or to characterize this entire period as an "age of anxiety."[118] Still this outlook did have deep roots in the educated elite of Rome, and it served as an ideal for most of the ruling class. And because of its prestige, at least some of its essential features would have to be included in any religious ideology that aimed to win the hearts and minds of the "best" men.

This elite world-view took a number of forms, and we shall have occasion to look at some of its variations as the discussion progresses. For the moment, let me mention just a few of its more common features.

At least since the first century A.D., many educated aristocrats and intellectuals had found the pragmatic religious consciousness of the masses inadequate. While they still participated in traditional cult aimed at enlisting the aid and avoiding the anger of the gods, they looked beyond it for something more. No doubt part of the reason for this was that wealth and leisure freed them from the immediate survival concerns that absorbed most people and so allowed new and less primary preoccupations. In particular, they were able to reflect on the seeming unreliability of the gods to ward off all evils and on the fact that human life, even at its most comfortable, remained subject to anxiety, suffering, pain and death.

There developed among these privileged few a different religious consciousness. They shared a sense of the human mind or soul as trapped in a body which is not its proper home. There was a feeling that the true abode of the soul is another realm, apart from the material world, and in close relation with a world soul or *Logos*, a realm of changeless and eternal reality. The soul, somehow "lost" or "fallen" from its proper home, has as its task to "free" itself from entanglements in this material world with its bodily needs and passions and to return to an original unity with that eternal reality.

This basic outlook was embodied in a number of varying accounts of the structure of reality and in a variety of programs for the liberation of the soul. It took root in pagan culture in some forms of Stoicism and varieties of Platonism; in the Jewish tradition in a figure such as Philo of Alexandria; and in the Christian tradition in the thought of a figure such as Origen, the most important Christian theologian prior to Augustine.

Those who worked within this outlook were frequently grouped together under the generic label "philosophers" or "lovers of wisdom," since in most cases there was agreement that the liberation of the soul must come somehow through a pursuit of "knowledge" within the soul that would re-establish the soul's link with eternal Wisdom. By the fourth century, it had long since been established that the "highest" and "best" life for a man was one centered in "philosophy" and the leisured pursuit of "Wisdom." And virtually every aristocrat and intellectual yearned for an existence in leisured retreat (or *otium* as it was called) to seek the liberation of the soul.

When Augustine left his native Africa to take his place among the intellectual elite in Rome and Milan, he found this outlook dominant among both pagan and Christian aristocrats. These were the ideological "gatekeepers" of the empire, and it was just unthinkable that any ideological system could win acceptance unless it spoke to their intuitions and needs.

In the following pages, I want to suggest that Augustine's search for an adequate conception of his God was in fact a search for a God that could meet both of the varieties of religious need mentioned above. He wanted a God of power and reliability who could be approached by the faithful in simple supplication and with the promise of reward for prayerful submission and service. But he also wanted a God who ordered the world by the divine *Logos*, whose eternal "light" was still to be found deep within the fallen soul and who promised those who "returned" to him the eternal bliss that comes only from the immediate vision of eternal Wisdom. And I would suggest that the irresistibility of his program rested largely on the fact that he was seen to have succeeded in basing his thought on a conception of God that accomplished both of these purposes. Whether or not his God does manage to blend all of these features into a consistent whole is another issue and one that will need some further discussion. But even if he was not altogether successful, two things do seem clear: first, that his conception of God struck a responsive chord in persons of all classes and promised to meet a variety of religious needs; and second, that there was no alternative conception that appealed so broadly or that met so many needs.

I believe that in the end, it was the power of this conception of God that did most to insure the success of Augustinianism. Though it cannot be argued within the scope of this work, I would suggest that the efforts of those, such as Pelagius and Julian of Eclanum, who attempted to avoid some of the conclusions of Augustinianism that seem such an assault on human dignity foundered on the fact that they felt compelled to accept the conception of God from which many of those conclusions followed. And when it turned out that Augustinian ideology was uniquely suited to serve as rationale and justification of a rigid social order and an imperial church, that seemed to many a further confirmation of the correctness of Augustine's conception of God.

By tracing Augustine's struggle to arrive at a satisfying conception of his God, I hope to make it clear that he was never engaged in any conscious effort to "cook up" a conception of God that could be "sold" to anyone or that could be used as an instrument of control or manipulation. Nothing could be further from the truth. Those who develop ideologies seldom see themselves as developing ideologies, and Augustine is no exception. In fact, what makes Augustine's development so interesting is that he developed an idea of God that would meet certain needs precisely because he felt those needs directly within himself. As a provincial small-town African, he brought with him the basic religious needs of the uneducated masses steeped in traditional cult. And as a young intellectual "on the make," he early developed the aspirations and needs of the aristocratic elite that he yearned to join. So in searching his own intuitions and sensibilities to find his God, Augustine was, at the same time, acting as a good representative of the society of the western empire in its search for a guiding ideology.

The development of Augustine's conception of God is fairly easy to trace because it was for him such an intensely self-conscious struggle. At least from the time of his later teenage years, Augustine himself clearly takes it as his most important task to develop a "right" conception of the nature of God. His progress toward that "right" conception consisted largely of the adoption and testing of a series of myths until he found one adequate for his intellectual, emotional and spiritual needs.

In putting it this way, I do not mean to deny that Augustine's search may have been guided by some "sense of the divine" or general awareness of spiritual reality. Augustine himself clearly believed that there is some sort of awareness of God implanted within every human soul, and he did come to see some aspects of his inner experience as manifesting the "light of God" within him (see, for example, *Conf.* VII. 10). I shall take no position on the question whether there is any such sense. What concerns us here is not any such general awareness, but the *content* of the concept of God, and it is very clear that Augustine never claims to have had any experience which would reveal to him that content. As we shall see, he spent many years working to develop an adequate concept of the nature of God, and even though he was confident that God was somehow "present within" him, this did not provide him with much content that would help him in that task. For this reason, in looking at the development of his concept of God, we can set aside the question whether there is a "spiritual dimension" of human existence or an innate awareness of the divine.

One final remark. In saying that Augustine proceeds by adopting and testing a series of myths, I *do* mean to call attention to the fact that he does not proceed by constructing arguments or proofs of either the existence or nature of his god. As we shall see below, he did finally come to think that there were good reasons for believing that there exists an eternal and changeless reality that is the source of both being and knowledge in the world. But whatever we may think of that argument, two things about it may be noted: first, that at best the argument establishes the existence of some eternal reality, not the existence of the "full-blooded" personal God of Augustinianism; and second, even that argument was discovered only with his absorption of Platonism after his arrival in Milan. Through most of the years we shall be considering below, he gave little or no attention to arguments for the existence of God and clearly saw no need for them.[119] And while he did work hard to develop an internally consistent conception of the nature of God, he was at no time concerned to prove the existence of a being having just that nature. In considering how Augustinianism came to be developed and accepted, it is important to note that, at least in its fundamentals, it was not grounded in rational demonstration. And for those who may be concerned with whether Augustinianism is "true," the absence of arguments for the truth of basic premises is one factor to be considered.

I. The Original Myth

When Augustine was born in 354 A.D., the historical tendencies discussed in Part One were already well advanced. Constantine's active promotion of Catholic Christianity was continued, though with less fervor, by his three sons, the last of whom ruled until 361 A.D.

By the time Augustine was nine years old, the emperor Julian was dead, and with him died the last serious effort to stem the tide of Christianization. The condemnation of the Arian heresy at the Council of Nicaea in 325 had demonstrated the determination of the emperor and his bishops to enforce Christian unity throughout the world. The imperial court in the new capital of Constantinople (dedicated in 330) was officially Christian, and bishops were emerging as central influences both at court and in most major cities. Though it was not until 392 that the emperor Theodosius finally banned pagan worship under severe penalties, the alliance of church and state was solidly established and the triumph of Catholicism was no longer seriously in doubt.

But this does not mean that Catholic Christianity had won the hearts and minds of all or even most of the population. The old Roman senate, isolated from the imperial court, was still largely pagan, and its leaders were among the most influential and respected men of the society. In the western provinces, many leading families and even whole cities remained pagan for many years. In Augustine's Africa, where Christianity had long been exceptionally strong, there remained significant pockets of paganism, and pagan festivals and practices continued without much interference. And even where people were Christian, it was by no means certain that the Catholic Church had won their allegiance. Arianism, which challenged both the unity of God and the divinity of Christ, was almost unanimously condemned at the Council of Nicaea in 325. Still it held on for a long time. Constantine himself was baptized by an Arian bishop, and Arianism remained the dominant form of Christianity among many of the northern tribes that moved into the empire through the fourth and fifth centuries, losing its hold only with the conversion of the Visigoths and Lombards at the end of the sixth century.[120] In Africa, the Donatist church, which had split from Catholicism early in the fourth century, was extremely powerful. By the time of Augustine's birth, Donatists may already have been a majority in Numidia, and by 390 they were almost certainly a majority in most of North Africa.[121] There were Donatist bishops in many towns and cities, including Augustine's see of Hippo, and despite official persecution and Augustine's own long struggle against them, Donatists persevered tenaciously. Indeed, Donatism outlasted Catholicism in North Africa, and Augustine's own Catholic bishopric of Hippo disappeared within fifty years of his death.[122] And, finally, there were eastern religions (especially Mithraism), philosophies (Stoicism, Epicureanism, Platonism) and hybrid sects (Manichaeism) which were vying for the souls of Romans.

There are important ways in which Augustine's personal religious development mirrors this general cultural situation. On the one hand, there was an inevitability in that development, since it was always unlikely in the extreme that Augustine would not finally find himself a Catholic Christian. But since Catholicism did not yet offer a fully developed world-view and theological system that could answer all his questions, the lure of other and seemingly more sophisticated sects was considerable. Thus many years were spent on a journey from the provincial Catholicism of his mother and his youth through a number of experiments with competing sects and finally back to the cosmopolitan Catholicism of his maturity.

Augustine was born and spent his early youth in the small Numidian town of Thagaste, some seventy miles inland from Hippo Regius and about two hundred miles southwest of its administrative center of Carthage. While the area was of considerable economic importance to the empire, it was in many ways treated as a colony and cultural backwater by the emperor and his court. Attention was focused on the challenges to the empire in the north and the east, and Africa was only a tightly controlled source of taxes and olive oil.[123]

For most inhabitants, it was a brutal and impoverished existence maintained by terror.[124] The dominant culture is characterized by scholars as Libyan or proto-Berber, and Augustine's own Berber heritage shows itself in several ways. For example, his mother, Monica, was named after the goddess Mon; and Augustine followed the Berber practice of incorporating the name of the god Baal in the names of male children by naming his own son Adeodatus (the Latin version of Iatanbaal). The peasant majority who worked the land and who had the best part of their produce taxed away belonged to that culture. While those who labored in the towns might mix some Latin with their native tongue, the agricultural masses spoke little or no Latin and experienced Rome primarily as an occupying power and alien oppressor.[125]

The Africans had never taken to the traditional gods of Rome.[126] Their supreme god was the terrible Saturn, an implacable and demanding father who required constant sacrifice and ritual purity.[127] And as the Africans turned slowly to Christianity, their religion remained drastic. A century and a half before Augustine, the African church father, Tertullian (ca. 150–225), had broken with Catholic Christianity, denouncing its contamination by "the world" and its temporizing with worldly authority. And in the early fourth century, this same uncompromising attitude gave support to the Donatist church.

Briefly, the Donatist movement had its origin just after the last great persecution of Christians under Diocletian in 303–305. At that time, the vast majority of Christians had "lapsed" and offered sacrifice to the pagan gods in order to escape punishment. Included among these were some priests and bishops who had "handed over" the scriptures to imperial authorities and so were branded as *traditores*. Some African Christians were outraged at the willingness of the Catholic Church to restore these defectors to full participation in the life of the church. In particular, it was claimed that Caecilian, the bishop of Carthage, had been ordained by a *traditor* and so held office without validity. In 311, a group of Numidian bishops elected one of their number, Majorinus, in place of Caecilian; and in 316, Majorinus was succeeded by Donatus, whose name came to be associated with the new movement. The emperor Constantine, eager to promote a unified church, endorsed the Catholic bishop Caecilian, and the radicals were further enraged at the willingness of the Catholics to tolerate lay interference in church affairs. And so began a struggle that was to endure until Christianity was overwhelmed entirely in the Islamic conquest of the seventh century. By the mid-fourth century, the Donatist church had won the loyalty of most Numidian peasants, although the leadership of the church was drawn from more educated strata.

Standing above this mass of peasants and urban laborers who are almost invisible to us from the sources we have available, there was a very small Romanized minority who owned most of the land, accumulated most of the wealth and administered affairs of state from their headquarters in towns and cities.[128]

On mosaics we can see the great country-houses of the African Romans: two-storied villas, surrounded by paddocks, fishponds, ornamental groves of cypresses. Their owners are shown, in the flowing robes of the age, hunting on horseback, and receiving the obeisance of a subservient peasantry. These men were the patroni, the 'protectors' of their community, in town and country alike. As they strode through the forum with their great retinues, the poor man was well-advised to rise and bow deeply to his lord.[129]

These were the men who collected the taxes, administered the law and enforced the norms of a rigidly controlled society. They were also the men who first filled the pagan priesthoods and later became the bishops and lay leaders of the Catholic Church. Their language was Latin and their cultural homeland was an idealized Rome. And despite the growing evidence of decay and imperial decline, "this world, on the edge of dissolution, had settled down to believe that it would last forever."[130]

Augustine himself belonged neither to the very rich nor to the very poor. His father, Patricius, was "moderately well-off," a member of the municipal curia and a man of modest property. His rank allowed him to aspire to providing his son with a liberal education, but his limited means meant that he was able to finance that education only with great effort and with several interruptions (see *Conf.* II. 3). And the young man would not have been able to pursue his later studies in Carthage had not his father secured the patronage of a local aristocrat, Romanianus, whose connections in Rome were to be important in launching Augustine's career (see *Ans. to Skep.* II. 2. 5).[131] Augustine's "middle class" origin is important for understanding the direction of his life and career. It meant, on the one hand, that he had little reason to feel any loyalty to his home town and that he needed to escape Thagaste and the burdens and demands of curial life if he was to enjoy the life of cultured leisure that was the ideal of every Romanized youth.[132] But it also meant, on the other hand, that there were avenues open for such an escape, avenues that were irrevocably closed to the poor majority.

While Augustine's class position may have been somewhat ambivalent, there is no question at all about the class allegiance of him or his family. Augustine spoke only Latin, and between his culture and that of the majority culture that surrounded him, "there stretched the immeasurable qualitative chasm, separating civilization from its absence."[133] One of his neighbors was a senator, and his friends and those of his family were rich men, such as Alypius, Romanianus and Nebridius (*Letter* 99). As a youth, he was unable to communicate with the peasant majority, and as priest and bishop, his Latin sermons could not reach them.[134] At no time in any of his writing does he give any indication of an awareness that there might be an alternative to the existing social order. And his own account of his early life gives no indication that he was more than barely conscious of the special misery of those who did the productive work of his world, though, of course, he was keenly aware that human life in general is filled with pain and tribulation. He did in later life sometimes urge masters to treat their slaves and other dependents justly (see, for example, *Letter* 247). But in the end, it seemed to him entirely proper to use whatever force was necessary to maintain the existing order and to bring the peasantry into the fold of Catholic Christianity (see *Letters* 58, 88, 112).[135] Seeing the obsequious good cheer of a poor beggar on the streets of Milan, the young Augustine was able to recognize that, in his own vain pursuit of earthly happiness, he was no better than the beggar; but at the same time, he is able to see in the beggar only that "he was free from care, while I was full of fear" (*Conf.* VI. 9). The man himself, the conditions of his life and the lives of those who made up most of the population were at best only on the very periphery of Augustine's reality.

Another indication of this class outlook is his attitude toward the woman with whom he lived for thirteen years and who bore his son, Adeodatus, while he was still an eighteen year old student in Carthage. Like any ambitious young academic, he thought nothing of taking a concubine who was "beneath his station," but he also never gave a thought to a proper marriage to such a woman. When, as a climbing Milanese professor, he was convinced by his mother that it was time to make an advantageous marriage to an aristocratic woman, he conceived of no alternative but to send the mother of his child back to Africa and to proceed with an appropriate betrothal. Not that the decision was an easy one: "My heart still clung to her; it was pierced and wounded within me, and the wound drew blood from it" (*Conf.* VI. 15). But so unquestioning was Augustine's class outlook that when the demands of status came, the woman disappeared from his life as completely as if she had never been part of it.

With this summary of the environment within which Augustine spent his youth, let me come now to say something more specifically about the influences that shaped his religious consciousness and his conception of a god. For this early period, the available information is sketchy, since Augustine begins his own detailed account of these matters only with his plunge into Manichaeism in his late teens. But from scattered remarks, it is possible to put together a probable reconstruction of at least the broad outlines of his early outlook.

First of all, I think we can safely say that paganism never held much attraction for him. Though his father was a pagan who did not convert to Catholicism until Augustine was seventeen, Patricius seems to have been an indifferent pagan who made little effort to influence his son or to undermine Monica's determined effort to bring Augustine up as a Catholic (see *Conf.* I. 11). In those earliest years, he seems to have had little contact with pagan cult, and by the time he did encounter it during his student years in Carthage, he seems to have viewed it more as a fascinating spectacle than as a serious contender for his allegiance.[136] On the other hand, while he did regard some of the pagan accounts of gods as no more than myths, he was certainly convinced later in his life that some of those gods were in fact evil spirits to be guarded against with the utmost care, and it seems likely this was something he learned at his mother's knee.[137]

Nor does Augustine seem to have been much affected by the Donatist church which held such sway in his part of the world. There seems to have been no Donatist church in Thagaste.[138] And Augustine seems to have had little concern about Donatism until much later when, as priest and bishop, he was forced to confront it as a political reality.

The god of Augustine's childhood was the god of his mother. As we saw above, it never occurred to him to doubt the existence of this god or his supremacy over the demons who posed as other gods (*Conf.* VI. 5). He tells us that from very early on, he was certain of the supremacy of this god for reasons similar to those we saw in Constantine: that god was a "winner."

> Next, I confess that I already believed in Christ and accepted what He said as true, even when my belief was unsupported by reason....I see that I have believed no one except the affirmed opinion and the widespread report of peoples and nations, and that the mysteries of the Catholic Church have everywhere taken possession of these peoples....In this matter, as I said, I believed a report which had the strength of numbers, agreement, and antiquity. (*Adv. of Bel.* 14. 31)[139]

By establishing the dominance of his church throughout the empire and driving the pagan gods from their temples, the Catholic God had left little doubt of his overwhelming power. To win the protection of this god, Augustine received the sign of the cross and was salted at birth to ward off evil spirits (*Conf.* I. 11). Seeking both to secure the rewards of ritual purity and to avoid the terrible wrath that would follow a death without that purity, Monica agonized over whether to baptize her child when he fell ill with a fever and begged for baptism. To baptize him too soon might risk his later contamination by even worse sins, but a death without that "cleansing" would surely result in eternal damnation (*Conf.* I. 11). In other words, this was a practical religion in the traditional sense, a religion based in the pursuit of favor and the avoidance of wrath. As Augustine says, he thought of his god as "some sort of mighty one who could hear us and help us, even though not appearing before our senses." And his first (largely unsuccessful) prayers were for protection from the terrible beatings of his schoolmasters (*Conf.* I. 9).

So it would seem that Augustine's earliest religious experience was guided by the myth of God as dominant among the gods, a father whose protection might be less than fully reliable on earth, but who offered to those who believed the perfect beatitude of a heavenly home removed from the pain of this earthly pilgrimage.[140] It was certainly a strongly anthropomorphic notion, and probably was so in the fullest sense. In particular, it seems certain that Augustine at this point conceived his god as a corporeal being with a body very like the human. Not only had God become flesh in the person of Jesus to take up the sins of the world, but God himself could only be thought of in anthropomorphic terms. So, for instance, God could still appear to his devotees in dreams, and he seems to have done so for Monica as he had for Constantine (*Conf.* III. 11).[141] Though Augustine never states this anthropomorphism explicitly, he does repeatedly assert, when discussing his Manichaean phase, that he was at that point still unable to conceive of God except as a body, and that he was attracted to the Manichees in part because their conception of God's material substance was at least superior to what he took to be the Catholic view "that in all your parts you were bounded by the form of the human body" (*Conf.* V. 10).

This was the God of Augustine's provincial youth, offering love and comfort to the faithful to be sure, but in most respects not so very different from the terrible Saturn of his mother's cultural tradition. And while Augustine and his family were certainly Catholic, their god was likely one that the poor Donatist majority would have found most compatible. What separated Augustine's religion from that of the North African masses was not its content but rather its identification with Rome. Augustine's god may have been virtually indistinguishable from the supreme god of the Donatists or of the cult of Saturn, but it bore the unique distinction of being the god of the empire. This was the god of Constantine, the god who had established dominion throughout the world and who was rapidly winning all people to his church. This was the triumphant deity who had defeated all pretenders to the throne and had established himself as alone to be feared and served.

This myth, which we may refer to for convenience as Augustine's original myth, was baked into his very bones by his zealous mother. From his youth, he never doubted the existence of this god, and it was thenceforth impossible for him to take seriously any religion unless it included "Christ's name" (*Conf.* III. 4). Whatever doubts and questions he might have, however he might struggle with apparent inconsistencies in the conception of God's nature, he carried this basic myth with him, and there was never any real doubt that it would finally form the core of his mature conception of God.

It was this myth that he took with him when he left his home town to receive his higher education in the relatively cosmopolitan atmosphere of Carthage. Still a boy of seventeen, he quickly found his original myth confronted with a host of skeptical questions and doubts from those he had been taught most to respect and emulate. It was that confrontation that set him on the road to his final conception of God and the system that would flow from it.

II. The Manichaean Myth

Augustine's father had already worked hard to secure for his son the best early education a provincial could receive, first in Thagaste and later in Madaura (*Conf.* II. 3).[142] Then at the age of seventeen, the wealthy Romanianus made resources available for him to finish his education as a rhetorician in Carthage (*Conf.* III. 1). Before going on to look at the development of his conception of God, it may be well to look briefly at the content and purposes of Augustine's education.

It was an education typical of that of the sons of ambitious provinicial parents. Designed to inculcate discipline and to immerse young men in the ideals of Roman culture, it was an extremely narrow, rigid and structured training. Augustine's teachers were mostly pagans whose focus was exclusively on a detailed mastery of a few classical authors, led by Virgil and Cicero. Texts were scrutinized line by line and often laboriously committed to memory in their entirety. It included almost nothing of science or philosophy, and in Augustine's case it included so little Greek that he was forever cut off not only from a long classical tradition, but from much of the Christian literature that was his legacy (*Conf.* I. 14). From his years of study, Augustine emerged with a love of words and careful turns of phrase, a prodigious memory and attentiveness to detail that would eventually enable him to use 42,816 uncannily accurate citations of the Bible in his works.[143] But more important to him in those early years, his education provided him with a grounding in the Latin classics that would gain him admittance to the cultural elite of the Roman world.

> Such a man could communicate his message to an educated Latin at the other end of the Roman world, merely by mentioning a classical figure, by quoting half a line of a classical poet. It is not surprising that the group of men who had, by their education, come to conform so successfully to this rigidly-defined traditional standard of perfection, should have come, by the fourth century, to stand apart as a caste of their own. Despite the humble origins of many of them, a common mastery of Latin literature had raised this class 'above the common lot of men' quite as effectively as that other class of 'superior men', the Mandarins of Imperial China.[144]

According to Augustine's own report, when he first arrived in Carthage, he was swept away by the glitter and debauchery of what must have seemed to him a wildly exciting new world (*Conf.* III. 1). Given what we know of the seriousness of the young man, we may doubt to what extent he "plunged headlong" into the "filth of concupiscence," as he reports. But he did enjoy the theater and and gladiatorial shows, and he fairly early settled down with the woman who bore him his son (*Conf.* III. 2 and IV. 2). What are certainly easy to believe are his admissions that he "took pride in being refined and cultured" and that as the leading student in the school of rhetoric, he was "swollen up with vanity" (*Conf.* III. 1 and 3).

But apparently this period of relative abandon was brief, and he soon found himself overwhelmed by the demands of his religious consciousness and the need to turn back to his god. Oddly enough, he credits not Christian teaching, but the pagan Cicero with returning him to his search for God. He says that upon reading the now lost *Hortensius* of Cicero, "all my vain hopes forthwith became worthless to me, and with incredible ardor of heart I desired undying wisdom" (*Conf.* III. 4).

One reason for thinking this source of inspiration odd is indeed that Cicero was not a Christian and it is not easy to see why the young man would immediately have identified the search for Cicero's "wisdom" with his own search for God. And in fact he does himself say that he was inspired by Cicero to pursue "not this or that sect, but wisdom itself, whatsoever it might be." Furthermore, he adds that he was checked in his admiration for Cicero's project by the fact that "Christ's name was not in it" (*Conf.* III. 4). And he remarks in another place that in the reading of Cicero, he was returning to "that religion which had been implanted in us in our boyhood," but that even though "that religion was drawing me to itself," at the time "I knew it not" (*Ans. to Skep.* II. 2. 5). From all this, it is perhaps best to gather that the reading of Cicero turned him away from the distractions of the city and his adolescent vanity to a new realization that there were more serious matters to be pursued, a realization that would inevitably put him in mind of his obligations to the god his mother had so solidly planted in him.

The other reason that the inspiration of Cicero seems somewhat odd is just that very little of the extant work of Cicero seems likely to inspire anyone to such an extent. An eclectic and rather superficial thinker, Cicero seems hardly a candidate for lifting someone to heights of religious and philosophical exhilaration. I make this remark not to disparage Cicero, but only to raise some question about the literalness with which we should take Augustine's recollection. Given the fact that Augustine would eventually see himself as led back to God in part by Platonist philosophers who would claim Cicero as one of their own, it is tempting to see in this early attribution of inspiration a dramatic "first call" that would eventually draw him home, and when read in that way, one wonders how seriously to take the recollection.

But be all that as it may, his reading of Cicero did not lead him at that time to plunge into the study of philosophy or the pursuit of what was commonly called "wisdom." Rather, by his own account, he was inspired to turn not to pagan philosophy, but to the Christian scriptures

(*Conf.* III. 5). In other words, whether by Cicero's inspiration, as he claims, or by the power of his childhood indoctrination, as may seem just as likely, he very quickly found himself turning to a search for the god and religion of his boyhood.

The problem he encountered—and here we may indeed see the influence not only of Cicero but of that whole elite culture into which he had been initiated—was that the god of his childhood would no longer "work" for him.

> When I first turned to that scripture, I did not feel toward it as I am speaking now, but it seemed to me unworthy of comparison with the nobility of Cicero's writings. My swelling pride turned away from its humble style, and my sharp gaze did not penetrate into its inner meaning. (*Conf.* III. 5)

The budding young provincial rhetorician, having been lately admitted to the exclusive world of aristocratic culture, with its love of carefully crafted style and elegant turns of phrase, found himself embarrassed by the crude and simple texts of his boyhood religion. Alongside Virgil, Terence, Sallust and Cicero, the prose of old Moses seemed crude and rustic indeed.

The lure of this elite culture was very powerful for Augustine, and it would be a mistake to underestimate it. He never lost the need to bring his religious life into harmony with that culture and to make it acceptable to the literary and philosophical tastes of the gentlemen who had accepted him into their midst. But as powerful as that lure was, it could not offset the ties that bound him to his Catholic upbringing. And his discomfort with the rough authorities of his youth did not in the least tempt him to turn to the pagan "philosophy" of the classical tradition. What he wanted was not to abandon his early belief or the original myth on which it rested, but to "elevate" that myth in a way that would make it more compatible with the intellectual and cultural sensibilities of his adopted class.

Many ambitious young Africans found themselves in Augustine's dilemma. Numidian Catholicism seemed inadequate for their cultured needs, they certainly could not identify with the Donatism that had captured their "rustic" countrymen, and yet neither could they reconcile themselves to the pagan "philosophers" and the quest for an abstract "wisdom" that still dominated the traditional aristocracy. They had learned to feel the presence of "sin" in the very core of their being, to tremble before the power and wrath of the Catholic god and to hope for redemption through the Christ who was the loving and providential face of that god. Their aim was not to abandon their god, but to clear away some of the crude anthropomorphic trappings that attached to him and to fit him with a more refined aspect that could be a proper object of contemplation for a cultured spirit. And it was in pursuit of this aim that many young intellectuals, including Augustine, found themselves attracted to the Manichaean sect that had taken root in Carthage.

Here is Augustine's own account of the appeal of Manichaeism:

> And so I fell in with certain men, doting in their pride, too carnal-minded and glib of speech, in whose mouth were the snares of the devil and a very birdlime confected by mixing together the syllables of your name, and the name of our Lord Jesus Christ, and the name of the Paraclete, our comforter, the Holy Spirit. These names were never absent from their mouths, but were only the tongue's sound and clatter, while their hearts were empty of truth. (*Conf.* III. 6)

The Manichaeans scoffed at the crude Catholic god and claimed for themselves not only a more exalted conception of God, but a strict rationalism that they contrasted with the naive credulity demanded of Catholic believers. To Augustine and his fellows

> they said we were terrified by superstition, and that faith was demanded of us before reason, while they, on the other hand, were forcing faith on no one without first hunting for and disentangling the truth. Who would not be enticed by these promises? And would there not be special enticement for a youthful mind desirous of truth, and yet haughty and talkative in disputations in the school of certain learned men? (*Adv. of Bel.* 1. 2)

But at the same time, Manichaeism was above all a cult of redemption, and the Manichees of the western empire grounded themselves in the writings of St. Paul and saw themselves as the most pure and refined of Christians.[145] They thus offered a powerful combination of seeming intellectual sophistication and redemptive hope. After only two years in Carthage, Augustine attached himself to the Manichaeans, and he remained with them for nine years.

The Manichaeans were an illegal and sometimes fiercely persecuted sect. In 297 the emperor Diocletian had issued an edict against them, primarily because he saw Manichaeism as an invasion by the hated Persians. And when Augustine himself moved to Rome in 383, he and his fellow Manichees were forbidden to hold public meetings.[146] But this official disapproval did not translate into real danger during Augustine's Manichaean period, and certainly ambitious young men did not feel Manichaean affiliation to be an intolerable burden. In Africa especially, Manichaeism had been well established at least since the end of the third century. Its followers were found almost exclusively among wealthy landowners, merchants and intellectuals, and it had little base among the urban or rural poor. In particular, Donatist Christians abhorred Manichaeism and avoided its followers like a plague. But among well-born young men and those aspiring to join the elite, conversions to Manichaeism were common. For example, in the year 400, former Manichaeans included not only Augustine himself, but his patron Romanianus, his friend Alypius, bishop of Thagaste, and another dear friend, Evodius, bishop of Uzalis.[147] In fact, many Catholic bishops had Manichaean sympathies, and Augustine himself was accused of being a closet Manichaean when he joined the struggle against the Donatists years later.[148]

For one with Augustine's background and pretensions, the Manicheans posed a number of very disturbing questions. Some of these grew out of the Manichaean rejection of the Old Testament as crude and repulsive:

- How can Christians accept as scriptural a book that calls upon people to slaughter innocent animals for sacrifice and urges the mutilation of male children through the barbarity of circumcision? (*Rep. to Faustus.* XVIII. 2)

- How can Christians claim to be heirs of the Old Testament tradition when they quite rightly ignore many of the foolish Jewish laws, such as abstention from pork (while eating other meat), observance of the sabbath and participation in the feast of unleavened bread? (*Rep. to Faustus.* IV. 1)

- How can Christians accept the primitive God of the Old Testament who is depicted with eyes and ears and, in general, a human form? (*Ag. Ep. Fund.* XXIII. 25)

- How can one honor those Old Testament patriarchs who are depicted as receiving divine favor despite living the most depraved lives? Abraham was an adulterer, who defiled himself with the full knowledge of his wife. That same Abraham twice sold his wife to the pleasure of kings in order to protect his own skin. Lot, Abraham's brother, committed fornication with his own daughters. Isaac misrepresented his wife Rebecca as his sister and was prepared to let other men sleep with her. Jacob had four wives who fought over him and paid each other for the privilege of a night with him. David had a number of wives, seduced the wife of his soldier Uriah and arranged to have Uriah killed in battle. Solomon had three hundred wives, seven hundred concubines and "princesses without number." Even Moses committed murder, plundered Egypt, waged bloody war and perpetrated many cruelties, in addition to having many wives. Who would want to go to the bosom of such an Abraham? And who can hold sacred the book that exalts these reprobates? (*Rep. to Faustus.* XXII. 5 and XXIII. 1)

Other questions cast doubt on the most basic scriptural foundations of the Catholic faith:

• Are we indeed to believe that the Son of God who was one with God himself was carried in the womb of a woman and underwent a fleshly birth? (*Conf.* V. 10)[149]

• Is it not obvious that someone has imported Jewish fictions into the gospel accounts? Not only is Jesus treated as a man born of woman, but the gospels of Matthew and Luke offer conflicting genealogies. (*Rep. to Faustus.* II. 1 and III. 3)

• Are we really to believe that the Son of God, the deity himself, suffered an actual bodily death on a cross? (*Conf.* V. 9)

But there were yet more fundamental questions that struck at the very heart of the original myth upon which Augustine's early religion was based:

• How can the Catholics believe that a single being is both the god of love and redemption and the terrible and angry dispenser of vengeance who condemns lost souls to eternal fire? Surely two competing forces are at work here. (*Rep. to Faustus.* XXI. 3)

• If creation is ruled by an omnipotent deity who cares for us, how is it that "perversity is so serious and widespread that it must seem unattributable not only to God's governance, but even to a hireling's management, if indeed such management could be entrusted to a hireling." Given the obvious pain, suffering and chaos of this world, we must believe "either that Divine Providence does not reach to these outer limits of things or that surely all evils are committed by the will of God." And given that choice, it is surely better to believe that God is unable to control evil than to believe that he is himself perverse, because at least "the imputing of negligence is indeed much more pardonable than the charge of ill will or cruelty." And it is better to believe that "the things of earth cannot be governed by powers divine" than to hold that God is either weak or malicious. (*Div. Prov.* I. 1. 1)[150]

- When we look at human action in particular, do we not find again and again that we fight a losing battle against our own fleshly desires? Do we not find, in fact, that we are forever acting in ways that we do not want to act but find ourselves unable to resist? We may hate evil and want with all our hearts to do good, but what we find is that we not only continue to do evil, but even take delight in doing what we hate. Is it not as though two souls were warring within us? Are not those same powers that struggle in the cosmos as a whole found by each of us to be struggling within ourselves? (*Contra Fortunatum* II. 20–21)[151]

Faced with such questions, Augustine became convinced that his boyhood religion was hopelessly primitive, unrefined and unreflective. He very quickly abandoned the original myth of his youth and turned instead to the Manichaean myth that was the foundation of that sect. And it was to be nearly a decade before his encounter with what seemed to him the greater sophistication of the Christian Platonism of Milanese aristocrats enabled him finally to leave Manichaeism behind.

Manichaeism was a sect with great staying power, and it endured in both the west and the Orient for over a thousand years. It had at its center a demanding mode of life rooted in an elaborate myth developed by Mani (216–277 A.D.), the Persian founder of the sect. This myth seems to serve three basic purposes: (1) it literally identifies good and evil and the struggle between them with objects and processes of the physical universe; (2) it further identifies those objects and processes with the corresponding good and evil aspects of each human being; and (3) it provides both a mode of life that seeks to maximize one's identity with the good aspects of the universe and the optimistic hope that such an effort will result in final redemption. Perhaps it will be useful to provide the bare bones of the myth, leaving out as much of its complex detail as possible, in order to give some idea of what it was that Augustine found himself able to embrace so quickly.[152]

The Manichaean myth, the second myth adopted by Augustine in attempting to find expression for his religious consciousness, is based on the notion of an incessant cosmic strife between two primary principles, the good (originally called Ohrmazd or Ahura Mazda, but often referred to by western Manichees as God) and the evil (called Ahriman or Ahura Mainyu). The good is also often referred to as light and the evil as darkness or matter (sometimes by the Greek term *hyle*). The actual physical manifestation of good or God is light and the divine homeland is the realm of light, which is unbounded on the north, east and west, but bounded on the south by the realm of darkness.

Now, the myth goes, in the beginning, the demons of the realm of darkness were jealous of the harmony of the realm of light, and so they launched an attack on it. In order to defend himself, God called into existence two beings of light, the father of greatness and the mother of life, and the mother of life in turn called into existence primeval man. This being of pure light plunged into the realm of darkness to do battle. But primeval man was defeated by the demons of darkness, and this defeat had two cosmic effects: in being defeated, primeval man had his being mixed with elements of darkness, and in victory, the demons of darkness stole and incorporated elements of light into their being.

In his condition of defeat and despair, primeval man sent up a prayer, to which the living Spirit of God responded by drawing primeval man back up into the realm of light, so that the suffering redeemer is himself redeemed. Having returned to the realm of light, the elements of light that are the being of primeval man must still be cleansed of the elements of darkness which befouled and fettered primeval man. The living Spirit does this work. Those elements that were still pure and undefiled are placed in the heavens and become the sun and the moon. Those that are partially sullied by darkness are made into the stars. And those that are most defiled seek purification as they are drawn up toward the moon and the sun in a "column of glory" that we see as the milky way.

With primeval man thus redeemed, God now seeks to recover those elements of light that had been absorbed by the beings of the realm of darkness. To accomplish this, God calls forth the beautiful messenger of light, who sails across the heavens and displays its naked form before the demons of darkness. To the male demons, it displays its female form, and in their resulting excitement the demons discharge the elements of light they had absorbed as sperm upon the earth, where those elements take the form of the buds of tender plants. To the female demons, it displays its male form, and in their excitement these demons abort the demon offspring they are carrying. These aborted offspring, in turn, eat the buds of the plants and so absorb elements of light.

The realm of darkness, now split into many beings and mixed with elements of light, seeks to concentrate all its strength for its contest with the realm of light. To do this, it selects two of the demons, one male and one female. The male demon devours all of its male fellows, and the female devours all the other female demons. These two great demons then join in intercourse and the result of their union is the begetting of Adam and Eve, the first human beings. As products of cannibalism and sexual lust, these human beings are mixed with elements of darkness and so are themselves driven by lust to act as agents of the realm of darkness. But they also contain the elements of light that had been captured, and so the realm of light eternally seeks to redeem them and to draw them up to the realm of light where they can be purified.

Adam remains blind, deaf and totally unaware of the light within him. So once again, primeval man returns to the realm of darkness, this time in the form of the redeemer, Jesus Christ, the Son of God. The redeemer rouses Adam from ignorance, reveals his twofold origin and nature, and instructs him in the redemptive knowledge needed to liberate the elements of light and to return to his higher identity with the realm of light. Now each individual human soul created by the propagation and diffusion of Adam's mixed nature is a part of that nature and as such is imprisoned by lust and in need of redemption. And so each soul must struggle to free that portion of its nature that is one with the sun and moon and to return to its proper abode in the realm of light.

If we now come to look at those North Africans who were bound into a single religion by this myth, I think we can agree with Brown that there were really two sorts of Manichaeans.[153] For the largely uneducated artisans and merchants who formed the backbone of the sect, Manichaeism bound them in a quite literal unity of nature with that great light, the sun, that ruled the universe and that the Romans had so long identified with Apollo, the highest of the gods. And Manichaean practice offered a way of life that could cleanse the soul and bring the rewards of peace and harmony with the divine. It was from among these faithful that the Manichees drew the "elect," those whose ascetic life of devotion made them so much admired by intellectuals such as Augustine and his friends.

For those intellectuals, on the other hand, Manichaeism had a somewhat different significance. While Augustine and his colleagues did indeed accept the Manichaean myth as literally true, they accepted it because they saw in it the most appealing way available to approach that "wisdom" that they had learned to admire and desire.[154] For such people, the commitment to the sect was never complete. They remained, as in the case of Augustine, only "hearers" who learned from the elect, but they did not surrender themselves to that demanding life. They brought food to the elect, believing that in digesting the food, the stomachs of the elect would liberate the particles of light trapped in the matter (*Conf.* III. 10; IV. 1). But they were content to wait for future incarnations to liberate the light in their own being. While Augustine certainly did take Manichaeism seriously enough to remain a hearer for nearly a decade, he seems never to have achieved the sort of conviction in it that he was seeking. It seemed to him superior to what the Catholicism of his original myth had to offer, but he never quite sold himself completely on it. While a Manichaean hearer, he also remained a Catholic catechumen, and though the sect was appealing enough to hold his allegiance for quite a long time, it appears that he began to have doubts about his new myth fairly soon.

The Manichaean myth and sect did have a number of strengths from Augustine's point of view:

First, it did not carry him too far afield from his spritual home. It was a religion that based itself in St. Paul almost as strongly as in Mani, and it incorporated at least the form of the god Augustine had known, including the Father, the Son and the Holy Ghost.[155] Thus a Manichaean hymn exhorted,

Let us worship the Spirit of the Paraclete.
Let us bless our Lord Jesus who has sent to us the Spirit of Truth. He came and separated us from the error of the world, he brought us a mirror, we looked, we saw the Universe in it.[156]

Also like Catholicism, it was a religion that emphasized the helpless-ness of mankind and the need to rely on God for redemption.

> Lo, the amnesty of the forgiveness of sins has come: it is Jesus, who giveth repentance unto him that repents.

> He stands in our midst, he winks unto us secretly, saying: 'Repent, that I may forgive you your sins.'

> He is not far from us my brethren, even as he said in his preaching: 'I am near to you, like the clothing of your body.'[157]

But while the Manichees offered much of Christianity, they offered what seemed to be a much more refined and uplifting form of that religion. In attacking the Old Testament, they not only made it possible for a young sophisticate to ignore that stylistic abomination, but they also eliminated some of the more unsavory aspects of Augustine's original god. The vengeful, angry and often terrible Yahweh of the Old Testament was exposed as a demon of darkness, and the true God remained as a being of pure goodness and light. Christ was identified with that pure God, but was freed from the entanglements of the flesh.

> Our Savior himself, your Only-begotten I so thought of as being some-thing extruded out of the mass of your pellucid substance for our salva-tion, that I could believe nothing of him except what I could picture by my own vain powers. I judged that such a nature as his could never be born of the Virgin Mary, without becoming intermingled in the flesh....So I feared to believe that he was born in the flesh, lest I be forced to believe him defiled by the flesh. (*Conf.* V, 10)

And finally, the Manichaean god, while still a corporeal being, seemed superior to the crudely anthropomorphic deity he had previously con-ceived.

> My God, to whom your own mercies make confession, I thought myself to be more truly religious if I believed you to be infinite in other parts, even though I was forced to admit that you are finite in that part where the evil mass stands in opposition to you, than if I thought that in all your parts you were bounded by the form of the human body. (*Conf.* V. 10)

Manichaeism could also claim a sort of intellectual respectability and sensitivity to the intuitions and needs of that cultured elite to which Augustine aspired. It not only attacked relentlessly the inconsistencies of Catholic belief, but it claimed to provide a single, comprehensive account of all phenomena.[158] Mani claimed not only that his myth incorporated and identified the cosmological and moral orders in a coherent way, but that his system was able to explain all astronomical events and to incorporate them into a single great conception of reality (see *Conf.* V. 5).

Manichaeism also appealed to that intuition of the cultured soul that it was in fact somehow "one with the divine" and carried the light of God within itself. And along with that, it appealed to the concomitant intuition that in this world, the soul is enslaved and sullied by the degradation of matter. So the Manichee spoke for the light that was his higher essence when he sang

> I am in everything, I bear the skies, I am the foundation, I support the earths, I am the Light that shines forth, that gives joy to souls.
> I am the life of the world: I am the milk that is in all trees: I am the sweet water that is beneath the sons of matter.[159]

But he spoke for that same essence when he lamented

> Matter and her sons divided me up amongst them, they burnt me in their fire, they gave me a bitter likeness.
> The strangers with whom I mixed, me they know not; they tasted my sweetness, they desired to keep me with them.
> I was life to them, but they were death to me; I bore up beneath them, they wore me as a garment upon them.[160]

Another clear appeal of the Manichaean myth was its ability to account for evil in a way that both fully acknowledged its obvious reality and also excused God from responsibility for it. So Augustine says that

> I believed that evil is some such substance and that it possesses its own foul and hideous mass, either gross, which they styled the earth, or thin and subtle, as is the body of the air, which they imagine to be a malignant mind stealing through the earth. Because some sort of reverence forced me to believe that a good God would create no evil nature, I postulated two masses opposed to one another, each of them infinite, but the evil one on a narrower scale, the good one larger....I thought it

better to believe that you created nothing evil…than to believe that a nature such as I thought evil to be could come from your hand. (*Conf.* V. 10)

In addition, Manichaeism provided an account of the particular evil called "sin" in a way that not only relieved God of responsibility, but that was appealing in other ways. For one thing, by depicting every person as a mixture of light and darkness, it made sense of the intuition that lust or fleshly desire must be a permanent and essential aspect of human being, since it is found from birth as an aspect of our nature.[161] And secondly, the myth really has the effect of absolving from responsibility for sin not only God, but humans themselves, since human evil is attributed to those elements of darkness with which we are soiled through no fault of our own.

> I still thought that it was not ourselves who sin, but that some sort of different nature within us commits the sin. It gave joy to my pride to be above all guilt, and when I did an evil deed, not to confess that I myself had done it, so that you might heal my soul, since it had sinned against you. I loved to excuse myself, and to accuse I know not what other being that was present with me but yet was not I. (*Conf.* V. 10)

And certainly, another appeal of Manichaeism was that it matched Catholicism in offering not only comfort in this world, but the hope of final redemption and the perfect happiness of the realm of light.

> The gates of the skies have opened before me through the rays of my Savior and his glorious likeness of Light.
> I have left the garment upon the earth, the senility of diseases that was with me; the immortal robe I have put upon me.
> Ferry me across to the sun and the moon, O ferryboat of Light that is at peace, above these three earths. O first-born
> I have become a holy bride in the bride-chambers of Light that are at rest, I have received the gifts of victory.
> O excellent toil wherewith I have toiled. O my end that has had a happy issue. O my eternal possession. O first-born
> Glory and victory to our Lord Mani and his holy elect and the soul of the blessed Mary.[162]

Finally, in determining the attraction of Manichaeism for Augustine, it must be mentioned that he was surely impressed with the ascetic lifestyle and moral purity of many of the elect. It is true that he would,

years later after returning to Catholicism, take pleasure in enumerating
the excesses and hypocrisy of some Manichaeans (see, for example,
Cath. & Man. II. 19. 67–68). Still at a time when adherence to
Catholicism was politically expedient and when a Catholic bishopric
could mean great wealth and political power, the young Augustine was
probably impressed by the selfless devotion of some of the simple men
of his adopted sect.[163] Even in writing his *Confessions* many years later,
he still remembered with warmth the humility and openness of the
Manichee Faustus, though he was utterly contemptuous of Faustus'
unlettered ignorance (*Conf.* V. 7). And in his *Reply to Faustus the
Manichaean*, although he now thinks that moral purity without Catholic
faith is empty, still he is able to put into the mouth of Faustus the following words, in which it is hard not to read some grudging admiration:

> The gospel is nothing else than the preaching and the precept of Christ.
> I have parted with all gold and silver, and have left off carrying money
> in my purse; content with daily food; without anxiety for tomorrow; and
> without solicitude about how I shall be fed, or wherewithal I shall be
> clothed: and do you ask if I believe the gospel? You see in me the bless-
> ings of the gospel; and do you ask if I believe the gospel? You see me
> poor, meek, a peacemaker, pure in heart, mourning, hungering, thirst-
> ing, bearing persecutions and enmity for righteousness' sake; and you
> doubt my belief in the gospel? (*Rep. to Faustus.* V. 1)

But despite all these attractions, it seems very unlikely, at least with
the clarity of hindsight, that Manichaeism could ever have held the
loyalty of an Augustine. It is true that for a time, he took a cocky pleasure in deriding the Catholics for their inconsistencies and reverence
for debauched patriarchs (*Conf.* III. 10). And when, two years after
joining the Manichees, he returned home to Thagaste to teach for a
year, he not only succeeded in enlisting a number of his friends from
the small-town "intelligentsia" to the sect, but he proselytized with sufficient brashness to get himself kicked out of his mother's house (*Conf.*
III. 11). But once he returned to the university in Carthage to pursue
his ambitions as a rhetorician, it was only a matter of time until doubts
about Manichaeism became pressing.

It is not easy to fix a precise timetable of events during this period.
Augustine first went to Carthage in 371, and he probably joined the
Manichaeans late in the year 373 or early in 374. He returned to
Thagaste in 375 and came back to Carthage from Thagaste in 376. By

383, when Faustus of Milevis paid a visit to Carthage, we know that he had already been filled with doubts for some time. Beyond that, it is impossible to know whether his doubts began immediately or grew slowly over the six or so intervening years. We do know that Manichaeism was very popular among Carthaginian intellectuals, so that Augustine would have felt little peer pressure to abandon or even examine his commitment. But at the same time, his continued reading of classical authors was bound to raise questions about the exotic Manichaean myth and its sweeping claims. As he mastered Aristotle's *Categories* and pressed ahead with his reading of Cicero and other classical authors, the pretensions of Manichaeism became first questionable and then embarrassing (*Conf.* IV. 16).

By his own account, his first doubts came with his reading of astrologers. Though he was warned by an older scholar not to place faith in the auguries and horoscopes by which those "nativity calculators" made their living, he could not help noticing that their astronomical predictions were extremely accurate and that they understood the movements of the heavens as operating according to strict and mathematically calculable laws (*Conf.* IV. 3 and V. 3).[164] Against the scientific accuracy of these "philosophers" he put the inflated claims of Mani, who incorporated all these astronomical events into his myth, but who was quite unable to make any such accurate predictions (*Conf.* V. 5).

He reports that this filled him with questions, which he was assured would be easily answered when the great Manichaean scholar, Faustus of Milevis, visited Carthage. But when this Faustus arrived and Augustine was able to question him, he found him unable to explain astronomical events in Manichaean terms. And what was even worse, this much ballyhooed Faustus turned out to be "unskilled in the liberal arts, with the exception of grammar, and with that only in an elementary way" (*Conf.* V. 6). While he admired Faustus as a humble and unpretentious man and an eloquent speaker, it turned out that Augustine, far from becoming a pupil of the great Manichaean, ended up taking him on as a student.

But all my efforts by which I had determined to advance in that sect collapsed utterly as I came to know that man. I did not as yet break completely with them, but as if unable to find anything better than what I had in some way stumbled upon, I resolved to be content with it for the time being, unless something preferable should chance to appear. (*Conf.* V. 7)

As we saw above, one of the great strengths of Manichaeism from Augustine's point of view was its claim to base its whole system on reason alone and its scorn of the Catholic demand for blind faith from its believers. Once such claims were made, Mani's inability to deliver on them came to seem to the young rhetorician an almost fatal flaw.

> He did not wish to be thought of small account, but tried to convince men that the Holy Spirit, the consoler and enricher of your faithful, was with full authority personally present in him. Therefore, when he was found out to have taught falsely about the heavens and the stars and the movements of the sun and the moon, although such things do not belong to religious doctrine, it would be quite clear that his were sacrilegious presumptions. (*Conf.* V. 5)

So it turned out, he thought, that Manichaeism demanded blind faith fully as much as the Catholics, with the difference that at least the Catholics avoided the arrogance of pretending to have full knowledge where they were ignorant (*Conf.* VI. 5). And once Augustine and his friends began to find kinks in the Manichaean armor, they took pleasure in finding and exposing the many inconsistencies that such myths invariably contain.[165]

It was in this state of doubt and uncertainty that Augustine sailed from Carthage for Rome in the year 383. He was an ambitious man, clearly the leading light of the Carthaginian intelligentsia and tired of dealing with the rude and undisciplined provincial students of his African homeland. And so he sailed for Rome, seeking "better order and discipline," "greater stipends" and "greater honors" (*Conf.* V. 8).

In going to Rome, Augustine left behind the world in which Manichaeism was dominant among the elite, and he found himself in a very different world, the world of the real ruling class of the empire. There were indeed Manichaeans in Rome, though they were forced to operate less openly, and Augustine lived with Manichaeans during his year there (*Conf.* V. 10). But Augustine had gone to Rome in hopes of catching the eye of some of the leading families of the empire, which was the only hope for an ambitious provincial, and Manichaeism did not have its strength among those old aristocratic families.

The great senatorial families were always on the lookout for able young men, and they were quite ready to patronize those who served their needs.

> They would be only too glad to patronize, and eventually to co-opt, a man such as Augustine. They needed teachers for their sons, well-trained spokesmen for their grievances, amateur administrators duly impressed by the vast prestige of their traditional way of life. These men represented the peak of Augustine's ambition as a young man.[166]

And so Augustine's move to Rome was in fact a move that was to carry him into the midst of the ruling class, where he would spend the remainder of his life.

Actually, the project did not get off to an altogether auspicious start. He had sneaked away from Carthage partly to escape the mother who constantly hovered over him and obsessed about his salvation (*Conf.* V. 8). To the guilt that he obviously felt about this subterfuge was soon added an illness that nearly cost him his life (*Conf.* V. 9). And finally, he found the more sophisticated students of Rome, while better disciplined, also much more clever and ruthless in finding ways to avoid paying their fees (*Conf.* V. 12).

Under these circumstances, it was no doubt a great relief to him that he managed to catch the eye of the great senator, Symmachus, prefect of the city. It happened that Milan was just then in need of a professor of rhetoric, and Symmachus recommended Augustine for the post. Apparently at least part of the reason Augustine was chosen was that Symmachus, a pagan, was hopeful that sending a bright young Manichee to Milan might help undercut the influence of Symmachus' cousin, Ambrose, who was the Catholic bishop of Milan (*Conf.* V. 13).

Augustine's appointment as professor of rhetoric in Milan moved him finally into the heart of the ruling circle of the empire. His position made him one of the most prominent academicians of the city, selected to deliver an annual ritual address to honor the young emperor Valentinian II, who was then living in Milan (*Conf.* VI. 6). It was not very long before he sent the woman who had loved him so long back to Africa and selected an aristocratic girl to marry when she came of age (*Conf.* VI. 13 and 15). And he found himself accepted among some of the most powerful and impressive men of his day.

Among his friends he still counted some of the provincial aristocrats who had long been friends and who now had the means to follow him to

Milan. These included, besides his hometown patron, Romanianus, close companions such as Nebridius and Alypius, both of whom would eventually return home to join him as Catholic bishops (*Conf.* VI. 10). But he also found himself moving among a traditional elite of a quite different order of prestige and power. Symmachus, the prefect of Rome who had recommended him for his Milanese position, was among the most lavishly wealthy senators, owning at least three townhouses and fifteen country retreats, including no less than three massive estates.[167] Another of his new friends was Manlius Theodorus, a powerful senator who had held a number of imperial posts before retiring to his country estate to study philosophy and who was to re-emerge as consul in 399.[168] There was Verecundus, a prominent and wealthy rhetorician, who made his country estate at Cassiciacum available to Augustine and his friends when they wished to further their own leisured pursuit of philosophy (*Conf.* IX. 3).[169] And there were a number of others, including Zenobius to whom he dedicated one of his early works (*Div. Prov.* 2. 4).

Alongside these men, some of whom were already Catholic Christians and some of whom were to convert only later, there were others who made an even deeper impression on Augustine. These were men who were certainly as much at the center of the ruling class as those mentioned above, and some of them came from the most powerful senatorial families. But they had cast their lot with the Catholic Church and had exchanged imperial authority and office for ecclesiastical power and office. Operating at the pinnacle of the hierarchy of the imperial church, they were among the most influential figures of the day, called on to advise and consult and sometimes even able to call the emperor himself to repentance.

The greatest of these and the man who most influenced Augustine at this stage was Ambrose, the senatorial aristocrat turned Catholic autocrat, who was bishop of Milan. In Ambrose, Augustine was able to find a new ideal, one that combined classical refinement and enormous prestige and power with a single-minded and radically activist devotion to his god. Son of a praetorian prefect of Gaul, educated in Rome, Ambrose had been governor of the great Italian province centered in Milan before he was thirty. When the Arian bishop of Milan died and Ambrose intervened as mediator between fighting Arians and Catholics, he had found himself drafted as bishop. He had taken this as a call from God and had quickly made the transition from civil authority to ecclesiastical authority.

In contrast to the unlettered and outlawed Manichaeans, Augustine saw in Ambrose the powerful and supremely confident Roman Catholic aristocracy that was taking control of the empire and establishing the church as its dominant institution. And against the suffering and largely passive Manichaean god of light who is defeated again and again and must eternally struggle to set free his own defiled nature, Augustine could now place the triumphant and omnipotent god of Ambrose who was establishing his authority throughout the world. With single-minded determination, Ambrose had fought off the efforts of Justina, mother of the child-emperor Valentinian II, to restore Arianism. And Augustine watched as Ambrose defeated the attempts of his cousin Symmachus to revive paganism by restoring the Altar of Victory to its place in the senate house of Rome.[170] This was a man who would later call the emperor Theodosius to penance for a massacre in Thessalonica.[171] And when Eugenius once again considered restoring pagan idols, Ambrose could write:

> The imperial power is great, but consider, O Emperor, how great God is. He sees the hearts of all; He probes their inmost conscience; He knows all things before they come to pass; He knows the inmost secrets of your heart. You do not allow yourself to be deceived; do you expect to hide anything from God? Has this thought not occurred to you?[172]

Here again was the god of his mother, and in Ambrose he saw not only the triumph of that god, but also a new way of life in a new aristocracy, an aristocracy of ecclesiastical service that combined enormous power and prestige with selfless devotion to God.

Augustine had been about ready to abandon the Manichaeans for some time. And when the preaching of Ambrose made it seem that there might be a figurative way of interpreting the Old Testament which would render it more acceptable, that was enough to persuade him to a final break with Manichaeism (*Conf.* V. 14).

But while he was ready to leave his old cult behind, Augustine could not yet commit himself to Catholicism. Two problems confronted him. One was certainly that he now felt that any commitment to the Catholic god must be a total commitment. Perhaps some gentlemen could pay lip service to the Catholic god while continuing to pursue classical learning and even to dabble in pagan rituals.[173] But for Augustine, the call of God was a call to abandon the "things of the world" and to devote his life exclusively to service. For him the Catholic god had never been an abstract "wisdom," but had been and remained the living Father who demands total obedience from his children. If he was to abandon the Manichaean conception of God and return to this god, the commitment could not be half-hearted. And while this did not necessarily mean a loss of power or prestige, it certainly did call for other sacrifices. It meant that instead of a prosperous career, marriage and eventual retirement to a life of leisured reflection, he would face a life of chastity, disciplined effort and service to the masses of the faithful. It was a decision that obviously provoked the most intense self-doubt and ambivalence.

> You took me from behind my own back, where I had placed myself because I did not wish to look upon myself. You stood me face to face with myself, so that I might see how foul I was, how deformed and defiled, how covered with stains and sores. I looked, and I was filled with horror, but there was no place for me to flee to away from myself. (*Conf.* VIII. 7)[174]

Alongside this very practical problem, there was, however, another that is more directly germane to the present discussion. While he was certainly impressed with the god of Ambrose and his conquest of the whole world, he was still confronted with many of the doubts about this god that had led him to Manichaeism in the first place. He was convinced that he would never be able to understand everything he needed to know before making a commitment. And he was also convinced that the very triumph of the Catholic god should itself be enough to establish the right of that god to his allegiance:

> Therefore, since we were too weak to find the truth by pure reason, and for that cause we needed the authority of Holy Writ, I now began to believe that in no wise would you have given such surpassing authority throughout the whole world to that Scripture, unless you wished that both through it you be believed in and through it you be sought. (*Conf.* VI. 5)

But at the same time, nagging doubts about this god kept him from making that commitment.

The god of Ambrose was the omnipotent, unchallengeable ruler of the universe, the lord of human destiny, the absolutely supreme being. This is what Augustine *wanted* to believe, what he knew *must* be true. The problem was to come to a conception of God on which these things could be consistently believed. So, for example, he knew that the god he was now called to must be impervious to harm from any source, absolutely inviolable and incorruptible, and yet neither of the myths by which he had so far conceived his god seemed to allow that possibility. Neither the anthropomorphic god of his youth nor the extensive being of light of the Manichaeans who finds his being mixed with matter seemed to measure up to the new standard, and yet these were the only conceptions available. So he reports that

> I believed with all my soul that you are incorruptible, and inviolable, and immutable. Not knowing whence or how, I clearly saw and was certain that what can be corrupted is inferior to what cannot be corrupted, and what cannot be violated I unhesitatingly placed above what is violable, and what suffers no change I saw to be better than what can be changed. (*Conf.* VII. 1)

But how could he think of God in this way when he could conceive God only as a corporeal being?

> Hence, although I did not think of you as being in the shape of a human body, I was forced to think of you as something corporeal, existent in space and place, either infused into the world or even diffused outside the world throughout infinite space....For whatever I conceived as devoid of such spatial character seemed to me to be nothing, absolutely nothing, not even so much as an empty space. (*Conf.* VII. 1)

He reports that he tried to think of God as "a great corporeal substance, existent everywhere throughout infinite space, which penetrates the whole world-mass, and spreads beyond it on every side, throughout immense, limitless space." He knew that this could not be so, since in that case "all things would be filled with you, in such wise that an elephant's body would receive more of you than would a sparrow's," but he was unable to think of God in any better way (*Conf.* VII. 1).

Perhaps more importantly, he still had no answer to the question of why an omnipotent and perfectly good god would create or even allow evil in his creation. Still under the sway of the Manichaean myth, he thought again of his god as an infinite being of light that fills all things.

> 'Behold God and behold what God has created! God is good. Most
> mightily and most immeasurably does he surpass these things. But
> being good, he has created good things. Behold how he encircles and
> fills all things! Where then is evil, and whence and by what means has
> it crept in here? What is its root, and what is its seed?...Whence, there-
> fore, is evil, since God the good has made all these things good? He,
> the greater, the supreme good, has made these lesser goods, yet both
> creator and all created things are good. Whence comes evil? Was there
> a certain evil matter, out of which he made these things? Did he form
> and fashion it, but yet leave within it something that he would not con-
> vert into good? Why would he do this? Was he powerless to turn and
> change all this matter, so that no evil would remain in it, even though
> he is all-powerful? Lastly, why should he will to make anything at all
> out of it, and not rather by that same omnipotence cause that it should
> not exist at all? Or forsooth, did it have the power to exist against his
> will? (*Conf.* VII. 5)

And when he turned to look at his own being, he found evil in the very
heart of it, and that too needed an explanation. The god of Ambrose
was not only the omnipotent creator, but he was the absolutely just
judge of each soul. But how can there be justice in God's punishment
if, as seems so clear, evil is built into the very nature of human beings
and stands against God as an alien power?

> But then again I said: 'Who made me? Was it not you, my God, who are
> not merely good, but goodness itself? Whence then comes it, then, that I
> will evil, and do not will the good? That there may be a reason why I
> should justly be punished? Who has placed this in me and ingrafted in
> me this seedbed of bitterness, since I have been fashioned whole and
> entire by my most sweet God? If the devil is its author, whence comes
> the devil himself?'...By such thoughts I was again crushed and stifled.
> (*Conf.* VII. 3)

Confronted with the problem of evil, he found himself unable even to
begin thinking about it constructively. And again, what stood in his
way was the dominance of the Manichaean myth that shaped his conception of God. He puts this explicitly in an earlier passage.

> To me it seemed a most base thing to believe that you have the shape of
> our human flesh and are bounded by the outward lines of our bodily
> members. I wished to meditate upon my God, but I did not know how
> to think of him except as a vast corporeal mass, for I thought that any-

thing not a body was nothing whatsoever. This was the greatest and almost the sole cause of my inevitable error. As a result, I believed that evil is some such substance and that it possesses its own foul and hideous mass....Because some sort of reverence forced me to believe that a good God would create no evil nature, I postulated two masses opposed to one another, each of them infinite, but the evil one on a narrower scale, the good one larger. (*Conf.* V. 10)

It is important to be clear about just what Augustine's difficulty was at this stage. His concern was not at all to try to establish by reason the existence or nature of the Catholic god. His experience with the rationalistic pretensions of the Manichees had convinced him that the basic truths of religion are not accessible to reason, and in fact he had, for a brief time, thought that the most rational men were the academic skeptics who denied the very possibility of any certain knowledge (*Conf.* V. 10). After hearing Ambrose, the Catholic demand for a commitment of faith seemed to him no longer irrational, but modest and sensible.

From that time forward I preferred Catholic teaching. I thought that on its part it was more moderate and not at all deceptive to command men to believe what was not demonstrated, either because it was a matter that could be demonstrated, but perhaps not to everyone, or because it was indemonstrable, than for others to make a mockery of credulity by rash promises of sure knowledge, and then commanding that so many most fabulous and absurd things be accepted on trust because they could not be demonstrated. (*Conf.* VI. 5)

And now, having seen the Catholic god establishing his church at the very heart of the empire, he had no doubt that this was the god to be worshiped. Even as he struggled with the questions discussed above, he never doubted that the Catholic god was the true god.

Yet in none of those wavering thoughts did you let me be carried away from that faith in which I believed both that you exist, and that your substance is unchangeable, and that you have care over men and pass judgment on them, and that in Christ, your Son, our Lord, and in the Holy Scriptures, which the authority of your Catholic Church approves, you have placed the way of man's salvation unto that life which is to be after this death. These truths being made safe and fixed immovably in my mind, I asked uncertainly 'Whence is evil?' (*Conf.* VII. 7)

What Augustine was seeking was neither a demonstration of God's existence nor evidence of God's nature. What he was seeking was a basic idea of God that would enable him to develop a consistent conception of the nature of God and of God's relation to creation. What he needed, in short, was a new myth to replace both the anthropomorphic original myth and the Manichaean myth that still held his imagination despite his having rejected it.

In his search for a myth to make sense of what he knew must be believed, Augustine turned not only to Ambrose, but even more to those cultured and refined gentlemen among whom he moved in his profession. Many of these men were also Christians, but even where they had adopted Catholic Christianity, their focus was not on the triumphant Catholic god who was ordering the world through his church and who called all people before the bar of his justice. Their focus was on a leisured pursuit of "Wisdom," on a "philosophy" that would lift their souls out of the degradation of this world and the body that entrapped it and lift them back to that source of being and truth that they were sure was the true home of all noble souls. And to guide them in their quest, these men had also found and developed a supporting myth, one that they called by the name of "Platonism."

> These men thought of themselves as taking part in a Renaissance of philosophy. A century before, the authentic doctrine of Plato had been rediscovered: the clouds had parted, and this, 'the most refined and enlightened' teaching in philosophy, could shine out in its full brilliance, in the works of Plotinus—a soul so close to his ancient master that in him Plato seemed to live again. Such men even had dreams, in which philosophers expounded 'Platonic maxims' to them in their sleep. We call this movement 'Neo-Platonism': but the participants called themselves 'Platonists', *Platonici*, pure and simple—that is, the direct heirs of Plato.[175]

These men introduced Augustine to their myth, which I shall call the Plotinian myth (because Augustine absorbed it primarily through his reading of the philosopher Plotinus), and it played a crucial role in the development of his idea of God (*Conf.* VII. 9).[176] The next section will review this myth and Augustine's absorption and use of it to develop the conception of God that finally came to dominate his religious consciousness.

III. The Plotinian Myth

Augustine was appointed professor of rhetoric at Milan in the autumn of 384, but by his own account, he was not introduced to the "books of the Platonists" until the spring of 386. This chronology is somewhat difficult to accept, since we know that by the time of his conversion to Catholicism and his retreat at Cassiciacum in September of 386, he had so completely absorbed the Platonist outlook that he was able to speak and write from that perspective with the ease of an old hand. It seems likely that even if his formal reading of Plotinus did not begin until June of 386, he had probably been moving among men who used Platonist modes of expression and thought for some time.

In fact, Platonism was, to a greater extent than any other system of thought, associated with the gentlemanly life of leisure, withdrawal and the "turning inward" of the soul in contemplation, so it would have been difficult for Augustine not to encounter it in the circles he frequented. A constant feature of elite ideology for a thousand years had been the pretension of a special "happiness" available only to the "best" men who enjoyed the free time and the "cultivation" to realize the most "noble" and complete fulfillment of the "life of the soul." Indeed, at times there had been an explicit connection made between this leisured cultivation of the soul and fitness to rule.[177] And although Plotinus and his disciple Porphyry no longer put emphasis on such political implications, their thought was very much in this tradition.

For many a Roman gentleman, the life of *otium* meant not merely an opportunity for reflection, but freedom from official duties which allowed one to focus on the accumulation of wealth. It was among men such as these that the contemplative "inwardness" of Plotinus could secure purchase. And it was among such men that Augustine moved from the time he first came to Milan.

The "Platonism" that Augustine encountered is not easy to describe in a straightforward way, since it was more nearly a kind of mystical cult than a philosophical system. It is directed less toward a rational account of reality than toward a liberating and transforming "vision." Those who called themselves Platonists shared a sense that their souls were, at one and the same time, both alienated from an original source of being and yet still somehow essentially united with that source. And the Plotinian myth, as developed in *The Enneads* of Plotinus, was an elaborate, complex, obscure and often paradoxical attempt to provide a picture of reality that would capture that double sense of alienation from and identity with the source of all being, while at the same time providing guidance for those seeking a "return" to complete unity with the original source.

When Plotinus (205–270 A.D.) arrived in Rome in the year 244, he quickly became the leading cultural light of the city.[178] He was not only a close friend and adviser to many great senatorial families, but he was an intimate of the emperor Gallienus, whom he almost persuaded to build a city devoted to the study of philosophy and to be called Platonopolis.[179] He had studied in Alexandria with Ammonius Saccas, an enigmatic figure of great influence, and he presented himself to the Roman aristocracy not as in any sense a radical figure, but as a conservative Hellene, steeped in ancient tradition and conveying an ancient truth.

For a thousand years and more, many of the "best" men had found the material world, with all its mutability, irregularity and chaos, an unacceptable reality. They were sure that this world was grounded in an eternal, immutable and ultimately unitary reality. The ideas of beauty, order and goodness that they found in their own souls could not, they believed, have had their origin in this defective world and so must be referred back to that eternal reality in which perfect beauty, order and goodness had their home. And the fact that those ideas were, however imperfectly, found within their souls, they took as testimony both to the soul's original unity with eternal reality and to its present alienation from its proper resting place.

> Let us, then, go back to the source, and indicate at once the Principle that bestows beauty on material things. Undoubtedly this Principle exists; it is something that is perceived at the first glance, something which the Soul names as from an ancient knowledge and, recognizing, welcomes it, enters into unison with it.[180]

The aim of intellectual and spiritual endeavor, then, became first an effort of the soul to identify the eternal "light" within itself and then an "ascent" of the soul back to that original unity. It is this outlook that the Plotinian myth was designed to capture.

The Plotinian myth is paradoxical and internally contradictory at many points. I think the best way to approach it is to realize that it is designed to make sense of the two central aspects of the sensibility described above: on the one hand, a sense that true reality must be somehow unitary, harmonious and complete, and, on the other hand, a sense that one's own soul is somehow both linked to and part of that true reality, and yet, at the same time, separated and lost from it. When these two aspects are combined, what emerges is a sense that reality must be both one and many, both harmonious and chaotic, both united and divided. The aim of the Plotinian myth is to capture this sensibility in all its paradoxicality.

The first of the aspects mentioned above—that of unity, order and harmony—is centered in the Plotinian concept of the One, while the second aspect—that of alienation and separation—is centered in the concept of the individual soul. And one way of approaching the myth is by seeing it as attempting to describe reality from the "point of view" of each of these simultaneously.

Seen, as it were, from the "point of view" of the One, the whole of reality is a perfect and complete order. The One is the absolute first principle, sometimes referred to as the supreme, the good or even as God, in which case it may be thought of as a person and addressed by the pronoun "he."

> And yet this 'He' does not truly apply: the Supreme has no need of Being: even 'He is good' does not apply since it indicates Being; the 'is' should not suggest something predicated of another thing; it is to state identity. The word 'good' used of him is not a predicate asserting his possession of goodness; it conveys an identification. It is not that we think it exact to call him either good or The Good: it is that sheer negation does not indicate; we use the term The Good to assert identity without the affirmation of Being.[181]

Thus we use terms to designate the One since "sheer negation does not indicate," but we recognize always that "strictly no name is apt to it."[182] The One is wholly self-contained, dependent on nothing and is "the principle of its own satisfaction."[183] Since discursive thought requires both a subject and an object and since no object stands over against the One, it can be said that "the Supreme will know neither itself nor anything else but will hold an august repose."[184] But since the One is absolute perfection, it must not be thought to be without consciousness, so it may be regarded as having "an immediate intuition self-directed."[185] The One is, in short, "utterly perfect above all, the beginning of all power."[186]

But while the One is complete and perfect and sufficient unto itself, it is also, by its very goodness, such that it "emanates" outward and creates being.

> If the First is perfect, utterly perfect above all, and is the beginning of all power, it must be the most powerful of all that is, and all other powers must act in some partial imitation of it. Now other beings, coming to perfection, are observed to generate; they are unable to remain self-closed; they produce: and this is true not merely of beings endowed with will, but of growing things where there is no will....How then could the most perfect remain self-set—the First Good, the Power towards all, how could it grudge or be powerless to give of itself, and how would it still be the Source? If things other than itself are to exist, things dependent upon it for their reality, it must produce since there is no other source. And, further, this engendering principle must be the very highest in worth; and its immediate offspring, its secondary, must be the best of all that follows.[187]

So from this original unity proceeds all being. And the first "emanation" from the One, "the best of all that follows," is the intellectual-principle (*Nous*). The intellectual-principle is used by Plotinus to link the unitary and self-contained One with the world of beings. The intellectual-principle contains within itself the forms or ideas of all beings, and since true reality is identified not with material being, but with immaterial form, it can also be said that the intellectual-principle actually contains all being.

> We take it, then, that the Intellectual Principle is the authentic existences and contains them all—not as in a place but as possessing itself and being one thing with this its content. All are one There and yet are distinct....[188]

Since the intellectual-principle contains the form of each individual, and since the forms within the intellectual-principle are identical with the intellectual-principle itself, it follows that each individual is really one with the whole of being.

> Since in our view this universe stands to that as copy to original, the living total must exist There beforehand; that is the realm of complete Being and everything must exist There.[189]

As the representative of the One in the realm of being, the intellectual-principle is sometimes referred to as the *logos* or "utterance" (word) or "reason" of the One, that which not only is the source of being and intelligibility in the world, but is also that which acts as mediator in linking the world with the primal unity of the One.[190]

The next great emanation proceeds from the intellectual-principle and is referred to as soul. Soul is, as is all being, identical with the intellectual-principle, but it is also capable of "going forth" from the intellectual-principle and becoming divided by being embodied in matter. It is by this going forth and this division that soul, while remaining eternally undivided, becomes, at the same time, individual souls.

> In the Intellectual Cosmos dwells Authentic Essence, with the Intellectual-Principle (Divine Mind) as the noblest of its content, but containing also souls, since every soul in this lower sphere has come thence: that is the world of unembodied souls while to our world belong those that have entered body and undergone bodily division....The Intellectual-Principle is for ever repugnant to distinction and to partition. Soul, there without distinction and partition, has yet a nature lending itself to divisional existence: its division is secession, entry into body. In view of this seceding and the ensuing partition we may legitimately speak of it as 'divided among bodies'. But if so, how can it still be described as indivisible? In that the secession is not of the Soul entire; something of it holds its ground, that in it which recoils from separate existence. 'Formed from the undivided essence and the essence divided among bodies': this description of Soul must therefore mean that it has phases above and below, that it is attached to the Supreme and yet reaches down to this sphere, like a radius from a centre.[191]

Thus, still looking at reality from the "point of view" of the One, the entire structure of being is a single, ordered whole. The emanation of the entire structure from the One is timeless and eternal, a perfect and complete architectonic unity, in which each "level" retains its perfect unity, while also "overflowing" to generate the next "level."

> It is of the essence of things that each gives of its being to another: without this communication, The Good would not be Good, nor the Intellectual-Principle an Intellective Principle nor would Soul itself be what it is: the law is, 'some life after the Primal Life, a second where there is a first; all linked in one unbroken chain; all eternal; divergent types of being engendered only in the sense of being secondary.' In

other words, things commonly described as generated have never known a beginning: all has been and will be.[192]

But now let us turn and look at this reality not from the "point of view" of the One, but from that of the individual souls that have entered into matter and find themselves embodied. From this angle, the entire structure takes on a quite different aspect.

For one thing, when individual souls experience the world of matter, they experience not an eternal reality, but a world caught up in time and change.

> Hence, time is aptly described as a mimic of eternity that seeks to break up in its fragmentary flight the permanence of its exemplar. Thus whatever time seizes and seals to itself of what stands permanent in eternity is annihilated—saved only in so far as in some degree it still belongs to eternity, but wholly destroyed if it be universally absorbed into time.[193]

If we go back now, for just a moment, and look again from the "point of view" of the One, this world is seen to be an image of that perfect reality from which it flows, and it really makes no sense to ask *why* the world came to be or why it unfolds as it does. The One "overflows" because it is good, and the intellectual-principle gives rise to that image which reflects its own perfect order.

> The All that has emerged into life is no amorphous structure—like those lesser forms within it which are born night and day out of the lavishness of its vitality—the Universe is a life organized, effective, complex, all-comprehensive, displaying an unfathomable wisdom. How, then, can anyone deny that it is a clear image, beautifully formed, of the Intellectual Divinities? No doubt it is a copy, not original; but that is its very nature; it cannot be at once symbol and reality. But to say that it is an inadequate copy is false; nothing has been left out which a beautiful representation within the physical order could include.[194]

> To ask why the Soul has created the Cosmos, is to ask why there is a Soul and why the Creator creates. The question, also, implies a beginning in the eternal and, further, represents creation as the act of a changeful Being who turns from this to that.[195]

But if we look at it from the "point of view" of the world of individual souls, the world of time and change, what formerly appeared as a finished structure now appears as an historical reality, unfolding in time. And what formerly appeared as the finished image of a perfectly unitary reality now appears as a world of becoming in which all beings and events work together to fulfill the perfect plan of an omnipotent and benevolent being who orders the whole of history by his will.

> This Universe, too, exists by Him and looks to Him—the Universe as a whole and every god within it—and tells of Him to men, all alike revealing the plan and will of the Supreme.[196]

> Another point: (you hold that) God has care for you; how then can He be indifferent to the entire Universe in which you exist? We may be told that He is too much occupied to look upon the Universe, and that it would not be right for Him to do so; yet when He looks down and upon these people, is He not looking outside Himself and upon the Universe in which they exist? If He cannot look outside Himself so as to survey the Cosmos, then neither does He look upon them.[197]

But to say that creation is due to the will of the Supreme is not to suggest any element of capriciousness. As an absolute unity, the Supreme contains no distinction between its essence and its will, and since its essence is goodness, creation necessarily represents the perfect order that is its source.

> Our inquiry obliges us to use terms not strictly applicable: we insist, once more, that not even for the purpose of forming the concept of the Supreme may we make it a duality; if now we do, it is merely for the sake of conveying conviction, at some cost of verbal accuracy. If then, we are to allow Activities in the Supreme and make them depend upon will—and certainly Act cannot There be will-less—and these Activities are to be the very essence, then will and essence in the Supreme must be identical. This admitted, as He willed to be so He is; it is no more true to say that He wills and acts as his nature determines than that his essence is as He wills and acts. Thus He is wholly master of Himself and holds his very being at his will.[198]

When individual souls are seen as belonging to this world of time and change, it seems that they have "fallen" from their identity with true being and are now trapped in matter, dominated by bodily desire and yearning for their lost home.

> So it is with individual souls....In the Intellectual, then, they remain with the All-Soul, and are immune from care and trouble; in the heaven-

ly sphere, inseparable from the All-Soul, they are administrators with it...the Souls indeed are thus far in the one place; but there comes a stage at which they descend from the universal to become partial and self-centered; in a weary desire of standing apart they find their way, each to a place of its very own. This state long maintained, the Soul is a deserter from the totality; its differentiation has severed it; its vision is no longer set in the Intellectual; it is a partial thing, isolated, weakened, full of care, intent upon the fragment; severed from the whole, it nestles in one form of being; for this it abandons all else, entering into and caring for only the one, for a thing buffeted about by a worldful of things; thus it has drifted away from the universal and, by an actual presence, it administers the particular; it is caught into contact now, and tends to the outer to which it has become present and into whose inner depths it henceforth sinks far.[199]

Seen in this way, the soul is trapped by its own desires and choices. This turning away from unity is its "sin," and the perfect order of the universe, administered by the many gods as agents of the eternal One, is such that each soul must pay the penalty for its sin in suffering, isolation and continued rebirth, until it can be set free once more.

Our adversaries do not deny that even here there is a system of law and penalty: and surely we cannot in justice blame a dominion which awards to every one his due, where virtue has its honour, and vice comes to its fitting shame, in which there are not merely representations of the gods, but the gods themselves, watchers from above, and—as we read—easily rebutting human reproaches, since they lead all things in order from a beginning to an end allotting to each human being, as life follows life, a fortune shaped to all that has preceded—the destiny which, to those that do not penetrate it, becomes the matter of boorish insolence upon things divine.[200]

In this condition, individual souls dimly remember and yearn for a return to that perfect order from which they fell and to which they still feel remotely linked:

for all that exists desires and aspires towards the Supreme by a compulsion of nature, as if all had received the oracle that without it they cannot be.[201]

The soul of each person is, therefore, at once both united with eternal Soul and isolated in the misery of individuality. Plotinus insists that, despite its apparent contradictoriness, this dual status must be asserted, because that is the experience of the soul itself. The lived experience of each soul is at once both an aspect of the unfolding of perfect order and the freely chosen course of egoistic individuality.

> It is possible to reconcile all these apparent contradictions—the divine sowing to birth, as opposed to a descent aimed at the completion of the universe; the judgment and the cave; necessity and free choice—in fact the necessity includes the choice...in a word, a voluntary descent which is also involuntary. All degeneration is no doubt involuntary, yet when it has been brought about by an inherent tendency, that submission to the inferior may be described as the penalty of an act. On the other hand these experiences and actions are determined by an eternal law of nature, and they are due to the movement of a being which in abandoning its superior is running out to serve the needs of another: hence there is no inconsistency or untruth in saying that the Soul is sent down by God....[202]

The individual soul is both in bondage to sin and eternally united with its source. The original experience of simultaneous alienation from and yet linkage with true being, which the myth was generated to explain, is now reflected in the paradoxical assertion that Soul is simultaneously one and many, sinless and guilty.

> But if Soul is sinless, how come the expiations? Here surely is a contradiction; on the one side the Soul is above all guilt; on the other, we hear of its sin, its purification, its expiation; it is doomed to the lower world, it passes from body to body. We may take either view at will: they are easily reconciled. When we tell of the sinless Soul we make Soul and Essential-Soul one and the same: it is the simple unbroken Unity. By the Soul subject to sin we indicate a groupment, we include that other, that phase of the Soul which knows all the states and passions: the Soul in this sense is compound, all-inclusive: it falls under the conditions of the entire living experience: this compound it is that sins, it is this, and not the other, that pays penalty.[203]

This, then, in briefest summary, is the Plotinian myth. And along with the myth itself, there is, as in the case of the Manichaean myth, a program through which individual souls may strive to return to the unity they seek. It is a program available only to a few of the "noblest" souls and possible only for those able to pursue a life of leisured withdrawal.

The first step in the recovery of the soul is to master the "science" of dialectic, by which the mind is able to grasp the interrelatedness of all being and the relationship between the particulars of this world and the universal beings of the eternal order from which they come.

> But this science, this Dialectic...what, in sum, is it? It is the Method, or Discipline, that brings with it the power of pronouncing with final truth upon the nature and relation of things—what each is, how it differs from others, what common quality all have, to what Kind each belongs and in what rank each stands in its Kind and whether its Being is Real-Being, and how many Beings there are, and how many non-Beings to be distinguished from Beings. Dialectic treats also of the Good and the not-Good, and of the particulars that fall under each, and of what is the Eternal and what the not-Eternal—and of these, it must be understood, not by seeming-knowledge (opinion) but with authentic science. All this accomplished, it gives up its touring of the realm of sense and settles down in the Intellectual Cosmos and there plies its own peculiar Act: it has abandoned all the realm of deceit and falsity, and pastures the Soul in the 'Meadows of Truth': it employs the Platonic division to the discernment of the Ideal-Forms, of the Authentic-Existence, and of the First-Kinds (or Categories of Being): it establishes, in the light of Intellection, the affiliations of all that issues from these Firsts, until it has traversed the entire Intellectual Realm: then, by means of analysis, it takes the opposite path and returns once more to the First Principle. Now it rests: caught up in the tranquility of that sphere, it is no longer busy about many things: it has arrived at Unity and it contemplates.[204]

But this is only the first step. Ultimately, the aim is to transcend reason entirely in a direct experience of union with the One.

> But what must we do? How lies the path? How come to vision of the inaccessible Beauty, dwelling as if in consecrated precincts, apart from the common ways where all may see, even the profane? He that has the strength, let him arise and withdraw into himself, foregoing all that is known by the eyes, turning away for ever from the material beauty that once made his joy. When he perceives those shapes of grace that show in body, let him not pursue: he must know them for copies, vestiges, shadows, and hasten away towards That they tell of.[205]

This heroic work of self-elevation is carried out by the noble soul itself which makes itself fit for union and lifts itself up to that ultimate vision.

But how are you to see into a virtuous Soul and know its loveliness? Withdraw into yourself and look. And if you do not find yourself beautiful yet, act as does the creator of a statue that is to be made beautiful: he cuts away here, he smooths there, he makes this line lighter, this other purer, until a lovely face has grown upon his work. So do you also: cut away all that is excessive, straighten all that is crooked...and never cease chiselling your statue until there shall shine out on you from it the godlike splendour of virtue, until you shall see the perfect goodness surely established in the stainless shrine. When you know that you have become this perfect work, when you are self-gathered in the purity of your being, nothing now remaining that can shatter that inner unity, nothing from without clinging to the authentic man, when you find yourself wholly true to your essential nature, wholly that only veritable Light which is not measured by space, not narrowed to any circumscribed form nor again diffused as a thing void of term, but ever unmeasurable as something greater than all measure and more than all quantity—when you perceive that you have grown to this, you are now become very vision: now call up all your confidence, strike forward yet a step—you need a guide no longer—strain and see.[206]

The end of this quest and the hope of the Plotinian mystic is for the ultimate blessedness of a final union.

This is the life of gods and of the godlike and blessed among men, liberation from the alien that besets us here, a life taking no pleasure in the things of earth, the passing of solitary to solitary.[207]

But finally, it is worth noting that, despite the apparent implication of the above passage, Plotinus did not believe that the final union could be achieved in this life. The best hope was for a momentary vision that would give a glimpse of the final union after death.

Many times it has happened: lifted out of the body into myself; becoming external to all other things and self-encentered; beholding a marvellous beauty: then, more than ever, assured of community with the loftiest order; enacting the noblest life, acquiring identity with the divine; stationing within It by having attained that activity; poised above whatsoever within the Intellectual is less than the Supreme: yet there comes the moment of descent from intellection to reasoning, and after that sojourn in the divine, I ask myself how it happens that I can now be descending, and how did the Soul ever enter into my body, the Soul which, even within the body, is the high thing it has shown itself to be.[208]

But how comes the soul not to keep that ground? Because it has not yet escaped wholly: but there will be the time of vision unbroken, the self hindered no longer by any hindrance of body.[209]

To understand how this myth could be so easily accepted by educated gentlemen who were trained above all in clarity and precision of expression, we must recognize the extent to which a certain sort of experience had taken possession of the cultured Roman elite. These men intensely *felt* that their souls were "fallen," that there must be something *more* beyond this transient material world, some original whole from which they were lost. In their love of a pure beauty and order that they never found in this world, they sensed that there must be some dim "recollection" of a reality lost when the "true self" had been distorted or buried by the preoccupations of passion, sense experience and intercourse with the world. The paradoxicality of the Plotinian myth has its roots in this sense that the inmost essence of noble souls is both lost from and yet still linked to that perfect unity that is the ground of being. Brown remarks that this idea was "as basic to the thought of the age of Augustine as is the idea of Evolution to our own."[210] It was not an idea that was pervasive in the culture—indeed it had its place only in the minds of a small minority—but it certainly seems to have had that status among many Roman intellectuals and aristocrats.

When Augustine entered this privileged circle and was introduced to the Plotinian outlook, he was quite swept away by it. Almost immediately he accepted most of the attitudes and beliefs of the Platonists as fundamentally true (even if not the whole "truth") and as obviously superior to everything he had so far encountered. He wrote of the many things he "learned" from the "books of the Platonists," but this learning involved very little in the way of being convinced by evidence or arguments. Rather, this new myth, legitimated by the most ancient and venerable "philosophy" and endorsed by the "best" men of the empire, both pagan and Catholic, took possession of him under the aspect of self-evident truth. So deeply did it penetrate that within a few months of first hearing this new "truth," Augustine was interpreting his own inner experience from that point of view as though it were the only possible one.

Looking back on this period years later, Augustine describes the way the Plotinian myth infused his consciousness. God became very like the Plotinian One calling him back to primal unity.

> Being thus admonished to return to myself, under your leadership I entered into my inmost being....I entered there, and by my soul's eye, such as it was, I saw above that same eye of my soul, above my mind, an unchangeable light. It was not this common light, as it were, of the same kind....Nor was it above my mind, as oil is above water, or sky above earth. It was above my mind, because it made me, and I was beneath it, because I was made by it. He who knows the truth, knows that light, and he who knows it knows eternity....When first I knew you, you took me up, so that I might see that there was something to see, but that I was not yet one able to see it....I found myself to be far from you in a region of unlikeness, as though I heard your voice from on high: 'I am the food of grown men. Grow, and you shall feed upon me. You will not change me into yourself, as you change food into your flesh, but you will be changed into me.' (*Conf.* VII. 11)

And once he was initiated into this eternal reality "which the intellect of a few sound men beholds" (*Ans. to Skep.* I. 11. 32), he came to see the whole of reality from a new perspective. Under the authority of those "few sound men," he was able for the first time to "realize" not only that there may be immaterial being, but that true being is necessarily immaterial. Thus he was able to break free of both the Manichaean myth and the anthropomorphism of his original myth. He was able to think of God as omnipresent and infinite but yet as unextended.

> At that time, after reading those books of the Platonists and being instructed by them to search for incorporeal truth, I clearly saw your invisible things which "are understood by the things that are made." (*Romans* I. 20) Although pushed backwards in my search, I perceived what that was which, because of my mind's darkness, I was not permitted to contemplate. I was made certain that you exist, that you are infinite, although not diffused throughout spaces, either finite or infinite, that you are truly he who is always the same, with no varied parts and changing movements, and that all other things are from you, as is known by one single most solid proof, the fact that they exist. (*Conf.* VII. 20)

And he was able to think of the true being of all things in terms of the forms contained eternally in the mind (*nous*) of God.

> I looked back over other things, and I saw that they owe their being to you, and that all finite things are in you. They are there, not as though in a place, but in a different fashion, because you contain all things in your hand by your truth. All things are true, in so far as they have being, nor is there any falsity, except when that is thought to be which is not. (*Conf.* VII. 11)

In seeing true reality as the reality of immaterial form, he came to see this world as only "half real" and as utterly dependent on the eternal reality of God.

> I beheld other things below you, and I saw that they are not altogether existent nor altogether non-existent: they are because they are from you: they are not, since they are not what you are. For that truly exists which endures unchangeably. (*Conf.* VII. 11)

Perhaps most importantly, in coming to identify true being with form and to see all being as flowing from God, he was able to come to believe that there could not possibly be a malignant evil substance opposed to God, as the Manichaeans said. The things of this world may be corruptible, less than fully real, and so "deficient" in one sense. But insofar as they exist at all, they have form and so are good.

> It was made manifest to me that beings that suffer corruption are nevertheless good. If they were supremely good, they could not be corrupted, but unless they were good, they could not be corrupted. If they were supremely good, they would be incorruptible, and if they were not good at all, there would be nothing in them to be corrupted....If things are deprived of all good whatsoever, they will not exist at all....But evil, of which I asked 'Whence is it?' is not a substance, for if it were a substance, it would be good....Hence I saw and it was made manifest to me that you have made all things good, and that there are no substances whatsoever that you have not made. (*Conf.* VII. 12)

But even more fundamentally, it is not merely that there is no substance called evil, but it is not even the case that creation as a whole is deficient in any way. Looked at from a Plotinian perspective, all being flows forth from God as a perfect order, and each being and event contributes to the harmony of that order. Plotinus had held that although the world is only a copy of true reality, it is in no way an inadequate copy: "nothing has been left out which a beautiful representation within the physical order could include."[211] And Augustine could now see God's creation as similarly perfect.

> To you, nothing whatsoever is evil, and not only to you but also to your whole creation, for outside of it there is nothing that can break in and disrupt the order that you have imposed upon it. Among its parts, certain things are thought to be evil because they do not agree with certain others. Yet these same things agree with others still, and thus they are good, and they are also good in themselves....No more did I long for better things, because I thought of all things, and with a sounder judgment I held that the higher things are indeed better than the lower, but that all things together are better than the higher things alone. (*Conf.* VII. 13)

So, armed with the Plotinian myth, Augustine was now able to see God as immaterial and infinite, as the absolute creator of all being and as perfectly good. And he was able to see the universe as a perfect order wholly created by a perfectly good god and without defect.

Furthermore, when he looked into his own soul and found there ideas of beauty and order, he was now able to see this as a "light" which was linked to that original light which called him back. And throughout the remainder of his life. he forever took this "light" in his soul as indisputable evidence for the existence of his god. More particularly, he accepted, with little examination, the claim that the human soul contains concepts (beauty, unity, wisdom, justice, etc.) and eternal truths (that happiness is to be desired, that wisdom is better than foolishness, that the incorrupt is better than the corrupt, etc.) which could not possibly be derived from human experience in this world, where true beauty, justice, happiness, etc., are never found. The existence of those concepts and truths, then, he took as pointing to an original source in which the eternal and immutable forms of beauty, wisdom, etc., are to be found. This line of reasoning, which Plato had used to suggest the existence of a realm of pure forms and which Plotinus had used to posit the existence of *nous* and the One beyond, Augustine took, without further elaboration, as pointing to the Christian "Word" that is one with God.[212] He used this "exceptionally well-known argument" over and over throughout his writings, and it became, as best I can tell, the only reasoning that could pass as an argument for the existence of God in his work. The most elaborate form of the reasoning is in Book II of his early work *On Free Choice of the Will*, but it occurs in a more concise form in the *City of God*, where he is reviewing what portion of Christian truth the Platonists had managed to capture.

> Physical beauty, whether of an immobile object—for instance, the outline of a shape—or of movement—as in the case of a melody—can be appreciated only by the mind. This would be quite impossible, if this 'idea' of beauty were not found in the mind in a more perfect form, without volume or mass, without vocal sound, and independent of space and time. But even here, if this 'idea' of beauty were not subject to change, one person would not be a better judge of sensible beauty than another; the more intelligent would not be better than the slower, nor the experienced and skilled than the novice and untrained; and the same person could not make progress towards better judgment than before. And it is obvious that anything which admits of increase and decrease is changeable. This consideration has readily persuaded men of ability and learning, trained in the philosophical discipline, that the original 'idea' is not to be found in this sphere, where it is shown to be subject to change. In their view both body and mind might be more or less endowed with form (or 'idea'), and if they could be deprived of form altogether, they would be utterly non-existent. And so they saw that there must be some being in which the original form resides, unchangeable, and therefore incomparable. And they rightly believed that it is there that the origin of all things is to be found, in the uncreated, which is the source of all creation. Thus 'what is known of God is what he himself has revealed to them. For his invisible realities have been made visible to the intelligence, through his created works, as well as his eternal power and divinity'. (*Romans* I. 19–20) It is by him that the visible and temporal things have been created. (*City.* VIII. 6)[213]

Finally, it should be noted that, at least when he was first introduced to Platonist culture, Augustine was taken with the ideal of a gentlemanly life of philosophical contemplation. Once he decided to enter the Catholic priesthood, it is true that he gave up the ideal of leisurely *otium* and turned to a career of service. But for a short time, that ideal captivated him, and throughout his life it retained a wistful attraction.

Before his final conversion to Catholicism near the end of August in the year 386, Augustine and his friends dreamed of a communal "life of retreat" in which they would be sure to include at least some men of "ample wealth" (*Conf.* VI. 14). And just after his conversion, he actually withdrew with some friends to an estate at Cassiciacum for a period of preparation and contemplation (*Conf.* IX. 2 and 7). The four works he wrote during his seven or so months at Cassiciacum are full of the glorification of "noble" souls seeking "wisdom" in cultured leisure. There we see Augustine and his friends, meeting in the bath or lounging in a meadow, free from care, with slaves to meet every need and only minor duties of household administration, seeking to sail to "the hinterland of the happy life" from the "port of philosophy" (*Happy Life*. 1. 1).[214] And indeed it seemed at times that this life of gentlemanly leisure was already the happy life they sought.

> For—to be concise—if we could always live as it was granted to us to live yesterday, I see no reason why we should hesitate to call ourselves happy. We lived in profound mental tranquility, entirely free from the fever of inordinate desires, keeping the mind free from every bodily taint and devoting ourselves to reason insofar as that is possible for a man. In a word, we were living in harmony with that part of the mind which is divine. And it was definitely agreed among us yesterday that this is the happy life. (*Ans. to Skep.* I. 4. 11)

From their vantage point, these fortunate spirits had no doubt that "the souls of wise men are by far richer and greater than the souls of the uneducated" (*Happy Life*. 2. 8). Such souls are able to leave behind the cares of the sordid world and to "flee to the bosom of philosophy." And once there, they are taught by philosophy

> that we ought to have no concern for anything that can be discerned by mortal eyes, or reached by any of the senses, but rather that all such things are to be disregarded. It promises to give a lucid demonstration of the most true and distinct God; and even now it deigns to furnish a glimpse of Him, as it were, through transparent clouds. (*Ans. to Skep.* I. 1. 3)

The "philosophic" soul attempts to gaze upon "truth," and in doing so, it looks beyond truth to the "supreme measure, from which it emanates and into which it is converted when perfected" (*Happy Life*. 4. 34).

> This, then, is the full satisfaction of souls, this the happy life: to recognize piously and completely the One through whom you are led into the truth, the nature of the truth you enjoy, and the bond that connects you with the supreme measure. (*Happy Life*. 4. 35)

And shortly after leaving Cassiciacum, Augustine reports a conversation he had with his mother in which they both yearned for a union with the eternal that lies beyond both sensation and thought, but that can only be glimpsed in this life.

> Therefore we said: If for any man the tumult of the flesh fell silent, silent the images of earth, and of the waters and of the air; silent the heavens; silent for him the very soul itself, and he should pass beyond himself by not thinking upon himself; silent his dreams and all imagined appearances, and every tongue, and every sign; and if all things that come to be through change should become wholly silent to him—for if any man can hear, then all these things say to him, "We did not make ourselves" (*Psalms*. 99. 3), but he who endures forever made us—if when they have said these words, they then become silent...and God alone speaks, not through such things but through himself, so that we hear his Word, not uttered by a tongue of flesh, nor by an angel's voice...but by himself whom we love in these things, himself we hear without their aid—even as we then reached out and in swift thought attained to that eternal Wisdom which abides over all things—if this could be prolonged, and other visions of a far inferior kind could be withdrawn, and this one alone ravish, and absorb, and hide away its beholder within its deepest joys, so that sempiternal life might be such as was that moment of understanding for which we sighed, would it not be this: "Enter into the joy of your Lord" (*Matthew* 25. 21)? When shall this be? When "we shall all rise again, but we shall not all be changed" (*I Corinthians* 15. 51). (*Conf.* IX. 10)[215]

The admiration for the Platonists that Augustine absorbed so quickly in Milan remained with him throughout his life. By the time of his sojourn in Cassiciacum, he was already "confident that I shall find among the Platonists what is not in opposition to our Sacred Scriptures" (*Ans. to Skep.* III. 20. 43). Philosophy had its real beginning, he thinks, with Plato's discovery

> that there are two worlds—an intelligible world in which the truth itself resides, and this sensible world which it is manifest that we perceive by sight and touch; that consequently the former is a true world, and the present world is truth-like—made unto the image of the other; that the truth emanates from the intelligible world, and is, as it were, refined and brightened in the soul which knows itself....(*Ans. to Skep.* III. 17. 37)

But after Plato, this teaching was hard to grasp, and so it was kept secret, which allowed the materialism of the Stoics and Epicureans to catch hold and gave rise to the healthy skepticism of Carneades and the Academics. But finally, he says, Cicero was able to defeat the enemies of Platonism and to revive Plato's true spirit, after which "Plato's countenance" appeared suddenly in Plotinus.

> Indeed, this Platonist philosopher has been adjudged so like to Plato that they would seem to have lived together, but there is such a long interval of time between them that Plato is to be regarded as having relived in Plotinus. (*Ans. to Skep.* III. 18. 41)

And this way of seeing the Platonists never left him. He was always convinced that Platonism had come as close to Christian truth as it was possible to come without God's grace. In fact, by the time he wrote the *City of God*, he was convinced that Plato could not have come so close to the truth without some divine aid, and so he speculates on how Plato may have come in contact with the scriptures during his purported visit to Egypt (*City*. VIII. 11).

Augustine's easy acceptance of the Plotinian myth and outlook was no doubt principally influenced by the fact that those men he most respected and admired were themselves captivated by this way of seeing reality. Platonic language and concepts were a familiar part of the discourse of the educated Christians, including Ambrose, among whom he now moved.[216] And indeed this way of speaking was backed by a long theological tradition. Prior to the fourth century, there were very few Christians among the educated elite, but those few had produced most of the theological speculation of the new religion. Among such men, there had always been an eagerness to present their faith as backed by a theology as sophisticated as those associated with pagan cult or Jewish practice. And so early on there had developed attempts to present Christian belief in philosophical terms that could appeal to the educated Roman or Greek. Platonism, with its emphasis on a true world beyond material reality, seemed most suited to accomplish this purpose.

The early apologist, Justin Martyr (d. ca. 165) had already seen Platonism as the philosophy nearest to that ultimate philosophy that he found in the Hebrew prophets. And Origen (ca. 182–251), the greatest systematic Christian theologian before Augustine, had in fact studied with Ammonius Saccas, the teacher of Plotinus, and had constructed a system in which Christ has a part very like that of *nous* in the Plotinian myth. The concept of the *Logos* as a principle of intelligibility that orders the world and with which the human soul is identified was derived first from the Stoics, but it came to play a central role in Platonist thought. And the Christians very early took over the notion by identifying Christ as the *Logos* or "wisdom" of God and the mediator between the divine mind and the human soul. The fourth gospel attributed to the disciple John already identifies Christ as the Word (Logos) who is identical with God and is with God from the beginning. And St. Paul also sometimes speaks of Christ in terms that can be easily read in this way. For example, in his first letter to the Corinthians he speaks of Christ as the "wisdom" of God, and in the letter to the Colossians he describes Christ as the agent by which God creates the world.[217]

Just how much of this tradition Augustine was aware of at that period of his life is hard to say. It is very unlikely that he had read Origen, Justin Martyr or most other of his theological predecessors, almost all of whom wrote in Greek. On the other hand, he had certainly read the gospels and had studied Paul's letters. But how much he had read personally is not so important for present purposes as the fact that Platonic language and concepts were and had long been a familiar part of the discourse of educated Christians.

So Augustine was certainly captivated by the Platonist outlook and by the Plotinian myth, and there was never a time when this way of viewing reality ceased to shape his thinking. That myth and its outlook not only spoke to the yearnings of his own soul, but it made Christian teaching appear as the crowning achievement and culmination of the project that had occupied the minds of the "best" men for centuries. The Plotinian myth provided a way of seeing the Christian God as the immanent agent in the entire creation and direction of the world, while yet avoiding the "crude" anthropomorphism of the original myth or even the more rarified materialism of the Manichaean myth. It suggested a view of the Christian god as perfectly good and provident, without needing to posit a malevolent reality to account for the apparent evils of the world. And it not only offered a view of the soul as belonging to a higher spiritual realm, but it made it possible to identify Christian redemption with that "return" to primal unity that had for so long been the ideal of the "best" men.

But despite his identification with much of the spirit and mythology of Plotinus, the Plotinian myth was not the myth that finally shaped Augustine's consciousness, nor was the Platonist outlook his final way of seeing reality. Even as he adopted the yearnings and aspirations of his adopted class, Augustine remained dominated by older and more fundamental needs and perspectives that could not be ignored.

IV. From the Plotinian Myth
to the Imperial Myth

Remember the mind-set out of which Augustine approached the Plotinian myth in the first place. First of all, he was already absolutely sure of the existence and supremacy of the Catholic god. And he knew this god as an intensely personal being who ruled the world by his will and had established his church as the very foundation of the empire. This was a god who satisfied the needs of traditional cultic consciousness, a stern but loving Father whose favor brought the greatest fortune and whose displeasure was the worst of misfortunes. It was a god that could replace the old gods as the foundation of the state and the cement of social order. Not only had this god proved himself able to reward his devotees, but the triumph of his church left no doubt that the other gods (or demons) were impotent against him.[218] What this god demanded was not "wisdom" or contemplation, but strict obedience, total surrender and absolute faith.

This was the god who had made a covenant with Abraham, who had destroyed the wicked of Sodom and Gomorrah, who had led the children of Israel out of Egypt and brought pain and death to the Egyptians. This was also the god who had sent his Son as a personal representative and epiphany to redeem fallen mankind by taking upon himself the sins of the world.

This god might *also* be the timeless, eternal Plotinian being whose essence is wholly identical with its properties, who exists changelessly in the repose of timeless eternity and who may someday be the final object of pure contemplation. And the influence of the Plotinian myth is nowhere more obvious than in Augustine's easy and almost uncritical acceptance of the paradoxical notion of a god that is at once timeless and yet an agent in history and of a creation that is at once a finished order and an unfolding becoming.[219] But the conviction that God is above all a *person* who rules and orders a dependent reality by his *will* meant that some aspects of the Plotinian myth and program could not be accepted.

For one thing, Augustine could never view creation as, in any sense, identical with God, as Plotinus seems sometimes to suggest.

> You have also told me with a strong voice within my interior ear, O Lord, that you have made every nature and every substance, things that are not what you are but yet exist. (*Conf.* XII. 11)

God is the being who creates the world, on whom the world is wholly dependent, who sustains the world and whose will is carried out in the world. But there is no literal sense in which God *is* the world.

> You made heaven and earth, not out of yourself, for then they would have been equal to your Only-begotten, and through this equal also to you. But in no way was it just that anything which was not of you should be equal to you. There was nothing beyond you from which you might make them, O God, one Trinity and trinal Unity. Therefore, you created heaven and earth out of nothing....(*Conf.* XII. 7)

More particularly, Augustine cannot accept Plotinus' view of the soul as both of this world and as identified with eternal soul and so with the intellectual-principle (*nous*). For Augustine, *nous* is replaced by the Word, the Christ, who is at once identical with God and the mediator between God the Father and the world. The human soul is a mutable creature, made by God and yearning for a relationship with God. But the soul is in no sense to be identified with God or with the Word. Even the angels, who are eternal and live forever in the light of God, are in no way identical with God, and the pilgrim soul, lost and yearning, is infinitely removed.

> Again, you have told me with a strong voice within my interior ear that not even that creature is coeternal with you whose delight you alone are....From this may the soul, whose pilgrimage has become long, understand...how far above all times are you, the Eternal. (*Conf.* XII. 11)[220]

One particular feature of the Plotinian outlook was its ability to see the many traditional gods as manifestations of the unitary reality of the One. This enabled them to be quite comfortable paying cult to the gods. And there were even Christians, such as Marius Victorinus, the translator of Plotinus, who could justify cultic practice (*Conf*. VIII. 2). But for Augustine, God was always the wholly independent deity, and while he says he read in the Platonists that God could be represented in "the likeness of the image of a corruptible man," he never allowed himself to "feed upon" such lies (*Conf*. VII. 9).

Perhaps most importantly, Augustine's religious consciousness was very different from that of Plotinus, and his project was radically different. Despite some brief pretensions and hopes, he was not able to persist in seeing himself as a noble soul turning within itself to find that light which would establish its true identity. His God was a stern but provident Father calling him to repentance. He saw himself as the creature of that omnipotent god, lost in sin and carnal desire, needing above all to surrender himself in total dependence in the hope of mercy. Even as he was searching the "books of the Platonists" for a more adequate idea of his god, his focus was on the redemption of his soul, not on the "philosophic" contemplation of Wisdom; and his deepest desire was to yield completely to the omnipotent deity, not to return to primal unity with an impersonal One. What he sought was the god who was establishing his dominion throughout the world, not a transcendent first principle that contemplates itself and serenely awaits the return of those who have gone forth.

According to the account in the *Confessions*, written more than a decade after his conversion to Catholicism, his love affair with the Platonist religious project was very brief. He reports that there were only a few months, during which he "prated as if I were well instructed," before he came to despair that the insights of the Platonists would ever bring him the redemption he sought (*Conf*. VII. 20). On this telling, he realized, apparently within two or three months of first reading Plotinus, that contemplation of the divine would never bring peace, so long as one could not get rid of carnal desire and surrender the will to God. It was at this point that he turned to the letters of St. Paul and learned that only a yielding of the will in faith aided by God's grace, only an embrace of Christ as savior, could bring the peace he sought.

> All this those writings of the Platonists do not have. Their pages do not have this face of piety, the tears of confession, your sacrifice, a troubled spirit, a contrite and humbled heart, the salvation of your people, the

city that is like a bride, the pledge of the spirit, the cup of our redemption. (*Conf.* VII. 21)

In short, he realized almost immediately that what he sought was not contemplative union with the One, but surrender to and salvation by the omnipotent God of the Catholics in the person of the mediator Christ Jesus.

> It is one thing to behold from a wooded mountain peak the land of peace, but to find no way to it, and to strive in vain towards it by unpassable ways....It is a different thing to keep to the way that leads to that land, guarded by the protection of the heavenly commander, where no deserters from the heavenly army lie in wait like bandits....In a wondrous way all these things penetrated my very vitals when I read the words of that least of your apostles, and meditated upon your works and trembled at them. (*Conf.* VII. 21)

At this point, he tells us that he went to the aged Simplician, the teacher of Ambrose, and asked his help. Simplician told him the story of Marius Victorinus, who was finally able to break with cultic practice and humble himself in public confession only when advancing years and the fear of hell broke his pride (*Conf.* VIII. 2). And as Augustine heard this and other accounts of those who had put aside the things of this world and turned to God, he felt more and more ashamed.

> What was there that I did not say against myself? With what scourges of self-condemnation did I not lash my soul? (*Conf.* VIII. 7)

His problem had nothing to do with the Platonist mastery of dialectic or the vision of a light above the soul. It had to do with the demand for total surrender to a personal God and the inability of the sinner to make that surrender.

> The enemy had control of my will, and out of it he fashioned a chain and fettered me with it. For in truth lust is made out of a perverse will, and when lust is served, it becomes habit, and when habit is not resisted, it becomes necessity....A new will, which had begun within me, to wish freely to worship you and find joy in you...was not yet able to overcome that prior will, grown strong with age. Thus did my two wills, the one old, the other new, the first carnal, the second spritual, contend with one another, and by their conflict, they laid waste my soul. (*Conf.* VIII. 5)

In this state of anguish, he reports that he rushed into his garden weeping, fell on the ground, heard the voice of a child telling him to "take up and read," whereupon his eyes fell on a passage from St. Paul and he was able to surrender his will to God (*Conf.* VIII. 8 and 12). Thus God's grace brought him the peace that the Platonists could never offer, and he withdrew to Cassiciacum to prepare for baptism.

We may doubt whether the surrender of his will and the abandonment of "prating" came so easily or so quickly. As we have seen, the books that he wrote from Cassiciacum are still full of hope for the project of philosophic contemplation by noble spirits in the peace of leisured *otium*. At times he even seems to entertain hope that the soul may rise to a pure contemplation of God. He writes to Nebridius of the comfort he finds in that "reasoning" which reveals that the realm of mind is so far superior to that of sense experience.

> After I had refreshed myself with it for some time, and after I had called upon God for help, I began to be lifted up to Him and to those things which are most completely true. I was so penetrated with a knowledge of eternal things that I wondered how I had ever needed to reason about them, since they are as intimately present as a man is to himself. (*Letters.* 7, written from Cassiciacum in 387)

But while he was still enamored of the spirit of the Plotinian project, it is also true that the books he wrote at that time already show a marked departure from that spirit. The *Soliloquies* begins with a long appeal to God for aid and an admission of helplessness to find the way to God alone (*Sol.* I. 1. 2–6). And only a few pages later, he explicitly says that Plato and Plotinus never knew God at all.

> If those things which they said are true, it does not of necessity follow that they knew them. For many people speak at length of things they do not know, just as I myself said I desired to know all those things for which I prayed. I would not desire them, if I already knew them. Was I not able, nonetheless, to speak of them? Indeed, I spoke, not of those things which I grasped with my intellect, but of the things which I had gathered from many sources and committed to memory, the things which I believed as much as I could. But to *know*—that is something else. (*Sol.* I. 4. 9)

Even when he was most hopeful of reaching the truth by reason, he was sure that reason must begin from the acceptance of Christ and his authority.

> Certainly, no one doubts that we are impelled toward knowledge by a twofold force: the force of authority and the force of reason. And I am resolved never to deviate in the least from the authority of Christ, for I find none more powerful. But as to what is attainable by acute and accurate reasoning, such is my state of mind that I am impatient to grasp what truth is—to grasp it not only by belief, but also by comprehension. Meanwhile, I am confident that I shall find among the Platonists what is not in opposition to our Sacred Scriptures. (*Ans. to Skep.* III. 20. 43)

At this point, he sometimes still talks as though "philosophy" might liberate a few of the highest souls, but even then he recommends the "mysteries" as an alternative—and in some ways more complete— avenue to the fullest truth.

> When the obscurity of things perplexes us, we follow a twofold path: reason, or at least, authority. Philosophy sends forth reason, and it frees scarcely a few. By itself it compels these not only not to spurn those mysteries, but to understand them insofar as they can be understood. The philosophy that is true...has no other function than to teach what is the First Principle of all things—Itself without beginning—and how great an intellect dwells therein, and what has proceeded therefrom for our welfare, but without deterioration of any kind. Now, the venerated mysteries, which liberate persons of sincere and firm faith...these mysteries teach us that this First Principle is one God omnipotent, and that he is tripotent, Father and Son and Holy Spirit. (*Div. Prov.* II. 5. 16)[221]

But while he still believes at this point that reason may bring at least some of us to the truth, it cannot do so, unless the mind is "cleansed" and prepared by faith.

> Yet I—Reason—am in minds as the act of looking is in the eyes. To have eyes is not the same as to look, and to look is not the same as to see. Therefore, the soul needs three distinct things: that it have eyes which it can properly use, that it look, and that it see. The mind is like healthy eyes when it is cleansed of every taint of the body, that is, detached and purged of the desires for earthly things—which cleansing it obtains, at first, only by *Faith*. (*Sol.* I. 6. 12)

Augustine made the decision to abandon his career and devote his life to the Catholic god in the late summer of 386, and after some months at Cassiciacum, he returned to Milan for baptism by Ambrose in the spring of 387. He left Milan with his mother some months later to return to Africa, but was delayed by a naval blockade mounted by the usurper Maximus, who was challenging the emperor Theodosius. He remained in Ostia and then in Rome for just over a year, during which time he was devastated by the death of Monica. Then in the latter part of 388, he returned to Thagaste by way of Carthage.

During his time in Ostia and Rome, his principal writings were *The Immortality of the Soul*, *The Magnitude of the Soul*, Book I of *On Free Choice of the Will* and *The Catholic and Manichaean Ways of Life*. He also continued work on *On Music*, which he had started in Milan while awaiting baptism. These works reflect a continuing ambivalence about the Plotinian myth and project, but they also let us see the development of his own priorities as he moves away from the contemplative attitude of the Platonists.

In a number of ways, the Plotinian myth continues to be absorbed as a part of Catholic truth. Thus he devotes many pages to discussing the soul as the true self of the human being and in emphasizing its immateriality. He continues to see human reason as linked essentially to eternal Reason, and he uses that relationship to develop the theme that knowledge is by "memory" of truths in the soul and to argue for the immortality of this soul that is essentially living and knowing. He returns to the theme of the perfect order of creation and the unreality of evil and uses this aspect of the Plotinian myth to bludgeon the Manichaeans. In short, those aspects of the Plotinian myth that support the omnipotence and goodness of God and the nature of the soul as an immaterial "pilgrim" seeking its eternal home become codified in these works as a permanent part of Augustine's own myth.

On the other hand, there is little indication in these works that the "pilgrim" soul is to find its way back to God through dialectical reasoning or mystical contemplation. What God demands of us is not understanding, but love and obedience, and while ignorance may separate us from God, it is sinful lust for temporal things that stands as the real barrier. While it is, of course, true that we should strive to develop reason and to have it rule over our passions, it is not by any special development of reason that we return to God. It is the *will* and the will alone that chooses either to love what is eternal or to love what is temporal, and the turning of the soul to God is a matter of fundamental choice for every person, not the ultimate attainment of a few select souls.

> ...whoever wants to live rightly and honorably, if his will for this surpasses his will for temporal goods, achieves this great good so easily that to have what he wills is nothing other than the act of willing. (*Free Choice.* I. 13. 97)

The knowledge of God that the Platonists, in their pride, strive to reach by unaided reason is in fact to be achieved only as a reward for those who love God, not as a way to lift the soul to God. It is love, obedience and submission that save us, not the arrogant pursuit of wisdom.

> Eternal life, then, is the knowledge of truth itself. See then from this how confused and perverse those individuals are who suppose that, by imparting to us a knowledge of God, they can make us perfect, when this knowledge is the reward of those who have attained perfection. What, then, must we do, what I ask, if we wish to know Him, if not to love Him first with complete devotion? This brings us back to what we have insisted upon from the beginning, that there is no sounder principle in the Catholic Church than that authority should precede reason. (*Cath. & Man.* I. 25. 47)

Once back in Africa, Augustine quickly found himself drafted as a soldier in the army of his god and in defense of God's Catholic Church. For over two years, he settled with friends on his family estate at Thagaste and led the life of an honored and much sought-after "Servant of God."[222]

During this time, some of his writing, such as his dialogue *Concerning the Teacher*, still focuses on Platonist themes such as the need for truth to be sought "within the mind," rather than in sense experience or even from spoken words. And when he writes in this way, Christ continues to play the role of the Plotinian intellectual-principle, that is, the role of the Word or the Teacher who is the Wisdom of God and who speaks directly to the individual soul (*Teacher.* XI. 38).

He also continues to use this perspective on knowledge as a reason to believe in a realm of eternal being that can be plausibly identified with the Catholic God. In *Of True Religion*, he again uses the "extremely well-known argument" that our ideas of beauty, unity, equality, etc., point to the existence of an eternal being which contains the exemplars of those ideas (*True Rel.* XXIX–XXVI. 52–66).

But while such themes continue to play a role, there is a dramatic and unmistakable shift in attitude and priorities when compared with the comfortable philosophizing of Cassiciacum. Back in Thagaste, Augustine was faced not with abstract ruminations and debates, but with an everyday reality in which the Catholic god and his church were locked in combat with Manichaeans and pagans (and Donatists as well, though they do not yet command his attention). The call that he heard now was not to turn inward and seek unity with the self-contained source of being, but rather to join that combat and insure the triumph of his god.

When Nebridius writes to him at this time and tries to engage him in discussion of some of the abstract issues that might have fascinated the little circle at Cassiciacum, Augustine dismisses him and sternly directs him to matters of practical moment (*Letters.* 8, 9 and 11). A pagan grammarian from his old school-town of Madaura writes to appeal to the liberality of Augustine's cultured spirit. He agrees that, of course, there is "one supreme God," but that God is worshiped throughout the world in many forms, since "none of us knows his true name." Is it not better, he asks, to worship this god in the forms of the "throngs of saving deities" displayed "by daylight" in the forum of the city than to reject all these lovely manifestations and insist on exclusive worship of a faceless deity to be sought "in hidden places" (*Letters.* 16)? But Augustine's reply is brutal. He ridicules every aspect of pagan religion and utterly rejects the notion that the petty and often immoral deities of the pagan cults could be manifestations of the true god. He wants to leave no doubt that allegiance is due solely to the Catholic god and to no other.

> Finally, let this be very clear to you, and let it keep you from falling into blasphemous insults, that we Christian Catholics, whose church is established in your town, adore no one of the dead, and worship nothing as a divinity which is made and fashioned by God, but we adore the one only God who made and fashioned all things. (*Letters.* 16)

During this time, the overriding theme of his writing becomes the primacy of authority and belief over "philosophy" and reason. The focus of his attack is often the Manichaean claim to base their religion on reason alone, but it is clear that he has the rationalist pretensions of the Platonists in mind as well. He writes to his old friend and patron Romanianus of all that he had learned from "Plato" about immaterial reality and contemplation of the eternal. But he adds that while all of this is very attractive, none of it is any longer necessary, since Christ has made it possible for all men to believe these things, even if they cannot be grasped by reason.

> However philosophers may boast, anyone can easily understand that religion is not to be sought from them. For they take part in the religious rites of their fellow-citizens, but in their schools teach divergent and contrary opinions about the nature of their gods and of the chief good, as the multitude can testify. (*True Rel.* III. 3)

Even when he makes use of Platonist reasonings, he is careful to emphasize their limitations. Thus in *Of True Religion*, after using the "exceptionally well-known argument" mentioned above to conclude that there must exist an eternal reality, he quickly adds that the most this reasoning can do is point us *toward* God. The argument tells us, he says, only that there exists *something* that is eternal and immutable, not that that something is the very God: "God is not offered to the corporeal senses, and transcends even the mind" (*True Rel.* XXIX. 67). Reason is at best a pointer toward the truth, not a means of access to the truth.

> Do not go abroad. Return within yourself. In the inward man dwells truth. If you find that you are by nature mutable, transcend yourself. But remember in doing so that you must also transcend yourself even as a reasoning soul. Make for the place where the light of reason is kindled. What does every good reasoner attain but truth? And yet truth is not reached by reasoning, but is itself the goal of all who reason. (*True Rel.* XXIX. 72)

In fact, many years later, Augustine will refer back to the reasoning of this passage as a proof that the existence of God cannot be demonstrated by reason (*Letters.* 162).

Furthermore, it was during these years, in Book II of *On Free Choice of the Will*, that he developed his most complete version of this argument that there must exist something eternal to account for our concepts of beauty, wisdom, number, etc. But even there, he concludes only that either this eternal "something" is God or that, if there is something even higher, then that something higher is God. As a demonstration of the existence of his God, he sees it as a "sure though somewhat tenuous form of reasoning," which is nevertheless "sufficient for the immediate question" of whether every being receives its form from *some* eternal source (*Free Choice*. II. 15. 155).

Plotinus would no doubt agree that the ultimate attainment of truth depends upon transcending reason in mystical contemplation. But Augustine now insists that the place to turn is not to mystical flight, but to the authority of the Catholic Church. The pursuit of truth begins not with dialectical investigations, but with unconditional acceptance of the Catholic god as the true God and of the Catholic Church as the bearer of his truth. Then whatever one finds by reasoning or reading of the philosophers, one will be able to interpret in the light of Catholic truth.

> Hold fast whatever truth you have been able to grasp, and attribute it to the Catholic Church. Reject what is false and pardon me who am but a man. What is doubtful believe until either reason teaches or authority lays down that it is to be rejected or that it is true, or that it has to be believed always. Listen to what follows as diligently and as piously as you can. For God helps men like that. (*True Rel*. X. 20)

And once we have accepted the authority which tells us of the triune Catholic God who is the source of all being, we are able to accept all the teachings of the Catholic Church, even where those transcend our understanding.

> Hence, all those things which to begin with we simply believed, following authority only, we come to understand. Partly we see them as certain, partly as possible and fitting, and we become sorry for those who do not believe them, and have preferred to mock at us rather than to share our belief. The Holy Incarnation, the birth from a virgin, the death of the Son of God for us, his resurrection from the dead, ascension into heaven and sitting at the right hand of the Father, the forgiveness of sins, the day of judgment, the resurrection of the body are not merely believed, when the eternity of the Trinity and the mutability of created things are known. They are also judged to be part and parcel of the mercy of the most high God, which he has shown to the human race. (*True Rel*. VIII. 14)

The philosophers may pretend to truth, and reason may indeed point toward truth, but "piety begins in fear and is perfected in love" (*True Rel.* XVII. 33).

Augustine left Thagaste in 391 and traveled to Hippo Regius, where he was soon drafted as a priest by popular demand. By this time, his direction was clear and his attitude was firmly set. Trying to win over his friend Honoratus, who was still attracted to the Manichaeans and their emphasis on reason, Augustine is willing to grant that some small number may learn of God's truth by reason. But the thing to remember is that there is just one Catholic Church to which all must be brought. And the acceptance in faith of that church and its truth is necessary for all (*Adv. of Bel.* 8. 20 and 10. 24). In fact, it is only by faith and acceptance of authority that souls can come to health.

> For I not only judge it most healthful to believe before using reason (since one is unfitted to comprehend reason), and, with faith itself, to prepare the ground to receive the seeds of truth, but I believe that such is the way, generally, by which safety can alone return to sick souls. (*Adv. of Bel.* 14. 31)

The Catholic god has left no doubt of his supremacy and authority. He has united people the world over and his scriptures are ancient. His truth carries "the strength of numbers, agreement and antiquity," and his authority is attested by "the widespread report of peoples and nations," as well as the fact that "the mysteries of the Catholic Church have everywhere taken possession of these peoples" (*Adv. of Bel.* 14. 31).

Reason doubtless has its place in helping us to understand. But religion rests not on understanding, but on submission to God and acceptance of his authority. Until we turn to God in loving submission, all attempts to see the truth are the emptiest vanities.

> It is authority alone that moves fools to hasten on to wisdom. So long as we cannot understand pure truth, it is indeed wretched to be deceived by authority. But surely it is more wretched to be unmoved by authority. For if the Providence of God does not preside over human affairs, there is no point in busying one's self about religion. But if both the outward appearance of all things (and they surely must be believed to come from some spring of purest beauty) and some, I know not what, inner conscience exhorts all better souls, both publicly and privately as it were, that God is to be sought and served, we must not give up hope that God has established some authority, on which, if we rely, just as on a sure step, we will be raised up to God. But, laying aside reason, which in its

purity is very difficult, as we have said, for fools to understand, this authority moves us in two ways, that is, by miracles, and by the crowds who follow it. No one of these is necessary to the wise man. Who denies the fact? But this is now our concern—that we be able to be wise, that is, to cling to truth. Surely, the sordid soul cannot do this. And the sordidness of the soul, to sum it up briefly, is love of anything whatsoever save the soul and God; in so far as anyone is more completely freed from these vices, he will the more easily gaze on truth. But it is surely perverse and preposterous to wish, then, to see truth in order to purge out the soul, since it is purged out for this very purpose that one may see. (*Adv. of Bel.* 16. 34)

What has happened here is far more than merely a shift of emphasis or priority. The Plotinian myth is inextricably bound up with the Plotinian project of return to the One, and when Augustine abandoned that project, he had also abandoned the accompanying myth. The Plotinian One overflows by the necessity of its nature and gives rise to intellectual-principle and soul which, since they are an emanation of unity, retain that unity as a duality which is at once an identity. The individual soul, in turning to matter, forgets its own identity with eternal Soul and the intellectual-principle. But while that identity is forgotten, it is never lost, and the soul, in its higher being, remains eternal and complete, even as it searches for completeness in its lower being. Because of this essential completeness and identity with eternal Soul, the soul lacks nothing that it needs to return to awareness of itself and, though the struggle may be long, the soul need only turn "inward" and employ its higher powers in order to recover its "true self." The struggle may require many reincarnations and perhaps only the "best" souls may reach the goal after long preparation, but there is no urgency, since all will surely return finally to the One with the same necessity that all things came forth.

When Augustine came to believe that authority alone can "hasten fools to wisdom," and that the *love* of God is the indispensable precondition of seeing the truth, he was implying a distinctly non-Plotinian view of the nature of God, the nature of the soul and the relation of God to souls and the rest of creation. God may be similar to the Plotinian One in a number of ways—eternal, immutable, good, omnipresent and omnipotent. But God is in no sense identical with his creation, and his "omnipresence" does not give creatures any part in his being. Similarly, the soul may contain some "light" of God, some knowledge given by the grace of God, but the soul is in every way a temporal creature, utterly distinct from God. Augustine was always able to speak of a "higher self" whose home was with God, but leaving aside a possible brief period of complete infatuation with Plotinus in Milan, this never meant for him that the soul was in any way ontologically united either with God or with any eternal reality flowing from God. The Augustinian soul is not a fragment of an eternal whole that is seeking to hasten an inevitable return to integrity. Rather it is the artifact of an omnipotent maker, cut off from that maker by its own sinful choices, helpless to remedy its condition without the merciful aid of the maker and with only dim memories of the happy life that it has thrown away. And though he had by this time incorporated into his idea of God some of the attributes of the Plotinian One, Augustine's god remains, above all, the omnipotent ruler of the universe who demands obedient service.

In short, while Augustine certainly used the Plotinian myth for a number of purposes—to evade problems with his earlier myths, to bring his conception of God into line with the outlook of the "best" men and to satisfy the personal needs and feelings he had developed in being assimilated to elite Roman culture—the Plotinian myth was not, in the end, Augustine's own. The myth he finally adopted was much closer to his original myth than it was to either the Manichaean myth or the Plotinian myth. That final myth I shall call the *imperial myth*, since his God was now much more like the perfect emperor than he was like the light of the Manichaeans or the One of the Platonists.

V. The Imperial Myth

By the time he became a priest in 391, Augustine's religious consciousness was dominated by the imperial myth. And certainly, by the year 395, his conception of God was complete. In that same year, he finally finished his dialogue *On Free Choice of the Will*, which was his first work of systematic philosophical theology. And though he does not anywhere set forth the imperial myth directly, it is clear in this dialogue that it is the operative outlook that shapes his thought.

At the time he completed *On Free Choice of the Will*, Augustine had not yet reached what were to be his final positions on some issues, such as original sin and the relation of grace to free choice of the will.

But his basic view of the nature of God and of God's relation to humankind was fixed and would not change throughout his life.

As we have seen, Augustine never really abandoned the conception of his God that he had absorbed in childhood and that was encapsulated in what I have called his original myth. He never doubted the existence of the Catholic god, nor the supremacy of that god over all others. Nor did he ever doubt that the appropriate attitude toward that god was one of humble and reverent obedience. Throughout his Manichaean and Plotinian adventures, he remained a Catholic catechumen, though a sometimes very confused one. What confused him was not the question of God's existence nor the need to approach God in fear and trembling. What confused him was the difficulty he encountered in conceiving his god "properly." The Manichaeans and many of the pagans he met in Carthage ridiculed the god of his original myth as crude, anthropomorphic and unsuited to the spirit of cultured gentlemen. But even the Manichaean myth, while it freed him from conceiving God in human form, still left him with a god that seemed seriously limited. The god of his youth was a "superman" among "supermen," a conquering commander constantly battling against the many demons that stood over against him and resisted the establishment of his church. The god of the Manichees was the omnipresent light that filled all things, not a single "god" among "gods." But unless that god was to be identified with all things evil as well as all things good, a second being of darkness had to be accepted as constitutive of being and as an everlasting boundary to the power of God.

When the gentlemen of Milan introduced Augustine to Plotinus, he saw his new outlook not as turning to a new god, but as shaking off the limitations of his own god. However obscure we may today find many aspects of the Plotinian myth, it incorporated a view of reality that had been adopted by many of the "best" men for centuries and that had even found a home among educated Christians. And so Augustine "learned" that true reality is not material reality, but is a timeless, extensionless and eternal realm of being, that the material world is of a lower "degree" of reality and that all material things owe their being to the forms of that eternal realm. Thus Augustine was assured that it *is* possible to conceive of God as omnipresent and yet as in no place, to conceive the entire universe as dependent on and formed by God and yet as an entirely different kind of being from God, and to conceive

God as both omnipotent and perfectly good and yet as the author of all that is, since evil is precisely what is *not*. And perhaps most important of all, Augustine "learned" from the Platonists that it is perfectly acceptable, when speaking of the eternal and its relation to the temporal, to speak in paradoxical and inconsistent ways, since the height of "reason" comes precisely in the recognition that ultimate truth "transcends" reason. Indeed, he was assured that the "best" men are those who speak in just that way.

Armed with the Plotinian outlook and its legitimation by the "noblest" minds, Augustine returned to the god of his youth with absolute certainty and unswerving commitment. And he used the Plotinian myth to reshape the Catholic god in a way that could satisfy both the religious needs of the provincial boy of Thagaste and the intuitions of the Milanese professor.

According to the imperial myth, which was to dominate the religious consciousness of the west for centuries, God is the absolute emperor of the universe, at once creator and provider, whose care and attention extends from the lowliest of material objects to the choirs of angels.

> For to hold God supreme is most truly the beginning of piety; and no one holds Him supreme who does not believe Him to be omnipotent and absolutely changeless, Creator of all good things which He Himself transcends in excellence, and the most just Ruler, as well, of all that He has created. And He has not, like one who is not sufficient unto himself, been aided by any nature in His creation. From this it follows that He created everything from nothing. From Himself He did not create Himself; rather He begot what was equal to Himself, whom we call the only Son of God. When we try to describe the Son of God more clearly, we name Him the Power of God and the Wisdom of God, through which God made everything that was made from nothing. (*Free Choice.* I. 2. 12–13)

So God is absolutely distinct from creation and creates all things not by his own "overflowing," but by a free productive act and with no dependence on any material. And the Son of God, like the intellectual-principle of Plotinus, is at once the direct expression of God (indeed, one with God) and the seat of the eternal forms through which all things are made and ordered.

God is both absolutely omnipotent and absolutely omniscient. His power has no limit, and his knowledge not only extends to all that is and has been, but even as regards the future, "it is proper to His fore-knowledge that nothing should escape His notice" (*Free Choice*. III. 4. 41). Nor is there any need in God to react to any event in creation. By a single, eternal act of will, "He has decided once for all how the order of the universe He created is to be carried out, and does not arrange anything by a new act of will" (*Free Choice*. III. 3. 25).106

The world that God has created is perfect, an ordered hierarchy of beings, in which each being has its place.

> But if, in the order of corporeal creatures, the beauty of good things is built by degrees from the very choir of stars to the hairs of our head, how unreasonably do men say, 'What is this? How is this?' For all things have been created in their proper order. (*Free Choice*. III. 5. 60)

Nothing is omitted from God's creation which could in any way add to the beauty, order or harmony of the whole.

> I warn you also to beware of this: you should avoid saying not only, 'It would have been better if they had not existed,' but also, 'They ought to have been made differently.' If, by true reasoning, you conceive of something better, you can be sure that God, the Creator of all good, has already made it. (*Free Choice*. III. 5. 45)

With an infinitely discriminating eye for detail, God has created every conceivable variety, type and level of being.

> Moreover, so great is the variety of earthly things that we can conceive of nothing which belongs to the form of the earth in its full extent which God, the Creator of all things, has not already created. For you may pro-ceed by degrees through intermediate types of land, from the most fruitful and delightful to the most treacherous and sterile, so that you would not dare to find any fault except in comparison with what is better. Thus you would ascend through all degrees of praise until you found the highest type of land—which, nonetheless, you would not want to be the only type in existence. How great is the distance between the whole earth and the sky? There lies between them a watery nature and an airy one. From these four elements we derive a variety of forms and species which God has numbered, although we cannot count them. There can exist in nature things which your reason is incapable of con-ceiving. It cannot be, however, that what you conceive with true reason cannot exist. You cannot conceive of anything better in creation which has escaped the Maker of the creation. (*Free Choice*. III. 5. 47–49)

Only the envy and pride of a sinful creature would presume to question the complete perfection of God's order.

> If he says, 'It would not have been difficult or troublesome for an omnipotent God to have created everything so that each would have its own place in the order of creation, in such a way that no one would be wretched; for it is impossible that omnipotence lack power, or that goodness be spiteful, my answer is as follows: the order of creation from the highest to the lowest occurs by just degrees. The man who speaks in such a way is simply envious when he says that this should have been different, or that that should not be. If he wishes something to be like something else which is higher, the very thing that he wishes to change is so great that it ought not to be changed because it is perfect. For the man who says: 'It should have been this way' wishes to add to a higher creation that is already complete....For example, if a man should say, 'The moon should not exist'...how could he dare assert that there should be no moon, but that the moon ought to be like the sun which he sees? He does not realize that he is simply saying that there should be two suns, not that there should be no moon. He errs in two ways: he wishes to add something to perfection when he desires another sun, and he wishes to diminish perfection when he wants to do away with the moon. (*Free Choice*. III. 9. 87–88)

In brief: "Wherever we direct our thoughts, we discover that God must be praised ineffably as the best Creator of all natures, and as the most just Ruler" (*Free Choice*. III. 12. 124).

Among the beings God has created are some (the good angels) whom he foresaw would cling to him in perfect and unalterable love forever. But also as a part of his order, he has created beings that he foresaw would turn from him in sinful love of temporal things. Some of these sinners-to-be he knew would retain at least enough memory of God so that it was still possible for them to turn back to him. But the order would not be complete unless there were other beings whose rebellion was so terrible that they had lost all touch with the light of God and all hope of redemption. To this last baneful lot belong Lucifer and his minions who rebelled against God and were cast out of heaven.

> You should then believe that there is a sinless creature in higher places and in the heights of the heavens; because if our Creator showed His goodness in creating a creature whose future sins He foresaw, He would by all means show His goodness in creating a creature who He foresaw

would not sin. Such a sublime creature has perpetual happiness and enjoys his Creator forever. He merits this because of his unalterable will to hold to justice. The sinful creature also has his own place in God's order, and although he has lost his happiness through sin, he has not lost the power to recover this happiness. He is surely better than the creature who forever wills to sin, and he is a kind of mean between this latter creature and the sinless creature we mentioned before, who forever has his will fixed on justice. (*Free Choice*. III. 5. 54)

But while the order created by God is perfect, it is not, as in the Plotinian myth, the only possible order. It does not flow from the nature of God by necessity, but it is a free act of creative will. Therefore, while God's perfect goodness assures that any creation will be a perfectly harmonious order, God is in no way bound to create this particular order. For example, in creating this world, God foresaw that humans would fall into sin, and so he created an order in which human sinfulness adds to the harmony of the whole. But God *could* have created a world in which he foresaw that humans would not choose to sin, and in that case, a perfect order would have just as easily taken account of that reality.

That objection is even less reasonable which says that if our unhappiness completes the perfection of the universe, then there would be imperfection in the universe if we were all happy; for then if the soul can come to happiness only by sinning, even our sins are necessary to the perfection of the universe that God created, and how could God be just in punishing sins? For if there were no sins, His creation would not be full and perfect.

In answer to this I say that neither sin nor unhappiness is necessary to the perfection of the universe; rather, it is the souls which simply because they are souls, are necessary to its perfection....In a house, what is so great as a man, and what so low and base as the house's sewer? Yet the slave caught in some offense, for which he has to clean the sewer, adorns the sewer even by his disgrace; both of these—the slave's disgrace and the cleaning of the sewer—are joined and reduced to a kind of unity. They are fitted and woven into the household order in such a way that, with their beauty, they suit its world with its own perfectly ordered beauty. Yet if the slave had not willed to sin, other provisions for cleaning the household necessities would have been made in managing the house. (*Free Choice*. III. 9. 96–97)

Even if the angels themselves were to decide to sin, the perfection of God's order would not be disturbed.

> Yet even though there is no order of the universe better than that in which angelic power, through the perfection of its nature and goodness of its will, is pre-eminent in governing the universe, still, even if all the angels were to sin, the Creator of angels would continue to rule His empire with no defect. (*Free Choice*. III. 12. 123)]

Let me turn now to consider the condition of human subjects and their relation to this eternal emperor. Human beings are, as are all beings, created as mutable things that derive their nature from the eternal forms in the mind of God.

> What more should we say concerning the mutability of body and spirit? Enough has been said above. We have established that body and spirit are given form by an immutable and eternal Form. To this Form it has been said: 'Thou shalt change them and they will be changed; but thou art the same, and thy years fail not'. (*Psalms*, 102. 26–27). The speech of the prophet has used 'years without fail' to mean 'eternity.' Concerning this Form, it has been said also that it is 'permanent in itself, it renews all things' (*Wisdom of Solomon*, 7. 27). (*Free Choice*. II. 17. 173)[224]

God, like the Plotinian One, is the source not only of our being, but of our knowledge as well, and if we look into ourselves, we find that the eternal law of God "has been impressed on our minds" and that "it is that law by which it is just that everything be ordered in the highest degree" (*Free Choice*. I. 6. 51).[225] Thus humans still have at least some knowledge of God and of what is required of them.

However, in a decisive break with the Plotinian myth, creatures are in no way one in nature with the source of their being and knowledge. God is not the One overflowing by the necessity of its nature, but the utterly autonomous artificer of a creation designed wholly to serve the purposes of its maker. Human beings are not "pieces" of the One lost to itself but destined to return to a primal unity. They are the products of a divine will and their whole destiny lies in carrying out the purposes of that will. They were created, in fact, precisely for the purpose of *loving* God completely and serving him with unmixed devotion: "The eternal law, therefore, orders us to turn our love away from temporal things, and to turn it in its purity to the eternal" (*Free Choice*. I. 15.

108). And all sin lies in "lust," i.e. in the love of anything other than the eternal God.

> All sins are included under this one class: when someone is turned away from divine things that are truly everlasting, toward things that change and are uncertain. (*Free Choice*. I. 16. 116)[226]

Since humans exist and are fulfilled in perfect submission to God, the love of anything other than God robs the soul of its true purpose and so enslaves it.

> Lust dominates the mind, despoils it of the wealth of its virtue, and drags it, poor and needy, now this way and now that; now approving and even defending what is false as though it were true, now disapproving what it previously defended, and rushing on to other falsities; now refusing assent and fearing clear reasoning; now despairing of fully discovering the truth and clinging to the deep obscurities of stupidity; now struggling into the light of understanding and falling back again from weariness. Meanwhile the reign of lust rages tyranically and distracts the life and whole spirit of man with many conflicting storms of terror, desire, anxiety, empty and false happiness, torture because of the loss of something he used to love, eagerness to possess what he does not have, grievances for injuries received, and fires of vengeance. Wherever he turns, greed amasses, extravagance wastes, ambition entices, pride bloats, envy twists, sloth buries, obstinacy goads, submissiveness harasses, and all the other things that throng and busy themselves in the kingdom of lust. Can we think that this is not punishment which, as you see, all must endure who do not cling to wisdom? (*Free Choice*. I. 11. 77–78)

Freedom lies in absolute dependence on God.

> Our freedom then consists in submission to the truth. It is our God Himself who frees us from death, that is, from the state of sin. (*Free Choice*. II. 13. 143)

Those who love God completely receive everything that the Plotinian intellectual-principle could offer, and because love is possible for all, the rewards are not reserved for a favored elite.

> When the will to enjoy is continually present, the beauty of truth and wisdom does not shut out those who have come to hear because of the large crowd; it does not pass with time, and does not move in space. It is not cut short by night or shadows. It does not depend on the senses of

the body. It is near to all men who have chosen it and love it. It is eternal for all. It is in no one place, yet it is never away. Without it advises; within it teaches. (*Free Choice.* II. 14. 151–152)

And the whole end and fulfillment of human life is to live in God's eternity.

> So great is the beauty of justice, so great the joys of eternal light, of the unchangeable Truth and Wisdom, that even though a man were not allowed to remain in its light for longer than a day, yet in comparison with this he would rightly and properly despise a life of innumerable years spent in the delight of temporal goods. Indeed, the following is neither false nor trivial: 'Far better is one day in thy courts than thousands' (*Psalms,* 83. 11). Yet it is also possible to understand this in another sense, namely that 'thousands of days' may be interpreted to represent the transience of time, while the term 'one day' represents the immutability of eternity. (*Free Choice.* III. 25. 265–266)

But from its earliest beginnings, mankind turned away from God to love of temporal things. What we have here are not individual souls severed from the unity of eternal Soul. What we have are distinct and autonomous beings, each with its own will. And the misery of those souls is not the yearning of Soul lost to itself, but the just suffering of creatures who have dared to turn their wills against that of the omnipotent emperor who is their creator and lord. The imperial God brooks no deviation from his will, and the sin of the first people, Adam and Eve, plunged the human race into darkness.

> God, the highest Ruler of the universe, justly decreed that we, who are descended from that first union, should be born into ignorance and difficulty, and be subject to death, because they sinned and were hurled headlong into the midst of error, difficulty and death. (*Free Choice.* III. 20. 186)

And now humans are so beset with ignorance and carnal desire that it is impossible for them to turn to God without help: "When we speak of the will that is free to do right, we speak of the will with which man was [first] made" (*Free Choice.* III. 18. 179). The present condition of humankind is utterly hopeless without the aid of God.

> If man were good, he would be other than as he is. Now, however, since he is as he is, he is not good, and does not have it in his power to be

good—either because he does not see what he ought to be, or because he does see, yet does not have the power to be what he sees he ought to be. Who would doubt that this is a punishment? (*Free Choice*. III. 18. 174–175)

In fact, those (such as the Platonists?) who seek to be like the angels, and to rise to look upon the face of God by their own efforts, are not only engaged in a hopeless quest. They are in fact victims of the most overweening pride.

Men who, because of their vain glory, want to be equal to the angels, do not really want to be equal to the angels; rather, they want the angels to be equal to them. If they persevere in this wish, they will be equal in punishment to the fallen angels who loved their own power rather than the power of God. (*Free Choice*. III. 9. 103)[227]

What all of this means is that mankind is saved not by reason or right conduct, but only by making a fundamental choice regarding the object of love: "The eternal law...established with immutable firmness the point that merit lies in the will..." (*Free Choice*. I. 14. 101). The good will is the will that loves God completely and submits itself to him totally. All other virtues are subordinate to this love.

Therefore, if we should love and embrace with our will the good will, and place it before all other things that we cannot keep even if we will to do so, then those virtues...will dwell in our spirit, and to possess them is to live rightly and honorably. (*Free Choice*. I. 13. 97)

The soul, trapped and seduced by carnal desire, may not realize that its fulfillment lies in this pure love of God. And even if it does recognize that therein lies the better way, it is so enmeshed in the love of temporal things that it may not want to turn to God. But in at least one sense, nothing is easier to obey than the commandment to love God, since if one merely *wants* to love God, then one already does love God.

From this it is established that whoever wants to live rightly and honorably, if his will for this surpasses his will for temporal goods, achieves this great good so easily that to have what he wills is nothing other than the act of willing. (*Free Choice*. I. 13. 97)

All that is asked is that we love God and submit to him completely, not that we grasp the nature of all things by reason or lift ourselves up to a vision of the divine. That every human fails to do this simple thing is the most eloquent testimony to the enormity of our sinful depravity, and "it is just to suffer punishment for so great a sin" (*Free Choice.* I. 11. 77). And indeed, the just consequence of so profound a sinfulness is the eternal punishment of hell that awaits all those who do not throw themselves on divine mercy and hope for aid in turning to God.

Thus the proper religious attitude is one of total submission, surrender of the will and absolute dependence on the mercy and grace of God. While we may be sure of the perfection of God's order and plan for the universe, that order and that plan remain forever beyond our comprehension. Reason may do what it will, but reliance on reason or any human effort marks the person as a victim of sinful pride. Absolute humility and unconditional acceptance of the will of God hold the only hope of redemption, and the unchanging command of God is for unquestioning surrender of the will to the divine will. Augustine emphasizes the proper attitude when he says that even if God were to inform me that my destiny is to spend eternity in the unspeakable torment of hell, the proper response would be to rejoice that God's will is to be done and to be grateful for the role I am to play in completing God's perfect order.

> If it is unjust for you to be more unhappy after death, you will not be more unhappy. If, however, it is just, let us praise God by whose laws you will be unhappy. (*Free Choice.* III. 6. 65)

Summary

We have now arrived at Augustine's final conception of God and the myth that was to dominate his religious consciousness. It is also the myth that was to dominate western ideology for many centuries. In concluding Part Two, I would like to make some observations by way of summarizing what has been learned so far and focusing attention on some significant implications of the discussion to this point.

Observation 1: The existence of God not an issue. Perhaps it is well to begin by noting that Augustine clearly did not arrive at his beliefs about the existence and nature of his God by means of rational investigation, the marshalling of evidence or the development of arguments. It is true that once he became imbued with the Platonist outlook, he came to regard it as self-evident that the very existence in our minds of certain concepts and necessary truths testifies to a realm of eternal and immutable truth. But he discovered this argument only when he was over thirty years old, and he never claimed that his belief in the Catholic god was *based on* that argument, just that it provided corroboration for the belief. More exactly, he specifically repudiated the idea that that "exceptionally well-known argument" constituted a demonstration of God's existence, and he always insisted that God's existence is not demonstrable by reason at all.

The only evidence Augustine cites as support for his belief was what seemed to him the indisputable fact that the Catholic god had triumphed in the world, had established his church universally and had won the allegiance of people throughout the world. But while that evidence did suggest something to him about the nature of God (the all-conquering emperor), he never thought of it as evidence for the *existence* of God.

The fact is that Augustine, like most people of his day, saw no need to demonstrate the existence of his god, simply because there was no doubt whatever of the existence and activity of the gods or of the one he called God in particular. The triumph of the Catholic god was important not as evidence of his existence, but as evidence that he was the supreme god to whom exclusive cult could safely be paid. As the temples of the old gods were destroyed or converted to Christian uses, as their statues were broken or melted down and their wealth appropriated, what was clear to a youth of Augustine's generation was the *impotence* of the pagan gods. In the face of the obvious power of God, the old deities seemed no more than petty demons.

Observation 2: Augustine's search was for a satisfying myth. Augustine's difficulty in finally settling into his Catholic heritage had nothing to do with doubts about the existence of his god or even the superiority of that god over all others. His hesitation had to do with whether he could come to believe that his god was what he needed him to be, with whether God could be thought of as the being that could meet the needs of his developing religious sensibilities. Augustine was looking not for rational proof, but for a satisfying myth that could meet his felt needs, and it was those needs that drove his development.

The god Augustine learned of from his mother, the god of his original myth, was the ultimate deity of Roman tradition. This god was a superhuman being of human (though always hidden) form, an invincible commander and a demanding but provident Father. God's purposes and the reasons for his actions might be hidden, but there was none of the capricious anger of many other gods. The believer could be sure of both the justice and the providence of this god. Those who offered the exclusive and complete service and devotion he demanded could be as sure of divine favor as those who turned from him could be sure of terrible retribution. This god, who had brought "eternal Rome" under his sway, demanded the absolute submission owing to absolute imperial authority, but he offered in return boundless providence and perfect justice.

This god of his youth was never lost. Even as he toyed with Manichaeism and Platonism, Augustine remained a Catholic catechumen and was always aware that the Catholic god was calling him. But as he left his provincial home and sought entrance into the cultured elite of Carthage, Rome and Milan, he found himself faced with two sorts of problems. On the one hand, he came to doubt whether the god of his original myth could in fact satisfy the needs he had brought with him. In particular, could he regard God as at once omnipotent and perfectly good, when he was becoming increasingly aware of the presence and intractability of evil in the world and in his own soul? And on the other hand, he found himself developing new needs and sensibilities, which the god of his original myth seemed badly equipped to meet. That anthropomorphic warrior-king seemed hardly adequate to the needs of a cultured soul yearning for reunion with an immaterial and eternal source of being and wisdom. And the scriptures of that god, though they might have the authority of antiquity, seemed hopelessly crude beside the perfectly turned lines of the poets. Augustine's pilgrimage through Manichaeism and Platonism was then not an effort at rational investigation. It was an attempt to find a myth that could satisfy the needs he found himself to have. He wanted and needed God to be a being that could meet both his need for a perfect ruler and his need for an eternal ground of being. The question was whether there was any way of thinking of God that an African provincial turned aristocratic intellectual could find comfortable.

Seen in this light, his Manichaean period was one of transition and experimentation. The Manichaeans allowed him to think of God in non-human terms, to appreciate more fully the struggle of "light" and "darkness" in the world and especially the division of his own soul by warring desires. And so long as he remained in Africa, his adherence to the Manichees put him in the company of the brightest of provincial aristocrats and intellectuals. But the Manichaean myth offered a god that was in other ways a poor substitute for the god of his youth, a passive being condemned to an eternal struggle with a force of darkness that was in some ways more dynamic than the light.

It was Platonism and the Plotinian myth that provided him an alternative to Manichaeism and pointed him toward his own final conception of God. But that Platonism managed to do so much for him is remarkable in itself. While Augustine was scornful of the rationalist pretensions of the Manichees and felt that the Platonists embodied the highest standards of "reason," the fact is that the Plotinian myth is at least as full of paradoxes, logical inconsistencies and obscurities as anything the Manichees had to offer. The Platonists provided not evidence or arguments or sound reasons to persuade the intellect, but rather a "picture" of reality that seemed to them more "noble" and uplifting than the Manichaean myth. The Manichaean god who is literal light that all could see is replaced by a being that is not a being, a god that both acts and remains forever in repose, a god that acts both by necessity and voluntarily, a god that becomes all things and yet is distinct from all things, a soul that is at once a unity and a plurality and that is both lost from its source and identical with its source. Just why it seemed so obvious to Augustine that this description of reality was a model of rationality to be much preferred to Manichaeism may be something of a mystery.

What attracted Augustine to the Platonists was not its superiority as a rationally coherent system. He discovered Platonism at the same time that he both discovered the intellectual and cultural elite of the empire and himself joined that elite. Among the leisured "lovers of wisdom" who moved easily between high imperial or ecclesiastical office, intense concentration on the piling up of wealth and the reflective repose of "philosophic" *otium*, it was already self-evident that the truly noble soul was at once lost from and yet still distantly united to an eternal source. And even as such a soul bore the burdens of earthly duties, it yearned for a return to the source which was its true home. Such men (and they were all, in fact, males) *felt* the light of the eternal within them, they felt the chains of the body and the burdens that went with their station, and they felt the need of mystical transcendence that would set them free.

When Augustine joined that elite, he absorbed their outlook completely and almost instantly. This was, after all, the most ancient wisdom, the truth that the "best" men had taught for a millennium. Even among "philosophic" Christians, some version of this picture had long been accepted and used to mold their vision of God and the Christ. Augustine began to *feel* the light of the eternal in his own soul, to see his own yearnings for truth, beauty and goodness as pointing back to an original Truth, Beauty and Goodness. The Plotinian myth, for all its obscurity and paradoxicality, was not only acceptable, but seemed to express the obvious truth that had long been the possession of the most noble spirits. And armed with this new picture, Augustine was able to affirm his God as unlimited, the source of all being, perfect in goodness and the architect of a perfect order in which evil had no place.

The Plotinian myth did in this way enable Augustine to leave behind both the anthropomorpic God of his original myth and the passive divinity of the Manichees and to move to a vision of God as limitless in both power and goodness. But the imperial myth at which he finally arrived is really very unlike the Plotinian myth in many ways, and it is a testimony to the power of that elite outlook that Augustine, with his need for consistency and clarity, continued to hold onto much of the Plotinian picture when he really no longer needed it.

The imperial myth satisfied Augustine's needs by portraying God as an absolutely omnipotent and perfectly good ruler and Father. Inspired by the Plotinian notion of the whole of reality as a complete and perfect harmony ordered by the harmony of forms flowing from the unity of the One, Augustine came to conceive his God as the omniscient creator who orders all reality after the forms in his mind. What is essential to Augustine's conception is that his God is an absolutely perfect person, who brings all things into existence by his will and orders all things by his plan; who knows all that is, has been and will be; who directs all things to the ends he has appointed; who demands from his creatures total obedience and love; who aids and rewards those who love him purely with an unspeakable happiness; and who tempers the just punishment of the unfaithful with an inscrutable *noblesse oblige* that lifts up some who would otherwise be lost.

In order to develop this conception of God, Augustine no doubt needed to break free of the notion of God as bounded by a human form, located in space, and opposed by other corporeal objects. He needed to see God as transcendent, apart from this world, unbounded and utterly independent of all other beings. In other words, he needed God to be the perfect emperor, combining and perfecting all the qualities one would find in a perfect autocrat, but with none of the limitations of even the most impressive of humans. And the Plotinian myth helped him to reach this conception by freeing him from anthropomorphism and the materialism of the Manichees.

But did he need also to see God as "outside" time, with all the problems that creates for understanding how God can be active in history? For that matter, did he need to see God as utterly changeless, a dogma that made it almost impossible to make any sense of the notion that God *acts* at all? He certainly needed to see the whole of creation as completely dependent on the creating and sustaining power of God. But did he need to hold onto the perplexing Platonic notion that the world is not fully "real," a notion that was linked to the discarded idea that the world is an imperfect "participation" or "copy" of a perfect reality, rather than an artifact of a perfect architect? Certainly he needed to see all reality as controlled by the good God and so to deny the reality of evil, since everything has its place in God's order. But once the idea of a perfect order was developed, why did he bother to hang onto the useless notion of evil as a "defect" or "lack" of being? Once it is established that every being and every event contributes to the perfection of God's order and to the completion of God's plan, is anything gained by retaining the notion of each being as somehow "defective" and "incomplete"? If each thing is exactly as God wanted it to be and if each event is what God wanted to occur, there are no "defects" in any sense that matters for Augustine's theology, and the whole Plotinian notion of a "falling short" of perfect reality loses its point.

Yet Augustine *did* retain all these ideas, even though, as nearly as I can tell, they were superfluous to his project. In fact, most of these Platonist trappings were simply ignored as irrelevant by many of those who accepted the Augustinian view of reality. They were ideas that retained their power for Augustine because of their elite credentials and because of his taking for granted that the ideas of the "best" men *must* be consistent with and precursors to Christian wisdom. When

Augustine sees Platonist ideas everywhere in the Catholic scriptures and so supposes that Plato must have read the Bible, what he actually reveals is the extent to which he and other Christian theologians were eager to align their religion with the dominant direction of aristocratic ideology. Augustine needed a god who was a perfect ruler and Father, and he needed a god that could satisfy the longing of the noble soul for union with its eternal source. But beyond that, he also needed a god that would seem respectable to those gentlemen who yearned for the eternal repose of changeless being. Throughout his career, he had trouble reconciling the dynamic, creative, provident and directing deity that met his initial needs with the changeless, eternal being for whom all of history is a "frozen moment" with neither past, present nor future. And it seems to me that his determination to hold onto that latter conception of God is explained only by looking to the complex of *needs* that Augustine was trying to satisfy.

Observation 3: Augustine's conception of God was universally satisfying. When we are trying to understand the power of the Augustinianism and its ideological dominance, certainly one factor to be mentioned is the fact that when we talk about the needs that gave rise to Augustine's imperial myth, we are, at the same time, talking about needs that were widely shared by others. In fact, it seems to me that one key to the success of Augustinianism lies in the fact that Augustine's own personal needs spanned the religious needs felt by others of every rank and station in western Roman society. His god "worked" for so many at least in part because the conception of deity that met his needs also met the needs of so many.

In Part One I looked at the role of religion in Augustine's society. That overview yielded the conclusion that for the vast majority, religious consciousness was still very near the spirit of cultic practice. Religion was a matter, above all, of gaining favor and avoiding the unpredictable anger of the gods by means of appropriate service. There is no reason to think that that outlook changed fundamentally when people shifted their allegiance to the Christian god. In any case, it was only in the half century preceding Augustine's birth that significant numbers of ordinary people had moved toward Christianity, and for the masses, religious attitudes were deeply rooted. Christian bishops spent a good deal of time either combating vestigial pagan rituals among their flocks or finding ways to accommodate those practices. Augustine's mother continued at least one such practice herself, until she was told by Ambrose that it was unbecoming in a Christian (*Conf.* VI. 2.).

Nor was such an attitude restricted to the laboring masses. Merchants, civil servants, senators and even (sometimes especially) emperors were always eager to please the gods, to avoid their wrath and to carry out those practices that would assure benevolent regard. What was needed was a god who was provident and so wanted the welfare of his devotees, was just in rewarding service and in punishing disloyalty, and was omnipotent and so able both to care for his own people and to ward off the envy of other gods.

The tiny educated minority shared these needs with "lesser" people, but they also developed additional needs, needs for liberation of the soul from the body, for achieving the "greatest good" of man and for that bliss that can come only by grasping eternal "wisdom." They felt their alienation from the source of all being, and they yearned to return to identity with it.

Since Augustine himself had all of these needs and felt them so intensely, it is not surprising that his conception of God struck a chord in others. The imperial myth was satisfying in many ways. The masses were treated to the spectacle of the all-conquering Catholic god, who had established his church throughout the world and had even brought the emperors to devout and exclusive service. As the absolutely omnipotent ruler of the universe, he could rightly demand far more than the blood of victims or the rituals of feast days. He could and did demand absolute surrender and total devotion. But for those who gave that devotion and committed themselves to God and his church, he could promise great rewards. While one's fortunes in this world remained as unpredictable as ever, one could be assured that in the end, all things work together for those who love God, that the church of God will be triumphant and that the rewards of eternal bliss await the faithful.

At the same time, the needs of the cultured few were met as well. They were offered a single eternal source of being with its own intellectual-principle in the form of the absolutely eternal and changeless person who not only "begot" the "Word" which gives the world order and intelligibility, but who could guarantee the redemption of all who love him, whether or not they are able to mount up to him on the wings of "reason." Here was that ineffable being beyond the gods that beckoned noble souls to transcendent unity, peace and harmony. It offered all that the Plotinian One could offer and more. For even as that eternal principle remained in perfectly ordered repose, it acted also as the personal creator, designer and caretaker of all reality, the engineer of history and the personal guide to every questing spirit.

The key features of this deity, those that enabled it to meet so many needs, were its absolute omnipotence and its perfect goodness. Whether God's power was associated with his being the single assurance of the unified harmony of the universe or with his being the conquerer of all demonic pretenders, it was essential that that power be lacking in no way whatever. And whether God's goodness was associated with that very cosmic harmony or with that perfect justice that assures his reliability to his devotees, it was also essential that his goodness be certain. A god in any way limited in power would not be a secure object of exclusive cult, the ever present fear of malicious demons would undermine Catholic devotion, and the empire could not be safely entrusted to an alliance with God's church. Nor could God lack at least the power of the Plotinian One to assure perfect order and to be the single source of that wisdom and beatitude sought by fallen souls. And similarly, while God's purposes might remain beyond the comprehension of creatures, it was essential that those purposes be seen as good if God was to provide solace and hope to those souls. Augustine's own odyssey toward an adequate myth was powered by his need for a God of unlimited power and goodness. It was his difficulty in finding a way to conceive God as both omnipotent and good that both led him to the Manichaean myth and that finally led him to abandon it. And the central attraction of the Plotinian myth was that it offered him a way to think of God as absolute in both these respects. These were also the features that most people sought in their God, and the power of the Augustinian conception is due above all to the fact that it offered a god of unlimited power and goodness. From this time forward, the mere suggestion that God might be in the least limited in power or goodness would seem the most terrible blasphemy. Given the religious consciousness and needs we have discussed, once Augustine insisted that it is *possible* that God be both omnipotent and perfectly good, it was no longer thinkable that he be anything less. And those who were unhappy with aspects of the Augustinian system were forced to begin their attempts at refutation only after granting the two basic premises on which the system rested, those of the omnipotence and perfect goodness of God.

Having said this, I must now add that, as we shall see in Part Three, Augustine himself was, in the end, unable to sustain a consistent view of God as possessing both these attributes, and when he was pushed to the wall, it was to divine *omnipotence* that he finally clung. But Augustine himself never admitted this ultimate incoherence in his thought, though it seems he was almost certainly aware of it. And though it is beyond the scope of the present work, I shall suggest that when his Pelagian critics attempted to point out that Augustinianism seemed to compromise the goodness of God, they ran aground on the fact that they could not find a way of preserving divine goodness without falling into the much more unthinkable alternative of undermining divine power. In short, once the god of the imperial myth was fully developed, no lesser conception could be entertained.

Observation 4: Augustine's myth was conservative and served the interests of the dominant classes. Finally, we should note, as so many others have, that even if Augustine's imperial myth met the needs of people of all stations, it did not, in the same way, serve the material interests of all. It offered, in fact, powerful reinforcement for continued ruling-class domination.

To begin with, the very picture of God as the ultimate emperor whose instrument was his church not only strengthened the institutional church and the aristocrats who occupied the principal bishoprics, but it supported the alliance of church and imperial autocracy that was the principal source of political unity in the empire. That service to God entailed strict loyalty and submission to the church was not an implication of Augustine's system, it was an integral part of the imperial myth. As we have seen, his principal evidence for the supremacy of his god was the fact that the church of that god had triumphed throughout the empire. There might be people within the church who were not truly faithful to God, but there was no doubt whatever that the Catholic Church was the very presence and agent of God on earth.

Furthermore, the imperial myth, in its Platonic aspect, carried over the conception of the universe as a hierarchical structure in which each being had its proper place and in which the structure and direction of the whole was the unfolding of God's perfect plan. Whether by virtue of its original state or as a result of the sin which had entered the world and which now served God's purposes equally well, the whole of being, including human society, is ordered under the aspect of perfect harmony, with each person in her or his place, dependent on those above and destined to remain so.

It is true that Christianity had always preached an abstract equality of all before God, and Augustine preserves that egalitarianism. All are equally sinners, and all are alike in the eyes of God. Poor Lazarus may indeed wear a crown while the rich man burns in hell. But this sort of equality had never threatened the actual order of things, and it never occurred to Augustine that it would. In fact, this sort of egalitarianism actually served to reinforce existing structures. It is precisely because all are equal in the eyes of God, because one's station in this world is irrelevant to one's ultimate destiny, that it is pernicious and foolish to worry about whether one is landlord or serf, slave or free. It is not that the emperor or other superiors always (or ever) act justly or rule as God commands; it may well be that there is no justice on earth at all. What is just and perfectly ordered is the whole universe in its unity and intricacy. That order is unchallengeable not because those who rule are good men or even better men, but because their dominion, since it is a fact, must be due to the will of God. The only alternative would be to suggest either that God is not good or that some aspect of reality escapes his control.

These implications of Augustine's thought have often been noted and lamented. It is sometimes suggested that earlier Christians had a quite different view. They saw their own community as the instrument of God on earth, they saw the emperor and the whole political and economic order as corrupt and sinful and as not binding on Christians who owed their whole allegiance to God. They believed that the hierarchies of this world are artificial, that the true society is the society of believers who recognize their equality before God, eschew domination and share all goods and all power in the community freely among themselves.

This is, I think, a very idealized and one-sided picture of the attitudes of early Christians. The situation during the first four centuries of Christianity was much more complex and ambiguous. Nevertheless, there is some truth in the picture, and it is certainly understandable that Christians today would yearn for the sense of community and equality of primitive Christianity and regret the rigidity and acceptance of hierarchy that characterizes Augustinianism.

Without pursuing this complex question in detail, what I would suggest is that there is a much greater continuity of religious consciousness here than may at first appear. Before the beginning of the fourth century, Christians existed as a tiny minority, alternately tolerated and persecuted, but always virtually powerless. Their god could compete with others in producing miracles and exorcisms, and Christians always used miracle reports as a primary argument for conversion, but there was little evidence of the power of their god in directing the major affairs of the world.

In those conditions, two things above all bound Christians together and gave their religion staying power. One was the cohesiveness of their community and the spirit of brotherhood and unity it offered to people faced with a loss of a sense of place in the world. It was only natural that this communal sense should have been seen as the very spirit of God and that it should have fostered a spirit of equality. The other condition that strengthened the faith and justified paying exclusive cult to their god was the hope of heaven. Those powerless and without hope on earth could look to perfect bliss as a reward for complete devotion. And in those conditions, it was again natural to see the powers of this world as alien forces to which no Christian owed allegiance.

The change in Christian attitudes in the fourth century, a change that receives final expression in Augustine, was not a break with the earlier religious consciousness, but a development of it. The god who had offered heaven to the faithful had now also conquered the world and brought the state under his sway. The church which had earlier been an exclusive and tightly controlled, often clandestine and always suspicious fraternity was now a powerful and increasingly centralized organization that had the care of every soul in the world and that was allied with the emperor in extending God's control over earthly affairs.

Under these circumstances, it would have made no sense for Christians to retain their earlier "communitarian" attitudes. By bringing the emperors to his service and establishing his church throughout the world, God had made the old attitudes irrelevant. The state was no longer an alien pagan oppressor, but was God's very instrument. The church was no longer an assemblage of persecuted "saints" but was the agent of God's power and voice in bringing the world to Catholicism. The spiritual egalitarianism of the Christians had never challenged the real hierarchies of the world, and under the new circumstances there was certainly no reason to do so. The "democratic" attitude of early Christians who insisted that they were able to direct their own affairs had always been based on an attitude of submission to the will of God, rather than to that of the pagan state. Now, however, there was no reason to distinguish submission to God from submission to the Christian authorities of both church and state. Augustinianism does not represent some sort of triumph of authoritarianism over a spirit of democratic community, nor does it mark the defeat of an earlier exaltation of human autonomy. Christians had always been called to submit wholly to the will of God. What was new was only that the will of God now called all people to obey the Christian state and to accept the structures of Christian society.

In conclusion, then, I would suggest that the key to Augustinian ideology is the concept of the absolutely omnipotent and perfectly good God. This concept of God responded to needs that Augustine shared with the vast majority of people of every rank and station, though it served the interests of the ruling strata to a far greater extent than those of any other. And so, even though Augustine offered little in the way of rational support for this fundamental belief, it was not only easily accepted by most Christians, but it seemed blasphemous any longer even to question it. Augustine offered a myth that made sense of the view of God as the absolute and unchallengeable ruler of the universe on whom all were totally dependent, and once that conception was made plausible, it was unthinkable for any Christian to consider God anything less. Those who were unhappy with Augustine found themselves bound to agree with the basic conception of God that was the foundation of his thought, so that if they hoped to refute him, it would have to be by challenging the inferences that he drew from that basic conception.

In Part Three, I want to look at some of those inferences, the ones that constitute the heart of Augustine's system. What I think we shall find is that while Augustine's system does, in the end, fall short of complete consistency, it is nonetheless an impressive structure indeed, one that no other thinker was able to approach or effectively criticize. Hopefully, that discussion will both fill out an understanding of Augustinianism and help explain its power as a dominant ideology.

Part Three

AUGUSTINIANISM

In Part One, I reviewed in broad outline some of the social and economic conditions within which Augustinianism had its birth. Part Two discussed the development of the idea of God, which is the fundamental concept of Augustine's thought, with an eye to understanding both the content of that concept and the factors that influenced Augustine's evolution toward that concept. Hopefully, those discussions have given support to two general observations:

- that Augustine's own religious consciousness was in many ways a mirror of ideas, attitudes, and needs that were not only shared with most of his contemporaries, but that were so basic as to constitute a kind of "common-sense" framework that no sensible person would be likely to question;

- that Augustine's search for an adequate idea of his god was not, in any serious sense, an attempt to provide evidence or arguments for the existence or nature of his god, but was a search for a unifying myth that presented God and his relation to the world in a way that satisfied those basic needs.

At the end of Part Two, it was suggested that the power of the Augustinian ideology rested to a large extent on the fact that the god which was its centerpiece was one that most people yearned for and that few would want to deny. And at this point, I would like to state that point explicitly once more. Even pagans, who were by this time in full retreat, were drawn to a god of absolute power and universal providence, and many of them believed that behind the many appearances of the gods, there was a single supreme god. And among Christians, there seem to have been none who did not seek to ground their faith in the idea of an omnipotent and perfectly good god. For Catholics, the Nicene Creed stated explicitly both that God is "almighty" and that he is the perfectly just judge of all souls. Arian Christians questioned the unity of God and Christ, but there was no doubt about the absolute supremacy of God in both power and goodness. Pelagius and his followers, who saw some of Augustine's doctrines as a threat to human freedom and moral responsibility, never questioned the fundamental conception of God on which Augustine based those doctrines. And the Donatists, with whom Augustine battled to the end of his life, grounded their sect in a conception of a god of unchallengeable supremacy. Manichaeism, despite an appealing vision that united human nature with the universe and the very essence of God, never gained wide appeal, and it was condemned not only because it still bore the odor of the hated Persians, but because it reduced God to a passive omnipresence that failed to satisfy the need for a triumphant commanding deity.

So part of the reason for the dominance of Augustinianism was that it rested on a conception of God so satisfying that once it was established as a *possible* conception, it was almost impossible to reject, certainly impossible for a Christian to reject. And it confronted a dying paganism with what seemed the indisputable fact of an omnipotent deity who had already proved his supremacy by driving their gods from the place they had occupied from time immemorial.

A second reason for the success of Augustinianism, and one that cannot be adequately discussed here, was its scope and depth. No part of Christian doctrine or practice escaped Augustine's notice, and the sheer volume of his work and his almost incredible attention to detail mark him as undoubtedly the most comprehensive intellect in western history. In exploring every aspect of God's relation to creation, he developed an entirely new and astonishingly complete interpretation of history, a fairly complete metaphysics and a systematic theology. His examination of his own soul in its search for salvation yielded brilliant psychological insights, established a new literary genre of spiritual autobiography and set the highest standard for that genre. As the foremost ecclesiastic of his time, he defined the church more completely than ever before, gave it the structure that was to endure to the present day and established the relationship between the church and the secular world. And along the way, he redefined scriptural exegesis, monastic discipline, contemplative spirituality and the role of priest and bishop in Christian society. Reviewing the enormous body of work, the voluminous correspondence, the many sermons, it is hard not to agree with Isidore of Seville, who inscribed above the cabinet containing Augustine's works: "He who claims to have read all this is a liar." And to realize that all this was written while Augustine was an active pastor who preached to his flock every day, the most prominent and active churchman in the west and frequently an active Roman administrator as well, is apt to leave most of us simply awestruck.

But while the power of his intellect and the breadth of his work would surely have won Augustine an important place in the history of the church, those alone do not explain the dominance of the Augustinian outlook. It is a view of reality that was difficult and painful to accept, and its success must rest on more than admiration for Augustine's personal qualities.

The core of Augustinianism is its emphasis on the absolute supremacy of God and the accompanying absolute helplessness and dependency of the human soul on the grace of God. While it calls upon every soul to do its duty in obedience to God, it also rejects any notion of the significance of human accomplishments. And while it calls upon all people and states to seek justice and earthly peace, it also rejects any hope that either justice or peace is to be had in this world. It is a world-view under which any ideas of human dignity or autonomy take quite a beating and under which any illusions about the worth of human institutions are shattered. Neither happiness nor justice is to be found in this world, and strict obedience to church and state are demanded not because those institutions have intrinsic worth, but because they are God's instruments for establishing a measure of peace in a sinful world and of calling the "damned mass" of humanity to repentance.

Such an outlook was hardly assured of easy acceptance, no matter how eminent its author. And indeed many Christians found it distinctly uncomfortable. Many priests and monks saw in it a tendency to hopelessness that reduced religious striving to futility.[228] Augustine himself recognized that some implications of his system should be kept from the masses, lest they lose heart and abandon the church, and indeed, within a century, the church itself rejected some of those implications as too bleak for believers to accept.[229] And finally, there were the

Pelagians who mounted a full-scale assault on Augustinianism during the saint's own lifetime. In short, neither Augustine nor his contemporaries would have thought the triumph of his system inevitable.

In light of these considerations, what I now want to suggest is that another reason for the success of Augustininanism is just that it was a more complete and consistent theology than any other available. A comparison of Augustine's system with others developed by his predecessors and contemporaries is more than I can undertake here. But in Part Three, I do want to display some central features of that system and the way in which they follow from basic claims rooted in his conception of God. The purpose of this discussion is twofold.

The first aim is just to complete the "picture" of Augustinianism that is the reason for this study. What I think can be made clear is that Augustine is a remarkably insightful, coherent and consistent thinker who was deeply committed to a rigorous rational defense of his ideas. While it is true that he was extremely suspicious of "philosophizing" without the guidance of faith, those who take this to mean that he was an irrationalist or a blind dogmatist are simply wrong. The reason Augustine seems irrational or dogmatic to many today is that the basic ideology on which his thought rests has been replaced by another (or others), so that many beliefs that seemed simply evident to him now appear as groundless assumptions. But if a failure to examine critically or even to be explicitly aware of the ideological base of philosophical thought is taken as crucial, virtually all philosophical thinkers of every period will stand condemned. Augustine is at least clearly conscious of his basic beliefs regarding the existence and nature of God and the relation of God to creation. And he proceeds from those basic beliefs to develop their implications with a really remarkable honesty and rigor.

The second aim of the discussion in Part Three is to bring out that while Augustine's thought does, in the end, fall short of complete consistency, the difficulty is rooted in his basic conception of God and would have been very difficult to avoid. What this means is that those who wanted to reject Augustinianism were hard put to capitalize on this inconsistency, unless they were prepared to abandon the conception of God on which it rested. In particular, I want to suggest that the Augustinian system, including both its remarkable consistency and its final inconsistency, rests on the conception of God's goodness, on the one hand, and his absolutely unqualified control of his creation, on the other. And it is very hard to see how the inconsistency can be avoided without compromising either God's goodness or his active omnipotence. Perhaps, in the end, some ingenious way can be found of holding onto that conception of God and yet avoiding the inconsistency. But what does seem to me clear (though, once again, I must leave it to others to test this claim) is that none of Augustine's opponents, and especially not the Pelagians who were his main critics, even came close to finding such a solution. And since no one was prepared to weaken the conception of God by qualifying either his power or his goodness, what this meant was that the less powerful thinkers who challenged Augustine just ended up with other more numerous and more blatant inconsistencies. In other words, I think that if one takes the Augustinian system and compares it with actually existing alternatives, what will be evident is that while it is imperfect, it was certainly the strongest available candidate.

Logical consistency is certainly not the only reason Augustinianism won acceptance. Indeed it is not even the most important reason. Had not the basic ideas of the system met the felt needs of most people, had not the system served the interests of the lay and ecclesiastical ruling classes, it is impossible to believe that internal consistency would have sold it. It is easy to think of dominant ideologies that have lacked such consistency. And in fact, though this is another thing that cannot be argued here, it seems to me that the version of Augustinianism that was finally adopted by the early medieval church was a good deal *less* consistent than Augustine's original thought. But while internal consistency is hardly crucial, I think it did play an important role in this case. During his lifetime, Augustine was confronted with direct challenges to his system, and I am persuaded that his success rested in large measure on the fact that his ideas held together to a far greater extent than those of any of his critics. So it does seem to me that when it is asked what led people to accept such bleak conclusions as Augustine developed, at least part of the answer is that no one was able effectively to challenge his claim that those conclusions simply *followed* from premises that were accepted by all parties.

What I want to do here is to illustrate this point by examining five core doctrines of Augustinianism: (1) free choice of the human will, (2) divine foreknowledge, (3) predestination, (4) original sin and (5) the primal fall of humanity. In each case, I want to look at how and why he arrived at his final positions as a way of understanding some of the power of his system. While these doctrines are certainly not the whole of Augustinianism (which would include his views of the church, political life, spirituality, monastic discipline and other subjects), they are, I think, its most distinctive features and the basis for his ideas on most other subjects. His views of these matters come together to present a picture of the nature and place of the individual soul in its relation to God, a picture that has been central to the discussion of Augustinianism from the beginning and the picture that was challenged so ferociously by Pelagius and his allies during Augustine's lifetime.

Augustine's first extended discussion of the complex of issues I am concerned with here is in the dialogue *On Free Choice of the Will*, which he began work on during his stay in Rome after baptism and completed in 395, about the time of his ordination as a priest in Hippo. That dialogue leaves a number of questions unanswered and is probably not entirely consistent with the conclusions he finally reached some years later. But already at that stage, the discussion is grounded in a number of beliefs that would remain unchanged and that would determine his thought on these matters. Those basic beliefs were brought out in our discussion in Part Two, but it may be well to state them explicitly at this point, since they form the unvarying premises from which he departs.

For present purposes, the most important of those beliefs are:

• *The Omnipotence Doctrine.* God is the sole creator and ruler of the universe. It is absolutely impossible for God to lack control of any event or aspect of reality or for him to lack any knowledge needed for such total control. God's omnipotence means also that he is utterly independent, that none of his actions or decisions are dependent on actions or decisions of any other being—that is, that God's action is never *reaction*. It is impossible for God to do evil, to be ignorant or to be impotent, since perfect goodness, knowledge and power belong to the nature of God and without them God would not be God. But God is absolutely free to create any universe consistent with his nature, and no jot or tittle of any such universe could escape his attention or direction.

• *The Goodness Doctrine.* God is perfectly good, meaning that God possesses in perfect measure all of those attributes that are defining of personal goodness. He is perfectly loving, just and merciful, and he acts always to maximize the beauty of creation. While God's purposes may be hidden from us, we may be sure that every being and every event contributes in the best possible way to a creation that is perfect in the beauty of its order and that is the ideal expression of God's love, justice and mercy.

From these two most fundamental doctrines, Augustine thinks that there follows another which it will be well to include among the foundations of his system:

• *The Imperial Edict Doctrine.* Since it is impossible for God to lack power, it is impossible for any being or event to escape God's conscious control. Hence, it follows that God has decreed that all creatures must follow his will without question or deviation. The fulfillment of this decree means that, as a matter of fact, every event in nature and every action of every creature *does* occur by the will of God and *does* serve the purposes of God. In the case of creatures that are capable of understanding (i.e. angels, demons and human beings), the decree also takes the form of a *commandment* to obey the will of God just because it is the will of God, without a shadow of hesitation and with no motive other than a desire to do God's will. Or to put it in another way, such creatures are commanded to *love* God completely and to act always and only because of and out of the love of God.

And finally, there is one other basic doctrine that is taken from scripture and from Augustine's insight into his own soul. It is fundamental to the Christian faith:

• *The Sin Doctrine.* Creatures who are commanded to love God purely have not in the past and still do not always love God in that way or act out of a pure love of God. When they act out of any other motive, they are in a state of sin. In that state, they are *guilty* and so are deserving of punishment in proportion to the extent of their guilt. And in fact, we know from scripture that sinful creatures are often justly punished by God, though God's mercy does at times redeem some from deserved damnation, and by the sacrifice of the Christ, God offers redemption to all.

I think it is easy to see that these basic doctrines are at the heart of the imperial myth that was discussed in Part Two. At their core is an emphasis on the absolute perfection of God and the absolute dependence and sinfulness of creatures. And as we saw in that earlier discussion, they were accepted with little in the way of evidence or argument. They grew out of a shared perception of reality as controlled by the gods and out of the shared needs of a religious consciousness associated with that perception, and they were given cohesion by their incorporation into a unifying myth. It is from these few basic beliefs that almost all of what is now called Augustinianism proceeds.

Perhaps the best way to appreciate the unity of Augustine's thought is to trace its evolution in his own mind, the problems he encountered and his effort to develop an internally consistent system. In this way, it may be possible to understand both what remains constant and basic and what he thought had to be adjusted so as to conform to his most basic beliefs. Let me start with what is at once one of the most difficult and one of the most discussed aspects of his thought—his doctrine of the free choice of the will.

I. Free Choice of the Will

Modern and contemporary western philosophers whose thought is dominated by the individualism of the liberal ideology that serves the present economic system have been much preoccupied with the question of free will, individual autonomy and personal moral responsibility. So in looking at Augustine's thought from our historical perspective, it is important to remember that his concerns were not the same as those of modern philosophers and his priorities were very different indeed. Modern discussions have focused mainly on the question whether it is possible to find a place for individual autonomy and moral responsibility in a universe that operates according to strict causal laws. Augustine's universe operates exclusively by the will of God, and his focus is on developing a conception of free will that is consistent with total dependence of human beings on God and yet that preserves the goodness and justice of God in punishing sinners. Whereas modern philosophers are much concerned with individual dignity and autonomy, Augustine wants to show how the filthy and polluted soul remains an agent of God's will even as it richly deserves

God's wrath. The difference is considerable, and it must be kept in mind if Augustine's discussion is to be appreciated.

The difference shows up from the very beginning. For Augustine, that human beings act voluntarily or have free choice is not a basic postulate, but neither is it the least bit in doubt. It is a simple certainty, because it *follows* directly from the most basic beliefs of a Catholic Christian. By the sin doctrine, we know that humans do in fact sin and that they are punished by God; and by the goodness doctrine, we know that God's punishment is just. Unless people act voluntarily, it makes no sense to say either that they sin or that they live rightly, and because God's punishment is just, it follows that people *deserve* punishment and so are responsible for their actions.

> If man is a good, and cannot act rightly unless he wills to do so, then he must have free will, without which he cannot act rightly...It is sufficient for our question, why free will should have been given to man, to know that without it man cannot live rightly...Then too, if man did not have free choice of will, how could there exist the good according to which it is just to condemn evildoers and reward those who act rightly? What was not done by will would be neither evildoing nor right action. Both punishment and reward would be unjust if man did not have free will. Moreover, there must needs be justice both in punishment and in reward, since justice is one of the goods that are from God. Therefore, God must needs have given free will to man. (*Free Choice.* II. 1. 5–7)

So the fact of freedom follows from the fact of responsibility, and the fact of responsibility follows from the fact of divine goodness and justice. But now the question is: What exactly does it *mean* to say that human beings have free choice of the will? Only after getting clear that meaning can we go on to discuss the relation of freedom to the further fact of divine omnipotence.

While Augustine's discussions of human freedom and its relation to divine power became very complex and convoluted through the years, it does seem to me that he begins and ends those discussions with the same rather straightforward conception of what it means to say that humans have free will. And while he never precisely defines "free choice of the will" (*liberum arbitrium*), the meaning becomes clear in context.

Augustine's position is that human beings can be seen to have free choice of the will because there are at least some situations in which the doing or not doing of something is in the *power* of a person. And when he says that an action is in one's power, he means that one does that thing if she or he *wants* to and *chooses* to and does not do that thing if she or he wants not to and chooses not to. Or to put it slightly more concisely,

> I am free with respect to an action X if, and only if, X is in my power; and

> X is in my power if, and only if, conditions obtain such that if I want to do X and choose to do X, then I do X, and, similarly if I want not to do X and choose not to do X, then I don't do X.

As nearly as I can tell, every example of free choice in Augustine's work fits this definition. In *On Free Choice*, he gives a number of such examples, and while we shall need to look at some of these more closely later, it may be well at this point just to mention a few.

In Book III of that dialogue, Augustine asks his interlocutor Evodius whether he has the power to be happy, and Evodius replies

> Had I the power to be happy, I would surely be happy now. I wish to be happy now, and am not, because it is God, not I, who makes me happy. (*Free Choice*. III. 3. 26)

And Augustine uses this admission of Evodius to show him that "your happiness will come about in you, not by will, but by the necessity of God's action" (*Free Choice*. III. 3. 26). In other words, Evodius is saying (with Augustine's approval) that it would be in his power to be happy if conditions were such that his wanting and choosing to be happy would result in his being happy, but that in fact conditions are not such, since God's action is also necessary if one is to be happy. And Augustine then goes on to remark that for the same reason "we are right in saying that we grow old by necessity, not by will; or that we die by necessity, not by will, and so on" (*Free Choice*. III. 3. 27). And the point seems again to be that even if we want and choose not to grow old or die, these things are not in our power because conditions are not such that our wanting and choosing are sufficient.

A more interesting example occurs in Book I. There he notes that all men "want and desire" to be happy and also "will" (or choose) to be happy, but then adds that most are not happy because they do not also choose to "live rightly," when living rightly is a necessary condition of being happy. Thus he says that

> when we say that men are unhappy because of their will, we do not mean that they wish to be unhappy, but that they are in that state of will where unhappiness must result even if they do not want it. (*Free Choice*. I. 14. 102)

Here again, wanting and choosing to be happy are not sufficient because other conditions are not met, but the implication seems to be that while being happy is not now in one's power, it *could* be in one's power if one only wanted and chose to live rightly. So it would seem in this case that it might be even now in my power to be happy if it is now in my power to want and choose to live rightly. But more will need to be said about this below.

Turning now from actions that are not free and in our power to those that are, the most vivid examples for illustrating the very meaning of free choice are those having to do with the good will itself. The good will is, for Augustine, the very paradigm of that which is in our power, because it is the one thing that cannot possibly fail to be in our power. And while this too will require a good deal more discussion below, I want to take note of it at this point in order to make the meaning of free choice as clear as possible.

Augustine defines the good will as "a will by which we seek to live rightly and honorably and to come to the highest wisdom" (*Free Choice*. I. 12. 83). Ignorance and folly may make it impossible for us always to do the right and honorable thing, and the attainment of wisdom may be beyond our power in this life (e.g. *Free Choice*. III. 18. 179). But a good will which *seeks* to live wisely, rightly and honorably is not only in our power but is more so than anything else. I may have desires for the things of this world, and the lusts of the flesh may assault me, but "nothing can make the mind a companion of desire except its own will and free choice" (*Free Choice*. I. 11. 76). And why is it that the good will is always in my power? It is just that in this case, if I want to have a good will and *choose* to have a good will, then I *do* have a good will, and no other condition need be considered.

> Whoever wants to live well, if his will for that surpasses all others, achieves this good so easily that to have what he wills is nothing other than the act of willing. (*Free Choice*. I. 13. 97)

will for civil righteousness

Or as he puts it a few lines earlier: "to love one's good will and to esteem it as highly as we have said—is this not the good will itself?" (*Free Choice.* I. 13. 95).

In brief, then, I am free with respect to any action (or that action is in my power) to the extent that my wanting and choosing to perform that action are sufficient for my performing it. I may want and choose to forestall aging and remain young forever, but it is not in my power to keep my youth, since my wanting and choosing to do so have little to do with withstanding the ravages of time. On the other hand, if I want and choose to write a letter to my friend, it may turn out that this is in my power since conditions are such (paper and pen are available, I know how to write, etc., etc.) that my wanting and choosing are all that is needed to bring it about that I write the letter. Similarly, if I want and choose to do the right thing or to avoid making a mistake, whether I succeed depends very much on other conditions, such as the state of my knowledge. But, says Augustine, if what I want and choose is to try to live rightly and wisely (i.e. if I want and choose to have a good will), then that is as completely in my power as anything can be. In fact, he suggests, if I want and choose to have a good will, then I already *do* have a good will.

Given this conception of what it means to have free will, there arose immediately some concerns about how he was to reconicile free will so understood with the basic beliefs cited above. By the omnipotence doctrine we know that every event in the universe is known and controlled by God; by the sin doctrine we know that humans do sin and are punished by God; by the goodness doctrine we know that God's punishment is just; and by inference from those doctrines we know that since God's punishment is just, humans must be free and responsible for their actions. But now by the meaning of "free choice" just discussed, we learn that for humans to be free, their actions must be in their power. And how can it be both that our actions are in our power and that every event is under the absolute control of God?

Augustine was by no means the first to notice this problem. It had concerned both other Christians and many educated pagans as well. In Book V of the *City of God*, Augustine contrasts his own view with some of those others. He begins by considering those who saw the problem of determinism and freedom not in relation to a god, but as rooted in the regularity of the nature and genesis of human beings out of nature—those known as astrologers (*City*. V. 1–7).

Astrology was involved both with the study of the heavens and with the prediction of human fortune. Seen in the former way, it was the most advanced ancient science and a worthy forerunner to modern astronomy. Astrologers attempted to carry out the most precise observations and calculations in order to map the heavens and to predict as accurately as possible the movements and positions of heavenly bodies. But seen in the latter way, astrology attempted to function as a combination of genetic psychology and augury. It made the claim that essential features of individual personality and the course of events for both individuals and society were determined by the position and movements of the stars. And since those positions and movements operated according to fixed and mathematically calculable laws, it was further claimed that all events on earth, including all human events, were strictly determined by an inexorable fate. Thus it was claimed, in the most extreme versions, that the character and complete life history of every individual was fixed absolutely at birth by the position of the stars, so that nothing whatever could alter the outcome. And this was sometimes taken to entail a strict determinism that ruled out the possibility of human free will.

Augustine early on came to regard the more exaggerated claims of the astrologers as absurd. In the *Confessions*, he reports that even before his initial departure from Africa, he had rejected astrology, and that during his stay in Milan, he had come to see clearly that its claims were baseless (*Conf.* IV. 3 and VII. 6). He thought it easy to see that the very different life histories of persons could not possibly be correlated with the star charts, and he was especially struck that identical twins (his favorite example is of Jacob and Esau) could have such very different careers. And in the *City of God*, he ridicules the pretensions of the astrologers at length (*City*. V. 3–7).

Many eminent Romans agreed with Augustine in rejecting these astrological claims. But among at least some of them, astrology was replaced by a theology that they saw as equally restrictive of human freedom. While they rejected the view that the stars govern human destiny, they also thought that the perfectly orderly movements of the heavens needed an explanation. So they held that the perfectly calculable movements of the stars must be due to the ordering will of a supreme god. And having attributed the ordering of the heavens to this god, they could hardly deny that the same god must order all affairs on earth by his will. Augustine cites the Stoic philosopher Seneca as an example of a thinker who saw all events on earth as caused by the supreme god and on that basis denied the possibility of human freedom or of the efficacy of human action (*City.* V. 8). And he notes that Cicero struggled with this same issue and found himself, in order to save a place for human freedom, forced to deny that the supreme God controls or even knows the course of human events prior to its unfolding. For, thought Cicero, even if God does not actively *cause* events but only *knows* of them before they occur, then it is already certain what will occur and it is beyond the power of humans to affect the course of events (*City.* V. 9).

Now there was never a doubt in Augustine's mind as to where he would come down on these questions. That God is absolutely omnipotent and omniscient is fundamental, and that sinners are responsible and so justly punished by the perfectly good God is equally fundamental.

> For our part, whatever may be the twists and turns of philosophical dispute and debate, we recognize a God who is supreme and true and therefore we confess his supreme power and foreknowledge. We are not afraid that what we do by an act of will may not be a voluntary act, because God, with his infallible prescience, knew that we should do it. (*City.* V. 9)

The question was not whether all these things are true, but only *how* they can be held consistently. The question was: *How* can it be that God knows and controls all events and yet that we act freely and responsibly?

As mentioned above, Augustine's first extended discussion of the issues involved in this question was in *On Free Choice*. Both in that work and in all his later discussions, he sees the question as raising two quite distinct issues. One issue is whether God's *knowledge*, especially God's knowledge of all future events, can be made compatible with human freedom. A second issue is whether it is possible to maintain human freedom in the face of the fact that every event is determined by the will of God. And we need to look at these issues separately, since the course of his thought was not the same for both.

II. The Problem of Divine Foreknowledge

In *On Free Choice*, Augustine states this issue clearly by asking

> how can the following two propositions, that [1] God has foreknowl-
> edge of all future events, and that [2] we do not sin by necessity but by
> free will, be made consistent with each other? 'If God foreknows that
> man will sin,' you say, 'it is necessary that man sin.' If man must sin, his
> sin is not a result of the will's choice, but is instead a fixed and
> inevitable necessity. You fear now that this reasoning results either in
> the blasphemous denial of God's foreknowledge or, if we deny this, the
> admission that we sin by necessity, not by will. (*Free Choice*. III. 3.
> 21–22)

Augustine discussed this problem both in this early work and in his
most mature writing in the *City of God*, but his reasoning and conclusions about it never changed, and he never saw it as posing a serious
difficulty. He had no doubt, of course, that God is both absolutely
omnipotent and absolutely omniscient, and it never occurred to him to
deny that God has perfect knowledge of all events, past, present and
future. But because of his conception of what it means for persons to
have free will, it seemed to him clearly *irrelevant* whether God has
foreknowledge of all future events.

His view is that I am free with regard to an action (or the action is in
my power) if conditions are such that if I want and choose to do the
action, then I do it. And God's foreknowledge of my voluntary actions
is certainly no threat to freedom so understood. If God knows that I am
going to perform a certain action by choice, then what God knows is
that there will in fact be conditions such that if I want and choose to
perform that action, then I shall do so. Even more, God knows not
merely that I shall perform the action *if* I choose, but he knows that the
action will indeed occur and will occur by my choice. Thus God's
infallible certainty of what I shall choose to do is not only not a condition that undermines my freedom, but it is a condition that guarantees
my freedom.

> Now if there is for God a fixed order of all causes, it does not follow
> that nothing depends on our free choice. Our wills themselves are in
> the order of causes, which is, for God, fixed, and is contained in his
> foreknowledge, since human acts of will are the causes of human activ-
> ities. Therefore, he who had prescience of the causes of all events cer-

tainly could not be ignorant of our decisions, which he foreknows as
the causes of our actions. (*City.* V. 9)

Now the reader may think at this point that Augustine's conception
of free will seems to leave open an important question, and his way of
dismissing the problem of divine foreknowledge calls attention to that
question. If all that is required for an action to be in my power is that I
do what I do because I want to and choose to, then Augustine is right
in thinking that God's knowing that I shall do something because I
want and choose to is indeed a guarantee of freedom. But, one may
ask, is there not a prior question? If God's knowledge that I shall
choose to do a certain action guarantees that the action is in my power
in Augustine's sense, doesn't that knowledge also determine irrevocably *which* choice will indeed be made? If it is impossible for God to be
mistaken, then the choice that God knows I shall make tomorrow is
certainly the one that I shall make. And so even as God's knowledge
that I shall perform an action by choice guarantees that that action is in
my power (in Augustine's sense), it also seems to guarantee that the
decision as to which choice I shall make is *not* in my power, since I
shall certainly make the choice that God knows I shall make.

At the time of his initial discussion of this problem in *On Free
Choice*, it does appear to me that Augustine did not yet have it quite
straight in his own mind. In particular, in that discussion, he seems to
confuse having an *action* in my power with having the *choice* to
perform that action in my power. Thus he first states again his basic
claim that "you could not maintain that anything is in our power
except actions that are subject to our own will"—which is just to say
that an *action* is in my power if I do it when I choose to do it. But then
he proceeds to infer that "nothing is so completely in our power as the
will itself, for it is ready at hand to act immediately, as soon as we
will." But this seems to be a confusion. It is no doubt true that when I
choose an action, the choice is at that moment "ready at hand"—
indeed it seems trivially true that when I choose, there is a choice present. What is not so obviously true is that that *choice itself* is in my
power, i.e. that the choice itself is an action that I perform if I want and
choose to and do not perform if I want and choose not to.

The confusion here seems to be between *making* a choice and
choosing a choice. The following passage is a good example.

> When we will, if the will itself is lacking in us, we surely do not will. If it cannot happen that when we will we do not will, then the will is present in one who wills. And nothing else is in our power except what is present to us when we will. Our will, therefore, is not a will unless it is in our power. (*Free Choice*. III. 3. 32)

Again, it is no doubt true that when we will, the will is present, but what guarantees that an action is in our power is not merely that it is present when we will, but rather that it is present *because* we will. In order to be sure that an action is in my power, it must occur because I choose it, and similarly, to be sure that a choice is in my power, that choice would have to occur because I choose it. To establish that I act by choice is not at the same time to establish that the choices themselves are in my power. And what seems to be threatened by the doctrine of God's absolute foreknowledge is the claim that the choices are in my power.

But despite Augustine's confusion in this early work, his basic position was not immediately threatened by this problem. Given his analysis of what it means to say that an action is in my power, there is no more problem in asserting that choices are in my power than there is in asserting my power with regard to any other action. As in the case of any other action, a choice can be said to be in my power just in case conditions are such that if I want and choose to make that choice, then I do make that choice. And if God's foreknowledge is compatible with other actions being in my power in this sense, then it is compatible with choices being in my power.

In fact, this is exactly what Augustine has already said about one choice in particular—the choice to try to live rightly or to have a good will. His whole point was that while I may not be able to live rightly, I can certainly *choose* to live rightly, i.e. that choice is in my power. If I want to choose to live rightly and I choose to make that choice, then I do make that choice. And of course, if God knew beforehand that I would choose to make that choice, his foreknowledge once again certifies my power to make that choice and so certifies my freedom, rather than undermining it.

Augustine thinks that there seems to be a problem here only because people confuse *knowing* that something will happen and *causing* it to happen. In knowing that you will perform a certain action tomorrow, God simply happens to know a truth about the future. The fact that

God knows & has the power to cause, but does not cause.

God knows that truth lets us know that it is in fact a truth, since God couldn't *know* it if it weren't true. But saying that God knows it to be true is not at all the same as saying that God *causes* it to be true.

To make this clear, Augustine points out that the situation would be exactly the same if that truth about the future were known not by God, but by any ordinary person. Since only what is true can be known to be true, the fact that *anyone* knows that something is true entails that it is indeed true. But knowing that something is true does not cause it to be true, since it would be true whether anyone happened to know it or not. So if God's knowing that you will perform an action tomorrow robs you of your free will, then even if there were no God, your free will would still be lost simply because it happens to be true that you will perform that action, even though no one knows that truth. And Augustine thinks that it is ridiculous to deny free choice of the will just on the ground that there are facts about the future. Surely, he thinks, an action is in my power if I do it when I want to and don't do it when I want not to, and it is absurd to say that I am rendered impotent merely because it happens to be true that I shall or shall not exercise that power. And if I am not stripped of my power by a mere truth about the future, then neither am I stripped of it by the fact that someone, whether human or God, happens to know that truth. So he concludes that

> unless I am mistaken, your foreknowledge that a man will sin does not of itself necessitate the sin. Your foreknowledge did not force him to sin even though he was, without doubt, going to sin; otherwise you would not foreknow that which was to be. Thus, these two things are not con- tradictories. As you, by your foreknowledge, know what someone else is going to do of his own will, so God forces no one to sin; yet He fore- knows those who will sin by their own will....Your recollection of events in the past does not compel them to occur. In the same way God's foreknowledge of future events does not compel them to take place....You may understand from this, therefore, how justly God pun- ishes sins; for He does not do the things which He knows will happen. Besides, if He ought not to exact punishment from sinners because He foresees that they will sin, He ought not to reward those who act rightly, since in the same way He foresees that they will act rightly. On the con- trary, let us acknowledge both that it is proper to His foreknowledge that nothing should escape His notice and that it is proper to His justice that a sin, since it is committed voluntarily, should not go unpunished

by His judgment, just as it was not forced to be committed by his foreknowledge. (*Free Choice*. III. 4. 39–40)

Now the reader may not find this altogether satisfying. And indeed,
the issue seems to continue to attract discussion by philosophers even
today. But for the development of Augustine's theology, which is our
purpose here, it is certainly of minor importance. Because while
Augustine denies that God's mere knowledge determines our actions,
he also finally came to the conclusion that God's *will* does indeed
directly determine every human action. From his own point of view, it
is not divine foreknowledge that poses the real problem, but the fact
that every event in the universe, including every human action, is
subject to absolute divine *predestination*. So I want to set aside further
discussion of the problem of foreknowledge and go on to look at this
more fundamental problem that is at the very heart of Augustinianism.

III. The Doctrine of Predestination

It took Augustine some years to arrive finally at his mature doctrine
of predestination, and we shall need to look at some of his evolution
toward the doctrine in order to understand it clearly. But if we look
from the point of view of the mature doctrine at the kinds of considerations that finally led to it, I think we can see that Augustine finally
came to regard the doctrine of absolute predestination as supported by
three different types of evidence and argument. First, he thought that
predestination was well grounded in scripture. Second, he believed that
the doctrine of predestination *followed* from the most fundamental
Christian beliefs. And third, he believed that an analysis of human
choice, while it would not strictly entail the doctrine of predestination,
would reveal that free choice of the will is compatible with and even
lends support to that doctrine.

In what follows, I want to look at each of those attempts to support
the doctrine of predestination. But first, it may be well to state the
doctrine in at least a loose and informal way, so that we are sure what
we are talking about. Briefly then, I understand the doctrine of predestination as stating that *the creation of the universe and every event that
occurs in the universe occurs because of the conscious will of God.*
That is, every event occurs because God chooses to have that event
occur and wills that event to occur. God's will is *sufficient* for the

occurrence of any event, and even if God makes use of other causes to bring about an event, God's will is *necessary* for the event to occur. It is especially important to note that when it is said that every event occurs by the will of God, it is *not* meant merely that God permits every event to occur. That is, there is no event which is such that God *permits* it to occur but does not actively choose and will it to occur. Augustine's doctrine of predestination makes the strongest possible claim that God actively and directly brings about every event by conscious choice and will, and every event that occurs is precisely the event that God wants, chooses and wills to occur. I hope that I have now put this in the strongest terms, because I think that Augustine himself holds the strongest possible form of this doctrine.

And now with the doctrine stated, it is time to look at the support Augustine offered for it. I shall review in turn each of the three sorts of support mentioned above.

A. The Scriptural Basis of Predestination

I shall not say much about Augustine's grounding of the doctrine of predestination in his interpretation of scripture. There has been much discussion about whether his interpretation of some passages is sound, and certainly others have found scriptural support for contrary views. I am not qualified to add to a discussion of biblical exegesis, and I shall not pretend to argue either for or against Augustine's reading of the texts. And in one sense, it is not so important whether Augustine read every passage as its author intended, since the more important support for his doctrine of predestination comes not from this source, but from other sorts of evidence and argument to be discussed below. But on the other hand, Augustine himself not only believed every bit of the Bible to be literally true, but he regarded it as the most basic and authoritative truth. So it is worth at least mentioning some passages that he cited in support of a doctrine that he believed to be inescapably established on other grounds.

Augustine wrote a very great deal on the doctrine of predestination, and that writing is filled, as is most of his writing, with hundreds and perhaps thousands of scriptual citations (Brown reports that Augustine quotes the Bible 42,816 times[230]). Many of these are cryptic and could be seen as supporting his doctrine only within the context of his general discussion. But a number of frequently used citations can certainly be read plausibly as supporting the doctrine even when quoted in isolation. Perhaps by looking at a few of those, we can at least get some indication as to why Augustine regarded his doctrine of predestination as supported by the authoritative texts that he regarded as the very word of God.

Augustine cites many texts which assert that all events are brought about directly by God, as, for example,

> And there are diversities of operations, but it is the same God which worketh in all. (*I Corinthians* 12. 6)

More to the point, he believes that scripture clearly supports the view that even sinners who work directly against God's commandments do in fact inevitably carry out the will of God.

> For of a truth against thy holy child Jesus, whom thou hast anointed, both Herod and Pontius Pilate, with the Gentiles and the people of Israel, were gathered together for to do whatsoever thy hand and thy counsel determined before to be done. (*Acts* 4. 27–28)

One example of God's predetermination both of saints and sinners is that of Jacob and Esau, the twin sons of the patriarch Isaac. As he sees it, the apostle Paul leaves no doubt that the destinies of the twins were determined before they were ever born.

> For the children being not yet born, neither having done any good or evil, that the purpose of God according to election might stand, not of works, but of him that calleth, it was said unto her, The elder shall serve the younger, as it is written, Jacob have I loved, but Esau have I hated. (*Romans* 9. 11–13)

In fact, the apostle seems to state plainly that the salvation or damnation of every person is worked out before ever the universe was created.

> According as he hath chosen us in him before the foundation of the world, that we should be holy and without blame before him in love, having predestined us unto the adoption of children by Jesus Christ to himself, according to the good pleasure of his will. (*Ephesians* 1. 4–5)

Jesus Christ himself tells us that "many are called but few are chosen" (*Matthew* 22. 14) and that even among those who turn to Christ, "Ye have not chosen me, but I have chosen you" (*John* 15. 16). But again, it is Paul who leaves no doubt whatever that whether we are saved depends wholly on God's inscrutable will and not in the least on our own efforts.

> For he saith to Moses, I will have mercy on whom I will have mercy, and I will have compassion on whom I will have compassion. So then it is not of him that willeth, nor of him that runneth, but of God that showeth mercy. For the scripture saith unto Pharaoh, Even for this same purpose have I raised thee up, that I might show my power in thee, and that my name might be declared throughout all the earth. Therefore hath he mercy on whom he will have mercy, and whom he will he hardeneth. Thou wilt say then unto me, Why doth he yet find fault? For who hath resisted his will? Nay but, O man, who art thou that repliest against God? Shall the thing formed say to him that formed it, Why hast thou made me thus? Hath not the potter power over the clay, of the same lump to make one vessel unto honor, and another unto dishonor? (*Romans* 9. 15–21)

If we have the faith in God that will save us, that very faith is said to depend wholly on the will of God.

> For by grace are ye saved through faith; and that not of yourselves: it is the gift of God, not of works, lest any man should boast. (*Ephesians* 2. 8–9)

Or again,

> work out your own salvation with fear and trembling, for it is God which worketh in you both to will and to do of his good pleasure. (*Philippians* 2. 12–13)

If all humans are not hopelessly damned, if some few are preserved, only the will and mercy of God can be found as the reason.

> Even so then at this present time also there is a remnant according to the election of grace. And if by grace, then is it no more of works: otherwise grace is no more grace. But if it be of works, then is it no more grace: otherwise work is no more work. (*Romans* 11. 5–6)

In fact, in response to *any* human pretension to power over any aspect of reality, including one's own soul and good will, Augustine is fond of quoting the following:

> For who maketh thee to differ from another? And what hast thou that
> thou didst not receive? Now if thou didst receive it, why dost thou
> glory, as if thou hadst not received it? (*I Corinthians* 4. 7)

And finally, there are a number of passages that seem to state explicitly
the predestination of every event and every soul by God. One of those
was quoted above, but other representative examples are the following:

> And we know that all things work together for good to them that love
> God, to them who are called according to his purpose. For whom he did
> foreknow, he also did predestinate to be conformed to the image of his
> Son, that he might be the first-born among many brethren. Moreover,
> whom he did predestinate, them he also called: and whom he called,
> them he also justified: and whom he justified, them he also glorified.
> (*Romans* 8. 28–30)

> In whom also we have obtained an inheritance, being predestinated
> according to the purpose of him who worketh all things after the coun-
> sel of his own will. (*Ephesians* 1. 11)

Whether or not the reader thinks that these and other scriptural passages, rather enigmatic as they often are, do indeed contain a doctrine
of predestination of the Augustinian sort, it is at least easy to see that
Augustine could find plausible texts to support a doctrine that he
thought must be true on other grounds. So now without further ado,
let's turn to look at those other grounds.

B. Derivation of the Doctrine from Basic Beliefs

In most of Augustine's discussions of predestination, he freely
mixes the three sorts of considerations that I am trying to consider
separately. Not only does he constantly reinforce his arguments by
citations of scripture, but he backs up his derivation of the doctrine
from basic beliefs by a running analysis of the nature of human willing. In some respects, that way of discussing the problem is preferable,
since remarks made from one perspective often raise questions that
belong to another perspective. Nonetheless, I think that, on balance,
our presentation of his views will proceed most smoothly if we keep
the three sorts of support distinct and refer any questions that may arise
to the appropriate place.

In *On Free Choice*, Augustine already states clearly the two positions that he attempts in the end to reconcile by the doctrine of predestination.

The first position and the one that predominates in the dialogue, is the familiar claim that human beings are free and so responsible for their actions and deserving of the consequences that follow from their actions. He summarizes the findings of Book I of the dialogue by writing:

> We have established...that what each man chooses to pursue and to love lies in his own will, and that the mind cannot be deposed from the citadel of mastery or from right order by anything except the will. And it is clear that things themselves are not to be blamed when someone makes evil use of them; rather, the man who makes evil use of them is to be blamed. (*Free Choice*. I. 16. 114)

And near the end of Book III, he is still maintaining that

> the souls of sinners suffer punishment at the hands of the most perfect, the most just, the most steadfast and changeless Majesty and Substance of the Creator. These sins, as we said a while ago, must be attributed only to man's will. We need seek no further cause of sins. (*Free Choice*. III. 22. 216)

But in Book III, he also gives over several chapters to emphasizing that creation is perfectly controlled and ordered by God. He is at pains to drive home the point in the strongest possible terms. Nothing is omitted that could add to the completeness and perfection of God's order.

> Moreover, so great is the variety of earthly things that we can conceive of nothing which belongs to the form of the earth in its full extent which God, the Creator of all things, has not already created. (*Free Choice*. III. 5. 47)

He explicitly recognizes that one of the components of this perfectly ordered universe is the sin of fallen humans. But even these sinners and their sins add to the perfection of God's order.

> You should think about the difference in souls, in which you will find the unhappiness that grieves you, and you will recognize that they have the power to complete the perfection of the universe even though, since they will to sin, they must be unhappy. (*Free Choice*. III. 9. 91)

But this is not to say that God's order in any way *depends* on the existence of sin or sinners. The point is that *whatever* exists and *whatever* occurs will certainly fit into that perfect harmony.

> That objection is even less reasonable which says that if our unhappiness completes the perfection of the universe, then there would be imperfection in the universe if we were all happy; for then if the soul can come to happiness only by sinning, even our sins are necessary to the perfection of the universe that God created, and how would God be just in punishing sins? For if there were no sins, His creation would not be full and perfect. In answer to this I say that neither sin nor unhappiness is necessary to the perfection of the universe; rather, it is the souls which, simply because they are souls, are necessary to its perfection....If sin occurred and unhappiness did not result from it, then evil would violate order. As long as men who do not sin gain happiness, the universe is perfect. When sinners are unhappy, the universe is perfect....In a house, what is so great as a man, and what so low and base as the house's sewer? Yet the slave caught in some offense, for which he has to clean the sewer, adorns the sewer even by his disgrace; both of these—the slave's disgrace and the cleaning of the sewer—are joined and reduced to a kind of unity. They are fitted and woven into the household order in such a way that, with their beauty, they suit its world, with its own perfectly ordered beauty. Yet if the slave had not willed to sin, other provisions for cleaning the household necessities would have been made in managing the house. (*Free Choice*. III. 9. 92–97)

But now the question is: How are these two positions to be reconciled? How can it be both that humans act freely, that the will is the sole cause of sin and yet that every event is willed by God and has its place in the order that God decided before he created the world?

The main question being posed here is one that will be taken up in the next section. That is the question whether Augustine is able to provide an analysis of human choice which is such that it makes sense to say both that humans act freely and that God nonetheless completely determines their every action. But for the moment, we are concerned only to discuss what Augustine saw as following directly from those most basic beliefs mentioned above.

To get at this aspect of Augustine's discussion, we shall do well to leave the dialogue *On Free Choice* and move on to discuss his *Propositions from the Epistle to the Romans* (hereafter, *Propositions on Romans*), which was written in 395, the same year in which he finally completed *On Free Choice*. As we have seen, that dialogue does set the stage by emphasizing both human freedom and divine omnipotence. And it also contains a number of suggestive remarks concerning the nature of human choosing, the role of the devil and the problem of original sin. But *On Free Choice* does not yet provide the sort of systematic discussion of the implications of basic doctrines that we find in the *Propositions on Romans* and later works.

The *Propositions on Romans* was Augustine's first systematic attempt to interpret Paul's letter to the church at Rome. It was an effort that would occupy the rest of his life, and it is surely true that his theology centers more around this portion of the scripture than around any other. But we are concerned here not with his interpretation of Paul, but with his effort to deal with the consequences of those basic beliefs discussed above.

Seen from that point of view, Augustine's discussion in the *Propositions on Romans* can be seen as starting from the following problem: We know that human beings are free and responsible both for their sins and for their turning to God. But we also know that God is absolutely omnipotent and that he controls every event in creation. And among other things, this seems clearly to mean that if God *wills* that a person turn to God (or if, in theological parlance, God "calls" that person) then that person surely does turn to God. So all and only those who are "called" by God actually turn to God. These are the ones Paul calls the "elect" and says of them that "those whom he foreknew he also predestined to be conformed to the image of his Son" (*Romans* 8. 29)

> 'Those whom he called, these also he justified' (*Romans* 8. 30) can likewise lead to the question whether all who are called are justified. But elsewhere we read, 'Many are called, but few are chosen' (*Matthew* 22. 14). Still, since the elect have certainly been called, they obviously are not justified unless they have been called. But not all are called to justification, only those who are 'called according to the purpose,' as Paul said above (*Romans* 8. 28). This purpose, it must be understood, is God's, not theirs who are called. Paul explains 'according to the purpose' when he says: 'Since those whom he foreknew he also predestined to be conformed to the image of his son' (*Romans* 8. 29). For not all who are called are called according to the purpose, for that purpose pertains to the foreknowledge and predestination of God. Nor did God predestine anyone except him whom he knew would believe and would

follow the call. Paul designates such persons 'the elect.' For many do not come, though they have been called; but no one comes who has not been called. (*Prop on Rom.* 55)

So while God may, in some general sense, "call" all persons to return to him, he does not call them all "according to the purpose." Those called "according to the purpose" are the ones who will in fact turn to God—these are "the elect" or "the predestinate." So Paul is simply confirming what would follow in any case from the omnipotence doctrine, that whatever happens happens by the will of God. It is not possible for God to will that a person turn to him and yet for that person not to turn, nor is it possible for anyone to turn to God whom God has not willed to make the turn. So, for example, God already loved Jacob and hated Esau before they were born, because God knew that he would call Jacob "according to the purpose" and that Jacob would turn to him, while Esau, who would not be so called, would remain lost in sin.

But having stated what is dictated by the omnipotence doctrine, Augustine immediately finds that the position he has taken seems to conflict with both the goodness doctrine and the doctrine of human freedom. By "hating" Esau before he was ever born, God seems to be condemning Esau when he is not yet guilty and has done no wrong. And by determining which of the twins will be called "according to the purpose" before they are ever born, God seems to be taking away the free will of both to choose their destinies.

This moves some people to think that the apostle Paul had done away with the freedom of the will, by which we earn the esteem of God by the good of piety, or offend him by the evil of impiety. For, these people say, God loved the one and hated the other before either was even born and could have done either good or evil. (*Prop. on Rom.* 60)

If God's grace is to be a reward, then it must be a *response* to some merit on the part of the creature. But then how can the decision be made before people are born?

What then has God elected? For if he gives the Holy Spirit, through whom love works good, to whomever he wishes, how does he choose the Spirit's recipient? If he does not choose according to merit, it is not election, for all are equal prior to merit, and no choice can be made between absolutely equal things. (*Prop. on Rom.* 60)

The solution Augustine proposes to this problem in *Propositions on Romans* is one he would himself abandon as inadequate only a year or so later. Still, it will be helpful in understanding his final position to look at the solution he was forced to reject.

Basically, the position he took at that point was that God, by his foreknowledge, knows who will turn to him in faith, and so to that person he issues a call "according to the purpose," and the person is then enabled to do good works and follow God's will. Because of the ignorance and weakness of the human condition brought on by Adam's sin, no person is able to *act* consistently in a righteous way. Even those who *want* to follow God's commandments find that they are unable to do so without God's help.[231] So what God does is to look ahead and see who will truly *want* to follow him (i.e. who will have faith and believe in him), and then God gives the purposeful "call" to those who he knows will respond. In this way, Augustine thinks at this point, God can "elect" persons before they are born (indeed, before the creation of the world), he can assure that all and only those so elected will be saved, and yet he can also allow humans to make the free choice whether to turn to him in faith and can make his election a response to human merit.

> But since he gives the Holy Spirit only to believers, God indeed does not choose works, which he himself bestows, for he gives the Spirit freely so that through love we might do good, but rather he chooses faith. For unless each one believes in him and perseveres in his willingness to receive, he does not receive the gift of God, that is, the Holy Spirit, whose pouring forth of love enables him to do good. Therefore God did not elect anyone's works (which God himself will grant) by foreknowledge, but rather by foreknowledge he chose faith, so that he chooses precisely him who he foreknew would believe in him; and to him he gives the Holy Spirit, so that by doing good works he will as well attain eternal life....Belief is our work, but good deeds are his who gives the Holy Spirit to believers....Moreover, the nature of grace is such that the call precedes merit, reaching the sinner when he had deserved only damnation. But if he follows God's call of his own free will, he will merit also the Holy Spirit, through whom he can do good works. And remaining in the Spirit—no less also by free will—he will also merit life eternal, which cannot be marred by any flaw. (*Prop. on Rom.* 60)

It is not hard to see that this initial solution to the problem left Augustine with severe difficulties. For one thing, the so-called "gift" of the Holy Spirit which makes salvation possible turns out, on this account, not to be a gift at all, but rather a reward for faith. God does not freely dispense grace to whom he will, but rather he is bound by his just nature to grant the Holy Spirit to those who freely turn to him in faith and to withhold it from others. So this solution seems to threaten the power of the omnipotent God to dispense grace at his pleasure.

But the solution also contains a more basic element that undermines the omnipotence doctrine, and it was this that made it finally unacceptable in Augustine's eyes. If the gift of the Holy Spirit comes only to those who turn to God in faith, it seems perfectly possible that God's will might be thwarted. Indeed the necessity that God has to look into the future and see who will believe before deciding whom to call emphasizes God's dependency. For example, it might be that God truly *wants* Esau to be saved. But when he looks into the future, he sees that despite his wishes, Esau is not going to turn to him. So despite his wanting to save Esau, he finds that he must withhold saving grace from one who will be undeserving. God appears then as forced to *respond* to the actions of his creatures and so as something less than omnipotent.

It did not take Augustine long to see this problem and to change his position. In 396 he addressed a commentary on some passages in *Romans* to Simplician, the teacher of Ambrose and successor to Ambrose as bishop of Milan. In the *Confessions*, Augustine reports that it was to Simplician that he turned for advice when he was struggling to commit himself to Catholicism (*Conf.* VIII. 2). Now he wrote to Simplician as a newly ordained bishop himself and as an already recognized authority.

The most important part of this discussion comes in Augustine's commentary on *Romans* 9. 10–29, in which Paul emphasizes at length the total dependence of humans on God for salvation. It is there that Paul insists that it is not human will that saves, but it is the mercy of God, and God has mercy on whom he will and "hardens" whom he will, citing the case of Jacob and Esau for illustration. In responding to Simplician's questions about this passage, Augustine finds himself forced to change his view of predestination.

First, he notes that his earlier view that God's grace must be a response to human merit was completely wrongheaded. God is in no way *bound* to dispense grace to anyone. Grace is, by definition, a gift that God gives to whom he will.

> First, I shall try to grasp the apostle's purpose which runs through the whole Epistle, and I shall seek guidance from it. It is that no man should glory in meritorious works, in which the Israelites dared to glory, alleging that they had served the law that had been given to them, and that for that reason they had received evangelical grace as due to their merits....The Jews did not understand that evangelical grace, just because of its very nature, is not given as a due reward for good works. Otherwise grace is not grace. (*To Simpl.* II. 2)

But now just how *does* God decide who is to receive grace? How did he decide before Jacob and Esau were ever born that one was to be chosen for grace and the other not?

It is at this point that he reviews the position he had taken in the *Propositions on Romans* and rejects it. First he says that it is wrong to suppose that God elected Jacob because he foreknew that Jacob would have faith and Esau would not. For one thing, just as God foreknew that Jacob would have faith, so he also foreknew that Jacob would perform good works. So if grace is a pay-off for things that don't yet exist, it could be just as well a reward for future good works as for future faith (*To Simpl.* II. 5).

But it turns out that this is not the real problem. The problem lies in the idea that grace is a *reaction* of God to human doing of any sort. If grace is a reward for faith, then God must first passively wait to see who will turn to him in faith before he can dispense grace. But this is an insult to the omnipotent God. It is God who creates, moves and controls the universe and every event in it. And if faith in God is needed for salvation, then that faith itself must be a gift of God.

> But the question is whether faith merits a man's justification, whether the merits of faith do not precede the mercy of God; or whether, in fact, faith itself is to be numbered among the gifts of grace....No one believes who is not called. God calls in his mercy, and not as rewarding the merits of faith. The merits of faith follow his calling rather than precede it....Unless, therefore, the mercy of God in calling precedes, no one can even believe, and so begin to be justified and to receive power to do good works. So grace comes before all merits. Christ died for the ungodly. (*To Simpl.* II. 7)

So here we have the full-blown doctrine of predestination. And Augustine goes on to spell it out in detail. To be sure, God rewards a good will with help in doing good works. But it is absurd to think that anything in the world is so out of God's control that he must wait and hope for it before acting. And if that is obviously true, then it is just as obviously true that the will itself must depend on the grace of God.

> Clearly it is vain for us to will unless God have mercy. But I do not know how it could be said that it is vain for God to have mercy unless we willingly consent. If God has mercy, we also will, for the power to will is given with the mercy itself. It is God that worketh in us both to will and to do of his good pleasure. If we ask whether a good will is a gift of God, I should be surprised if anyone would venture to deny that. But because the good will does not precede calling, but calling precedes the good will, the fact that we have a good will is rightly attributed to God who calls us; and the fact that we are called cannot be attributed to ourselves. So the sentence, 'It is not of him that willeth, nor of him that runneth, but of God that hath mercy' (*Romans* 9. 16) cannot be taken to mean simply that we cannot attain what we wish without the aid of God, but rather that without his calling we cannot even will. (*To Simpl.* II. 12)

If we maintain that the will of a human being is not in God's power but is controlled wholly by the person, then it is possible for God to be frustrated. And that is just absurd.

> For the effectiveness of God's mercy cannot be in the power of man to frustrate if he will have none of it. (*To Simpl.* II. 13)

Having stated this inescapable conclusion in the strongest terms, Augustine then went on to give a number of examples from scripture to illustrate that the movement of faith is both unpredictable and undeserved. He mentions Simeon who came to a firm faith in God while still a child, and Nathaniel who turned to God after hearing only a single sentence. On the other hand, some remained skeptical after spending much time with Christ and even seeing the dead raised. The disciples who had served Christ for three years were terrified by the spectacle of the crucifixion and ran away. But a thief, a complete reprobate, who knew Christ only as a degraded fellow criminal hanging on a cross, surrendered himself completely on the spot. And many who did not believe when they heard Christ himself preach were able to turn to God when they heard the disciples much later (*To Simpl.* II.

14). So we see that while God does indeed call all to come to him in some general sense, not all are "effectually" (*congruenter*) called. And it is this "effectual" call that not only makes it possible to turn to God, but that makes it certain that that turning will occur (*To Simpl.* II. 13).

> Since, then, people are brought to faith in such different ways, and the same thing spoken in one way has power to move and has no such power when spoken in another way, or may move one man and not another, who would dare to affirm that God has no method of calling whereby even Esau might have applied his mind and yoked his will to the faith in which Jacob was justified? But if the obstinacy of the will can be such that the mind's aversion from all modes of calling becomes hardened, the question is whether that very hardening does not come from some divine penalty, as if God abandons a man by not calling him in the way in which he might be moved to faith. Who would dare to affirm that the Omnipotent lacked a method of persuading even Esau to believe? (*To Simpl.* II. 14)

It will be noted here that while Augustine thinks that the omnipotent God can call whomever he will, it is nonetheless likely that there is *some* reason for the choices that God makes. It seems likely, he says, that there is at work "a certain hidden equity that cannot be searched out by any human standard of measurement" (*To Simpl.* II. 16). And he suggests that the basis of God's choice lies somehow in the sin of Adam, which leaves all humanity a single "mass of sin" deserving of damnation (*To Simpl.* II. 16). But it will be best to save a discussion of this point until we can look at his doctrine of original sin.

Here then we have Augustine's doctrine of predestination. Hopefully, it is now clear that this was not for him a matter of "pessimism" or "fatalism." Rather, it was a direct inference from doctrines that he believed to be absolutely fundamental to the Christian religion. So perhaps it will be well to lay out the line of reasoning from those basic premises.

(1) God is omnipotent. (omnipotence doctrine)
(2) Every event in creation is brought about by the will of God. (imperial edict doctrine)
(3) God is perfectly good and just. (goodness doctrine)
(4) All human beings sin and are punished by God. (sin doctrine)
(5) Punishment is just if, and only if, it is deserved. (by definition)

(6) Punishment (or reward, for that matter) is deserved if, and only if, the agent is responsible for the action punished (or rewarded). (by definition)

(7) An agent is responsible for an action if, and only if, that action is in his/her power. (by definition)

(8) An action is in the power of an agent if, and only if, conditions are such that the agent performs that action if he/she wants and chooses to and does not perform that action if he/she wants and chooses not to. (by definition)

(9) The sinful actions of humans that are punished by God are in the power of those humans. (from (3)–(9))

(10) The sinful actions of humans, as events in creation, are brought about by the will of God. (from (2) and (4))

These steps lead at last to a final conclusion which is a statement of the doctrine of predestination:

(11) The sinful actions of humans (and all other actions for which humans are responsible) are both in the power of humans and are brought about by the will of God. (from (9) and (10)).

As we have seen, Augustine arrived at this doctrine of predestination by the time he became bishop of Hippo in 396, and as nearly as I can tell, he never deviated from it throughout his life. But obviously, as it stands, it appears to be a paradoxical doctrine. Even if one agrees that the doctrine (proposition (11) above) follows from his basic premises, it still appears to be an internally inconsistent doctrine. That is, it states both that human actions are in the power of humans and that they are brought about by the will of God. But it seems impossible that both be true: it seems that if an action is in my power, then it is brought about by my will, not by God's will; and by the same token, it seems that if an action is brought about by God's will, then the action is not in my power.

This brings us to the third line of reasoning Augustine uses in support of his doctrine of predestination. It would seem that the only way to salvage the consistency of the doctrine is to provide an analysis of human choosing on which it is possible that an action be *both* in my power *and* brought about by the will of God. And Augustine did in fact think that an honest look at what is involved in choosing will make it clear that it is perfectly possible for both of these to be the case. So to complete this discussion, let's now look at that analysis.

C. Confirmation of the Doctrine by an Analysis of Choosing

When we think of Augustine's doctrine of predestination, we are apt to think of it in contrast with Pelagianism. But it is important to realize that Augustine's ideas were complete in all essential aspects long before he even heard of Pelagius. He says himself that he had developed the doctrine by the time he wrote *To Simplician* and that it is clearly presupposed in the *Confessions*, which was completed by 401 (*Gift of Persev.* 20. 53). But even though Pelagius had been in Rome for many years, it is unlikely that Augustine had even heard of him before about 410, and he did not become acquainted with any of his ideas until 411. So when he began his assault on Pelagianism, it was grounded in an already worked out doctrine which he felt free to use without always reconstructing it. It is true, as many have pointed out, that his attacks on the Pelagians were often dogmatic and inflammatory. But it is important to realize that those anti-Pelagian writings presuppose a developed doctrine and do not constitute the development of that doctrine. It is a mistake to judge the merits of his debates with the Pelagians on the basis of those writings alone. What we want to do here, then, is to look at Augustine's reasons for holding the doctrine of predestination, quite apart from his concerns about the dangers of Pelagianism.

We have seen that Augustine believes that the doctrine of predestination follows from basic beliefs that must be held by any Christian. And we have looked at some passages of scripture that he thinks contain the doctrine. Now we want to ask whether the doctrine is after all internally inconsistent or whether he has some way of making sense of the claim that human action is both in our power and determined by God.

In his discussions of predestination, Augustine is really concerned not about human choosing in general, but about one particular choice—the choice whether to turn to God in faith and love or to remain lost in a state of sin. What concerns him is the issue of salvation and damnation and the roles played by freedom and grace in determining that issue.

But while Augustine's discussions are usually so focused, the question of predestination needs to be considered in broader perspective as well. For one thing, it is difficult to understand what he has to say about the crucial choice that concerns him unless it is understood in the context of a more general discussion of human choice and divine determination. But also, if I have understood Augustine's thought correctly, the doctrine of predestination must be very general in order to preserve the consistency of his thought. If God is indeed utterly omnipotent in the way we have indicated, then *every* event in creation is under God's control and subject to God's will. Furthermore, if God is perfectly good and just, then all punishments and rewards must be deserved, which means also that humans must be free and responsible for their actions. Therefore, it must be the case that *every* voluntary action is both freely chosen and determined by God, not merely that one that ends in eternal life or eternal death.

So even though this will lead us into a rather involved discussion, I think it is worthwhile looking at Augustine's position on freedom and divine determination in a general way, before going on to look at his discussion of sin and "saving grace."

(1) *Some Preliminary Distinctions.* In order to undertake these general remarks about freedom and determination, it will first be necessary to call attention to a few crucial distinctions and relationships without which Augustine's view is likely to be misunderstood. While this may be somewhat tedious, I think that the benefits in understanding Augustine's position will justify going into these details.

The first thing to take note of is a distinction between actions that are *in one's power* and actions that are *voluntary*. We need not only to distinguish these two but also to see the relationship between them.

The second distinction needed is that between *wanting* and *choosing* in voluntary action. And again we need both to understand each of these and to determine their relationship.

So let me begin with the first of these distinctions, that between actions in our power and voluntary actions.

We have already looked closely at Augustine's claim, in *On Free Choice*, that at least some human actions are in our power and that the will itself is surely in our power. We saw that by saying that an action (including choosing) is in our power he means that conditions are such that if we want and choose to perform the action, then we do perform it, and if we want and choose not to perform the action, then we do not perform it.

Now before proceeding, it may be well to note what may already be obvious, that voluntary actions are *intentional* actions, that is, that they are actions undertaken for some end or purpose. And so just as we speak of certain actions being in our power, we may also speak of it being in our power to bring about certain ends. So it can be said that a certain end is in our power just in case we bring about that end if we want and choose to and do not bring it about if we want and choose not to. An end is in our power in this sense if, and only if, an action that brings about that end is also in our power.[232]

Now what I first need to point out for future reference is that it may be in my power, in this sense, to bring about a certain end and yet it still not be the case that I bring about that end *voluntarily*.

Take a rather trivial case. Suppose that I am sitting at my computer keyboard, with my fingers resting on the keys, thinking about what I want to type next. In those circumstances, it seems appropriate to think that it is in my power to type the letter "k." But now, suppose that as I am sitting there lost in thought, I inadvertently allow my fingers to relax a bit, thereby depressing the key for the letter "k."

In this hypothetical case, I have now brought about an end that was in my power (the typing of the letter "k"), but I have not brought that end about voluntarily. And without getting too technical about it, I think we can see that the reason this was not a case of voluntary action is that I did not bring about the end *because* I wanted and chose to, but rather I did it accidentally.

So here is our first distinction. An action (or the bringing about of an end) is in my power in case I perform it (or bring about that end) *if* I want and choose to, while an action (or an end) is voluntary only if I perform it (or bring it about) *because* I want and choose to. And while every case of voluntary action is also a case of an action being in my power, it is perfectly possible for there to be actions in my power which are not voluntary.

Before leaving our example above, one further remark may prove to be helpful later. Notice that in the particular case of typing the letter "k" as described above, it may be unclear whether the typing of the letter "k" is "my fault." That is, it may be unclear whether, in Augustine's terms, God would justly hold me responsible for bringing about that end. After all, I may say, it was purely inadvertent and harmless.

But suppose for a moment that God has actually *commanded* that the letter "k" never be typed again. And suppose further that I have a lot of experience with this particular keyboard and that I know full well (though I may not be thinking of it at the moment) that if I sit there and let my fingers relax, the letter "k" is apt to get typed. In that case, it seems likely that God *would* hold me responsible for the typing of the letter "k," even though I did not type it voluntarily.

The point here is not that we are held responsible for *every* involuntary action that is in our power. But it does seem that there may be *some* actions (or the bringing about of some ends) which are not voluntary and for which we are yet held responsible.

And one further point in this connection. Note that I may similarly be held responsible for *failure* to bring about certain ends, even though the failure is involuntary. Suppose that what God has commanded is that the next letter to be typed is to be a "t," and suppose further that it is in my power to type a "t." Now when I let my fingers relax and inadvertently (i.e. involuntarily) type a "k," I have failed to bring about the required end, and it seems likely that God will hold me responsible for the failure.

A great deal more could be said about all this, but for present purposes, this may be enough to help us understand what Augustine will be saying. So let's go on to look at the second distinction mentioned above, that between *wanting* and *choosing*.

We have seen that an action is in my power in case I do it *if* want and choose to and that an action is voluntary in case I do it *because* I want and choose to. So there are actually at least three elements involved in voluntary action, since in addition to the action, we have the wanting and choosing that accompany the action. We have said something about the relationship between the action, on the one hand, and the wanting and choosing, on the other, and we shall want to say more about this below. But now we need to look briefly at the other two elements.

First, we need to note that Augustine does indeed distinguish between wanting and choosing in voluntary action. While choosing is always associated with wanting, choosing is not *reducible* to wanting.

The first point of distinction we need to note is that (at least where action is concerned), what is *chosen* is an action, while what is *wanted* is usually some object or end which it is believed the action will realize. So, for example, I may *choose* to eat less because I want to lose weight (or achieve thinness or health, etc.). Or, to use a favorite example of Augustine's, all people want to be happy, but they *choose* actions (e.g. pursuing pleasures of the flesh) that will surely lead to unhappiness, because, in their ignorance, they do not fully realize the consequences of their actions (see e.g. *Free Choice*. I. 14. 99–102).[233]

This brings us to the second point of distinction between wanting and choosing—that choosing involves, in addition to wanting, one or more *beliefs* (or, as philosophers might put it, voluntary action is *intensional* as well as *intentional*). One makes choices not only because one wants certain ends, but also because one *believes* that the action chosen will bring about the wanted end. Choices are based not only on wants, but on beliefs about the options available, about the likely outcomes of various actions, etc. And, of course, one may base one's choices on false beliefs and so be led astray. So even if voluntary action is always action based on what one wants, it is not the case that voluntary action need be action that does in fact lead to what one wants.

So, in summary, the general model of a voluntary action is one on which I *want* some end and *choose* an action that I *believe* will realize that end.

The reader will notice that in this account, I am deliberately using the general and vague term "want," rather than a great many others, such as "desire," "lust after," "yearn for" or "have a yen for." There are a couple of reasons for this. One is just that Augustine himself often speaks of voluntary action as a matter of "doing what one wants."[234] And this still seems to accord with our usual way of talking today. But the second reason is more important. It is that what one *wants* may not be what one desires, yearns for, lusts after or has a yen for. Augustine himself points out that every person, even the saint, is afflicted with bodily desire (*cupiditas*). The saint is one who *wants* the joy of service to God more than she or he wants to satisfy that desire (see e.g. *City*. XIX. 27). Acting voluntarily is doing what I want to do, but it may not be doing what I desire to do. So it seems advisable to stick with the general term "want," even though its content may vary in different life situations.

But this now brings us to the final remark that needs to be made regarding the relationship between wanting and choosing. As the above remarks may already suggest, Augustine seems to take it as simply self-evident that voluntary action is, by definition, a matter of doing what one wants. More particularly, since one may want several things at once, he seems to take it as obvious that to choose is to elect what one *most* wants and that it makes no sense to say that I choose an action that I believe will lead to a certain end even though I really wanted another end more.

He realizes, of course, that this may seem false at first glance, since it is just as obviously true that we sometimes make choices that we don't want to make ("I didn't want to hand over the money, but he had a gun on me" or "I didn't want to go to work this morning, but I had no choice"). But Augustine believes that if such cases are genuinely voluntary actions (if choices really are being made), then it is necessarily the case that people are choosing actions on the basis of what they most want. If you did in fact choose to hand over the money, it follows that you must have wanted to preserve your life more than you wanted to hold onto your money. And if you did choose to go to the hated job rather than sleeping in, it must be that you wanted to hold onto the job (or something of the sort) more than you wanted to stay in bed.

The following passage brings this out clearly. If a person is acting voluntarily, then he is doing what he is "willing" to do. Volition (*voluntas*) is derived from that which one is willing to do (*ab eo quod est velle*). Even if one acts "unwillingly" (*invitus*), still, if one is indeed acting and not merely being acted upon, one acts "voluntarily" (*quod quisque invitus facere cogitur, si facit, voluntate facit*). And even if one is an unwilling agent, in this sense, still the very fact that one is an agent at all entails that one is doing what one "prefers" (*malit*). One is said to have something in one's ability (*in potestate*, which we have been translating as "in one's power") if one does it if she or he wants to (*si vult*) and does not do it if she or he does not want to (*si non vult*).

> From the words themselves when sufficiently considered, we shall detect, in the very ring of the terms, the derivation of volition from willingness, and of ability from ableness. Therefore, even as *the man who wishes has volition*, so also the man who can has ability. But in order that a thing may be done by ability, the volition must be present. For *no man is usually said to do a thing with ability if he did it unwillingly*. Although at the same time, if we observe more precisely, *even what a man is compelled to do unwillingly, he does, if he does it, by his volition; only he is said to be an unwilling agent, or to act against his will*, because he would *prefer* some other thing. He is compelled, indeed, by some unfortunate influence, to do what he does under compulsion, wishing to escape it or to remove it out of his way. For *if his volition be so strong that he prefers not doing this to not suffering that,*

then beyond doubt he resists the compelling influence, and does it not. And accordingly, *if he does it,* it is not with a full and free will, but yet it is not without will that he does it; and inasmuch as the volition is followed by its effect, we cannot say that he lacked the ability to do it. If, indeed, he willed to do it, yielding to compulsion, but could not, although we should allow that a coerced will was present, we should yet say that ability was absent. But when he did not do the thing because he was unwilling, then of course the ability was present, but the volition was absent, since he did it not, by his resistance to the compelling influence. Hence it is that even they who compel, or who persuade, are accustomed to say, Why don't you do what you have in your ability, in order to avoid this evil? While they who are utterly unable to do what they are compelled to do, because they are supposed to be able usually answer by excusing themselves, and say, I would do it if it were in my ability. What then do we ask more, since we call that ability when to the volition is added the faculty of doing? Accordingly *every one is said to have that in his ability which he does if he likes, and does not if he dislikes. (Spirit and Letter.* LIII) (italics are mine)

One way of emphasizing Augustine's belief that choice is always of what one most wants is by looking at a problem that haunted him as he strove to commit himself to Catholic Christianity—the problem often characterized as that of the "divided will."

In the *Confessions*, Augustine reports that he early on became aware that he often found himself, in the words of St. Paul, not doing the good that he wanted but doing the evil he hated (*Romans* 7. 19). That is, he found that even though he *wanted* to do the right thing and to serve God, he was unable to leave behind those fleshly pleasures that bound him to the world. The Manichees had seen this also and had attributed it to a double nature—the soul of darkness within us wars with the soul of light that is striving for God.[235] But Augustine finally concluded that this would not do. Though it still seemed that when he acted "against his will," it was not so much something he did as it was "something done to him," yet it was also clear to him that he was *responsible* for those acts and justly punished by God.

I saw that what I did against my will was something done to me, rather than something I actually did. I concluded that it was not my fault, but my punishment, but I quickly confessed that I was not punished unjustly, for I thought of you as being just. (*Conf.* VII. 3)

But how could this be? If he was justly punished, then the action must be voluntary. And yet how could it be voluntary when he was not doing what he wanted to do?

His solution to this problem was found in his concept of "habit." It is by habit that we come to be bound so that we are victims, but habit itself is formed only because we are willing.

> Thus I understood from my own experience what I had read, how 'the flesh lusts against the spirit, and the spirit against the flesh' (*Galatians* 5. 17). I was in both camps, but I was more in that which I approved within myself than in that other which I disapproved within me. For now, in the latter, it was not so much myself, since in large part I suffered it against my will rather than did it voluntarily. Yet it was by me that this habit had been made so warlike against me, since I had come willingly to this point where I now willed not. (*Conf.* VIII. 5)

In his commentary on *The Lord's Sermon on the Mount*, written prior to the *Confessions* in 394, he had already developed this conception of habit and of the way in which it comes to be dominant. The first step he says is a "suggestion" which may give rise to an initial "pleasure." If the pleasure in question is one we are forbidden to indulge and if we nonetheless "consent" to it, then we commit a sin.

> For example, when we see food at a time when we are fasting, an appetite rises in the palate: that comes about only through pleasure; but on this occasion we do not fall in with the pleasure; we check it under the sway of reason. Were we to yield consent to it, we would commit sin surely, a sin in the heart known to God, though actually it may remain unknown to man. (*Lord's Serm.* I. 12. 34)

The initial suggestion, he says, is like the serpent in Eden which uses "suasion" to lure us, and "he who uses suasion does not compel." In fact, the initial suggestion may be so mild that "either there is no pleasure or it is so slight that there is hardly any" (*Lord's Serm* I. 12. 34). A few lines earlier he describes this initial pleasure as no more than "to be tickled" (*titillari*) (*Lord's Serm.* I. 12. 33). But if one consents to this initial pleasure and allows oneself to love and enjoy it, then the person commits a great sin "in his heart." And this initial consent is the first link in the chain that binds.

> If he goes further and puts this [love of pleasure] into action, his passion appears to be sated and quenched; but later on when the suggestion is repeated, there is enkindled a more intense pleasure; though this pleasure is still much less formidable than the pleasure that comes when repeated acts have formed a habit. To overcome a habit is most difficult. Yet one will overcome even a habit if he does not give up and does not dread a Christian's warfare against it under Him who is his leader and helper. (*Lord's Serm.* I. 12. 34)

So as we consent to a "suggestion" coming "either through memory or as sense perception," and as we act on that consent, we soon find ourselves confronted with stronger suggestions and pleasures. And as we continue to act on these, a habit is formed which is impossible to break without the aid of God. Once we find ourselves in that condition, we can only cry out:

> Unhappy man that I am, who shall deliver me from the body of this death? The grace of God, by Jesus Christ. (*Lord's Serm.* I. 12. 36, quoting *Romans* 7. 24–25)

This is the condition that he found himself in as he yearned to turn to Catholicism and yet could not break free of worldly pleasure and ambition. It was a condition from which only God's grace could save him.

> The enemy had control of my will, and out of it he fashioned a chain and fettered me with it. For in truth lust is made out of a perverse will, and when lust is served, it becomes habit, and when habit is not resisted, it becomes necessity. (*Conf.* VIII. 5)

His action was no longer voluntary, precisely because the action was not what he most wanted, but was driven by a compulsion.

> …it was not so much myself, since in large part I suffered it against my will rather than did it voluntarily. Yet it was by me that this habit had been made so warlike against me, since I had come willingly to this point where I now willed not. (*Conf.* VIII. 5)

Another way of putting it, making use of the role of belief in choice, would be to say that habitual action is not voluntary action because one no longer believes that the action performed is the one that will achieve the wanted end. Nonetheless, while the person performs such action involuntarily, he or she is still responsible for it because the chain that binds the will was itself forged by earlier voluntary actions.

We have now completed our discussion of those distinctions that we need to present Augustine's doctrine of predestination—(1) the distinction between actions in my power and voluntary actions, and (2) the distinction between wanting and choosing as components of voluntary action. We may now state by way of summary the principal outcomes of that discussion as follows: Whether we are free and responsible agents justly held to account by God depends on whether actions commanded or forbidden by God are in our power, that is, whether we perform them just in case we want and choose to and do not perform them just in case we want and choose not to. And it seems intuitively clear that many of our actions meet these conditions and so are in our power. But furthermore, among the actions that are in our power, some are in fact performed voluntarily and others are not. Those are voluntary in which the action is performed *because* we want and choose to perform it.

Derivative on this, we can also say that the end brought about by an action is in my power just in case the action is in my power. And the end is brought about voluntarily if the action is voluntary and if the action is performed in the true belief that the outcome of the action will in fact be the end in question.

And finally, Augustine takes it as a matter of meaning that there is an invariable connection between wanting and choosing. Every voluntary action is one that the agent believes is aimed at the end the agent most wants to realize in the given situation. And every end brought about voluntarily is the end that the agent most wants to realize in the situation.

With these distinctions made, we are ready to have a look at Augustine's argument for predestination based on his analysis of choice. But before going on to that argument in the next section, I want first to call attention to a more general form of the doctrine that seems to be implied by the general analysis of choosing that we have just completed.

(2) *A General Doctrine of Predestination.* As I indicated above, Augustine is concerned with just one set of voluntary actions, those by which persons act either to serve God or to pursue temporal ends. What concerns him is the issue of salvation and damnation, and his

focus is on the choices that are crucial to that issue. But the doctrine of predestination is really much broader than that. It has to do with whether (and, if so, how) there can be voluntary actions that are in fact determined by God. The omnipotence doctrine requires that *everything* be controlled by God. And the assertion of human autonomy (or free will) requires that there be voluntary actions. The required conditions will not be met unless *every* voluntary action is in fact determined by God. And although Augustine does not address the problem in this more general way, it will help us in understanding what he has to say about the choices that bear on salvation to address the problem in that way. So before going on, I want to take note of some more general consequences of his analysis of choosing. I think when we come to look at his discussion of predestination to salvation and damnation, we shall see that it is only a particular application of this more general position.

Remember, first, his axiom that voluntary action is always aimed at what one most wants. Or to put it another way, choice is always of action that one believes will more likely bring about what one wants than any other available action. So choice is always rooted in wants.

But now what of those wants themselves? Where do they come from? Is it in our power to bring it about that we have certain wants rather than others? Do we act voluntarily to bring it about that we have the wants we do have?

The answer would seem to be that at least some of our wants are in our power, and it may be that we actually bring about some wants voluntarily. For example, if I find it difficult not to smoke cigarettes (Augustine's own example is of trying to stop swearing) (*Lord's Serm.* I. 17. 51), I may voluntarily undertake a program that will bring it about that I no longer *want* to smoke. And it may turn out actually to be in my power to succeed in changing my wants in this way.

But now notice that, on Augustine's analysis of choosing, if I do change my wants voluntarily, that can only be because I *want* to accomplish that end more than others (say, because I want to be healthy more than I want the pleasures of smoking). So we now have a second want (wanting to be healthy) and we can also ask as to the source of that new want.

It may turn out that my wanting to be healthy is also a want that it was in my power to bring about and that I have voluntarily and painstakingly developed. But again, if that is so, it is only because I wanted to want health more than I *wanted* other things. So now we have yet another want, the source of which is to be asked after.

The point is no doubt clear. It is that even if (and this is a "big 'if'") each and every one of our wants is in our power, it is still impossible that *all* our wants be brought about voluntarily. Since every voluntary bringing about of a want is based on yet another want, the attempt to bring about all wants voluntarily would generate an unending series of wantings and choosings. It must, therefore, be the case that at least our initial choices are based on wants that we have but do not choose to have. That is, even if our most basic wants are in our power, in the sense that we could bring it about that we either have them or have others, still there must be some basic wants that are not *in fact* brought about voluntarily. The initial choices we make must then be based on wants that we do not choose.

If all this does indeed follow from Augustine's analysis of choosing, then at least two significant points may be noted.

The first is that we have here all that we need for a general doctrine of predestination. If we accept the omnipotence doctrine and the claim that God is the source of all things, and if there are basic wants that we do not bring about voluntarily, then it follows that God is the source of those wants. And since our most basic choices (including possible choices of other wants) are grounded in those basic wants, it follows that we shall in fact choose as God has determined that we *want* to choose. So even if all our wants were in our power, and even if we were to act voluntarily in every case, still God would determine our actions by determining the wants on which our choices are based.

The second point to be noted is that while Augustine's analysis of choosing does seem to imply predestination when it is coupled with the omnipotence doctrine, the implications of his analysis for the issue of free will are altogether independent of that doctrine. That is, given his analysis of choosing, the question whether humans are free has nothing to do with whether there is an all-powerful god or a god of any sort. If it is true that choices are based on wants, and if it is further true that our most basic wants are not chosen, then it is irrelevant to the question of freedom whether those basic wants come from God, genetic factors, cultural conditions or any other source. If one holds that our freedom is lost if choosing is ultimately based on wants that are not chosen, then our freedom is lost, whether or not there is a God that determines our actions.

Augustine clearly thinks that there is no threat to freedom in the realization that our choices are based on our own wants. If I am able to do what I want and I do what I do because I want to, then, in his view, I am free. I am free not only to do what I want, but to change my wants if I want to. Furthermore, if I do what I want because I want to and if I *can* both do and want otherwise if I want to, then I am not only free, but I am responsible and justifiably held to account by God's justice.

As I said above, Augustine himself does not develop the doctrine in this most general form. But this analysis does seem to be presupposed by his discussions of predestination, and indeed, his discussion is an application to particular cases of that general analysis. Also, as we shall see, the particular cases of choosing that he is concerned with involve a qualification that may tend to muddy the waters somewhat, so for that reason as well, it may be useful to have offered the above analysis in its most general form.

Finally, let me say that this most general statement of the doctrine may help us understand the task that confronted Pelagius or any other critic of Augustine's doctrine of predestination. It would not be enough simply to reject one or another of Augustine's theological claims or to insist on God's justice or on human responsibility. Augustine can quite agree that God is just and that humans are responsible. What must be shown is that Augustine's analysis of choosing is incorrect, that choice is not rooted in wants which are themselves involuntary. For if one accepts that analysis, then the only way to avoid the doctrine of predestination is to reject the doctrine that God is the source of all things and to leave the determination of those basic wants to an agent that is neither God nor the person whose wants they are. For myself, I find nothing of this sort in any of the Pelagian authors, but I leave it to the reader to investigate this matter on her or his own.

(3) *Augustine's Special Doctrine of Predestination.* With all these preliminaries covered, we are at last ready to look at the development of Augustine's own application of his analysis of choosing to the doctrine of predestination. We have already seen the scriptural basis of his concern, especially in Paul's letter to the Romans. And we have seen that it follows from his most basic beliefs both that humans are free and responsible and that all things (including human actions) happen

by God's will. What we want to do here is to see how he analyzes those particular choices by which humans turn toward or away from God and his effort to understand how it is *in fact* the case that human choosing leaves people both responsible and divinely determined.

It is not surprising that Augustine confines his discussion of predestination to those crucial choices. From his very earliest writings, Augustine was clear that the essence of Christian truth is that there is only *one* choice of importance for human destiny. The pagans (and, he would later add, the Pelagians) might put great emphasis on *obedience* to the gods as the way to win divine favor. But the god of the imperial myth cannot be won over so cheaply. That absolutely omnipotent deity demands not merely obedience, but total surrender of the self. What is required is that all action be based on a single motive—the motive of *love* of God.

> ...we have discovered that there are two kinds of things, eternal and temporal. Two kinds of men, as well, have been clearly and sufficiently distinguished: those who pursue and love eternal things, and those who pursue and love temporal things. (*Free Choice*. I. 16. 114)

Augustine believes, of course, that God commands many things and that humans are held responsible for many voluntary actions. But in the last analysis, actions are of no importance whatever. What matters is the *attitude* out of which the actions flow. If I believe, for example, that God commands me to tithe and I do so, but do so only because I am afraid of hell or because I hope for a reward or want to impress my fellows, then my action has no merit whatever in God's eyes.

So Augustine is really not concerned with human agency because of a concern for morality as such. Right and wrong actions scarcely matter to him. What matters is whether actions flow from and are motivated exclusively by a love of God. And since that is his focus, there is only one choice that matters—the choice whether to surrender ourselves to God in love or to remain in egoistic love of the self and its private needs and wants.

To put it another way, what matters to Augustine is not the actions of the soul, but the *state* of the soul. The soul that acts out of any motive other than the love of God is in a state of sin, and no collection of good deeds has any effect on that state. And even if a soul has acted repeatedly out of love of God (and it is doubtful whether any soul on earth ever does so), a single act motivated by love of the temporal plunges the soul once more into the state of sin.[236]

Thus while the choice whether to love God or to love the world is one that is made over and over countless times throughout life, still it is the *only* choice that matters. And Augustine's discussions of predestination are almost wholly limited to that single choice.

The best place to begin tracing Augustine's rather complex discussion of predestination is with the *Propositions on Romans*. There the first choice he considers is the choice faced by every person whether to live righteously by the law of God or to "pursue fleshly concupiscence." God commands us to be just, charitable, temperate and to seek those things that are eternal. But we are also driven by bodily lust to pursue the temporal and to live lives of sensuous degradation (*Prop. on Rom.* 13–18).

Now the question we may pose is whether it is in our power to live righteously and so obey God's law. That is, if we want and choose to live righteously, do we do so?

Augustine's answer to that question is a clear "No." It is *not* in our power to live righteously. Once we have received the law, we know what is required of us. But the desires of the flesh are too powerful for us. It is only with the aid of God's grace that we can have the strength to fight off the snares of this world and do the will of God.

> Therefore the Law is good, for it forbids what ought to be forbidden and prescribes what ought to be prescribed. But when anyone thinks that he can fulfill the Law by his own strength and not through the grace of his Savior, this presumption does him no good. Rather it so harms him that he is both seized by a stronger desire to sin, and by his sins is made a transgressor....Therefore let the man lying low, when he realizes that he cannot rise by himself, implore the aid of the Liberator. For then comes grace, which pardons earlier sins and aids the struggling one, adds charity to justice, and takes away fear. When this happens, even though certain fleshly desires fight against our spirit while we are in this life, to lead us into sin, nonetheless our spirit resists them because it is fixed in the grace and love of God, and ceases to sin. For we sin not by having this perverse desire but by consenting to it. (*Prop. on Rom.* 13–18)

So his position at this stage is that while we may recognize the precepts of the law and even want to obey them, we find that we do not have the strength to live as we ought unless God helps us. We have already looked at one reason for this position when we discussed the power of habit.[237] We saw that an initial voluntary response to the "tickle" of the flesh may lead to a strengthening of that desire, so that finally it becomes a compulsive habit that cannot be resisted and makes voluntary action impossible. Now in the *Propositions on Romans*, he goes beyond that. He still recognizes the power of habit and holds that "the law of sin holds everyone captive, entangled by carnal custom" (*Prop. on Rom.* 45–46). But now he also holds that even before habits are formed, fleshly desire is so powerful that no one succeeds in living righteously. This condition, he says, is our inheritance from Adam and his sin:

> But these desires arise from the mortality of the flesh, which we bear from the first sin of the first man, whence we are born fleshly. Thus they will not cease save at the resurrection of the body, when we will have merited that transformation promised to us. (*Prop. on Rom.* 13–18)

Here we have ventured into the topic of original sin, a topic that we are not yet ready to deal with. So for the moment, let me avoid the difficulty with just one remark. That remark is that while Augustine *may* indeed be saying here that we have actually inherited Adam's sin, so that we are born already guilty and doomed, he *need* not be making such a strong claim for present purposes. We shall see below that he does have an argument to support the view that we are actually born guilty.[238] But we are not yet in position to look at that argument. And for the moment, we don't need to look at that argument.

All that Augustine is clearly saying at this point is that, in fact, what we find when we look at human beings is that they are dominated by very powerful "desires of the flesh" and that they simply do not have the strength or perseverance to ward off those desires and follow the path of righteousness. But to say that we are all born *weak* is not quite to say that we are all born *guilty*. It is true that without God's help, we shall surely all fall into sin and incur guilt. But the position at this point need not be that Adam's sin left us all guilty, only that it left us weak and in need of help to avoid sin and guilt.

So for present purposes, let's set aside the issue of original sin and focus on what is most directly relevant to the doctrine of predestination. At a later point, we can return to the issue of original sin.

The position taken in the *Propositions on Romans* is then that we are not, in fact, able to live righteously without God's help. But while it is not in our power to live righteously, it is, he says, in our power to *want* to live righteously.

> For free will .existed perfectly in the first man; we, however, prior to grace, do not have free will so as not to sin, but only so much that we do not want to sin. But with grace, not only do we want to act rightly, but we can; not by our own strength, but by the help of the Liberator. (*Prop. on Rom.* 13–18)

He again empathizes with St. Paul's lament: "For I do not want to do what I do; but what I hate, this I do" (*Romans* 7. 15). But he quickly adds that "one must take care lest he think that these words deny our free will, for it is not so." And again the reason is that while I do not have it in my power to do what I want, I do have it in my power to *want* to obey God and to cry out voluntarily for God's help in obeying.

> The man described here [i.e. in the above passage from *Romans*] is under the Law, prior to grace; sin overcomes him when by his own strength he attempts to live righteously without the aid of God's liberating grace. For by his free will man has a means to believe in the Liberator and to receive grace so that, with the liberating assistance of him who gives it, he might cease to sin. (*Prop. on Rom.* 44)

This then brings us to the initial position on predestination taken in the *Propositions on Romans* and discussed in the previous section.[239] It is in the power of every person to seek God's help and to cry out to him. God looks into the future and foreknows who will in fact cry out for help. He then responds in advance to this act of faith by deciding to grant the grace of good works to all and only those who cry out. So once again,

> God indeed does not choose works, which he himself bestows, for he gives the Spirit freely so that through love we might do good, but rather he chooses faith. For unless each one believes in him and perseveres in his willingness to receive, he does not receive the gift of God, that is, the Holy Spirit, whose pouring forth of love enables him to do good. Therefore God did not elect anyone's works (which God himself will grant) by foreknowledge, but rather by foreknowledge he chose faith, so that he chooses precisely him whom he foreknew would believe in him; and to him he gives the Holy Spirit, so that by doing good works he will as well attain eternal life. (*Prop. on Rom.* 60)

Or as he puts it a few lines later,

> Belief is our work, but good deeds are his who gives the Holy Spirit to believers. (*Prop. on Rom.* 60)

We have already seen that he very quickly abandoned this version of the doctrine of predestination. Within two years, he had developed what was to be his final view. In the previous section, we looked at the change in light of his realization that this initial position was inconsistent with his basic beliefs in the power and goodness of God.[240] But now we need to see that his analysis of choosing also led him to move to the new position.

By the time he wrote *To Simplician*, he had abandoned the view in the *Propositions on Romans*. There he had held that while living righteously is not in our power, it is in our power whether we call out to God for help. But now he clearly recognizes that the calling out itself is a gift of God.

> No one believes who is not called. God calls in his mercy, and not as rewarding the merits of faith. The merits of faith follow his calling rather than precede it. (*To Simpl.* II. 7)

And again,

> Clearly it is vain for us to will unless God have mercy. But I do not know how it could be said that it is vain for God to have mercy unless we willingly consent. If God has mercy, we also will, for the power to will is given with the mercy itself. It is God that worketh in us both to will and to do of his good pleasure. If we ask whether a good will is a gift of God, I should be surprised if anyone would venture to deny that. But because the good will does not precede calling, but calling precedes the good will, the fact that we have a good will is rightly attributed to God who calls us, and the fact that we are called cannot be attributed to ourselves. (*To Simpl.* II. 12)

Those who cry out to God for help in living righteously are those who have a good will. That is, in the words of our earlier analysis, they are those who truly *want* to live righteously. But now what is the source of that want? Augustine's answer is that it can only be God who so turns the heart that some want righteousness in the first place.

It is in the power of every person either to believe in God and seek

God's help or to pursue the things of this world. That is to say, every person seeks God's help *if* she or he *wants* to live righteously. But whether in fact a person wants to live righteously—whether that want is stronger than others—is decided by God, who grants it to whom he will.

> 'Many are called but few are chosen' (*Matthew* 22. 14). Many, that is to say, are called in one way, but all are not affected in the same way; and those only follow the calling who are found fit to receive it. It would be no less true that 'it is not of him that willeth, nor of him that runneth, but of God that hath mercy' (*Romans* 9. 16). For God calls in one way that is suited to those who follow his calling. The call comes also to others; but because it is such that they cannot be moved by it and are not fitted to receive it, they can be said to be called but not chosen. (*To Simpl.* II. 13)

Here then we have Augustine's final doctrine of predestination. We are free and responsible because it is entirely in our power whether we turn to God in faith or remain steeped in sin. But we do make that choice just in case we want to live righteously more than we want the pleasures of the flesh. And it is God who determines who has that want without which the redeeming choice is never made.

Augustine believes that the doctrine of predestination is affirmed by scripture, that it follows from the most basic beliefs of any Catholic Christian and that it is confirmed by a careful analysis of human choosing. This was the arsenal against which Pelagius and his followers had to contend. Whatever one's judgment of that contest may be, it should now be clear, at least, that a refutation of Augustine's doctrine would need to be complex and sophisticated.

But this is not quite the end of the matter. There is one final point concerning the doctrine that we need to consider if it is to be clear. Because at least at first glance, there seems to be an inconsistency still lurking in his view. Examining that problem will not only complete the discussion of predestination, but it will help us see why he was convinced of the truth of the doctrine of original sin as well.

To see the problem here, remember that the doctrine of predestination asserts both that humans are fully responsible for the actions that lead to salvation or damnation and also that God determines those actions. We have seen that God's determination is explained by saying that choosing is ultimately based on wants that are not themselves chosen but are brought about by God. But it also seems that while there may be wants that are not *in fact* chosen by the person, it must at least be *in the power* of the person to choose those wants, otherwise responsibility would seem to be undermined. If my voluntary actions are based on wants, and it is not in my power either to bring about those wants or to change them for others, then how can it be said that the actions themselves are in my power? And how can I be held responsible if I am a victim of wants over which I have no power?

Now what one would *expect* Augustine to say in response to this problem is quite different from what he does say. One would expect him to reply that all of the wants relevant to salvation are in our power, though some of them are not in fact chosen. So it would be said that it is not only in my power to cry for God's help in living righteously, but it is also in my power to *want* to live righteously, to *want to want* to live righteously, etc. And if all those wants are in my power, then I am responsible, even though *in fact* God does determine some basic wants, since otherwise there would be an endless regress and no choices would ever occur.

But this is not the reply Augustine gives. What he does say is that while it is indeed in my power to call on God for help, it is *not* in my power whether I *want* to issue that call.

> Who has it in his power to have such a motive present to his mind that his will shall be influenced to believe? Who can welcome in his mind something which does not give him delight? But who has it in his power to ensure that something that will delight him will turn up, or that he will take delight in what turns up? If those things delight us which serve our advancement towards God, that is due not to our own whim or industry or meritorious works, but to the inspiration of God and to the grace which he bestows. (*To Simpl.* II. 21)

But if it is not in my power whether I want to cry out to God, how can I be held responsible for not crying out, since I cannot even *want* to do so?

There are two perplexities here. First, we need to take a closer look at just what is involved in the choice to turn to God, in order to see why he became convinced that it is not in our power whether or not we want to make that turn. And second, we need to see how Augustine attempted to reconcile this apparent inconsistency in his view.

To deal with the first issue, it will be best to turn to his work *On the*

Spirit and the Letter, one of the very first of his anti-Pelagian works, written in 412.

In that work, he speaks of the turn to God in general terms as a matter of belief. He asks whether it is in our power to believe that only God can "justify" us, and he replies that that certainly is in our power. Those who want to live righteously certainly have it in their power to seek God's help. They do so if, and only if, they want to do so.

But it is a bit more complicated than it appears. Not all those who choose to seek God's help have the same ends in view. That is, those who turn to God may *want* very different things.

> But there is another distinction to be observed—since they who are under the law both attempt to work their own righteousness through fear of punishment, and fail to do God's righteousness, because this is accomplished by the love to which only what is lawful is pleasing, and never by the fear which is forced to have in its work the thing which is lawful, although it has something else in its will which would prefer, if it were only possible, that to be lawful which is not lawful. These persons also believe in God; for if they had no faith in Him at all, neither would they of course have any dread of the penalty of His law. This, however, is not the faith which the apostle commends. He says: 'Ye have not received the spirit of bondage again to fear; but ye have received the spirit of adoption, whereby we cry, Abba, Father' (*Romans* 8. 15). (*Spirit and Letter.* LVI)

So there are two possible wants on which a turn to God might be based. The person might either (a) want to avoid punishment and win reward (the fear motivation), or (b) want God's will to be done for its own sake with no thought of self (the love motivation). Here again, then, we are back to that fundamental choice—the choice to love God—which is, in the last analysis, Augustine's exclusive concern, the unconditional choice demanded by the imperial deity.

It is only the second of these wants (the love motivation) that leads to salvation. It is only by completely surrendering our will to God, by losing all egoistic self-will and wanting only for God's will to be done that our cry will receive God's response. So long as we seek God's help out of fear or in hope of reward, we do not yet want God's will to be done, but rather we are still motivated by our own private interests.

The fear, then, of which we speak is slavish; and therefore, even though there be in it a belief in the Lord, yet righteousness is not loved by it, but condemnation is feared. (*Spirit and Letter*. LVI)

Those who think that they have been obedient to God and so deserve reward have missed the essence of Christian truth. Christianity, unlike all other religions, rests not at all on propitiation of its god by ritual practices or even moral conduct. The heart of Christianity is the atonement, by which humans are saved only by recognizing their sinful condition and surrendering their creature will wholly to God. Those who have not surrendered wholly to God may obey, but their obedience is rooted in self-love.

'But,' they say, 'we do praise God as the Author of our righteousness, in that He gave the law, by the teaching of which we have learned how we ought to live.' But they give no heed to what they read: 'By the law there shall be no flesh justified in the sight of God.'(*Romans* 3. 20). This may indeed be possible before men, but not before Him who looks into our very heart and inmost will, where He sees that, although the man who fears the law keeps a certain precept, he would nevertheless rather do another thing if he were permitted. (*Spirit and Letter*. XIV)[241]

But couldn't it be that by initially obeying the law out of fear, one might eventually come to the pure love of God which is the ultimate command? Augustine's answer is that this is impossible. It is not possible, by acting again and again out of self-love, to rid oneself of self-love. The falling away of self-love, the real fulfillment of the command to love God with all one's heart, mind, soul and strength—that cannot be won by egoistic striving. It must be a gift.

Must then the unrighteous man, in order that he may be justified—that is, become a righteous man—lawfully use the law, to lead him, as by the schoolmaster's hand, to that grace by which alone he can fulfill what the law commands? Now it is freely that he is justified thereby—that is, on account of no antecedent merits of his own works; 'otherwise grace is no more grace' (*Romans* 11. 6), since it is bestowed on us, not because we have done good works, but that we may be able to do them—in other words, not because we have fulfilled the law, but in order that we may be able to fulfill the law. (*Spirit and Letter*. XVI)

We are, Augustine thinks, egoistic beings by nature. We are born with innate desires and we strive to satisfy those desires and to avoid the pains that afflict us. We may come to see that only by obedience to God can we ever hope to attain true happiness. We may even come to understand that we must lose self-love in the love of God. But given our nature, the very effort to obey and to overcome self remains rooted in self-interest, so that our striving not only does not save us but mires us ever more deeply in self-love. Indeed, because this sinful character is so deeply rooted, those who live in the Christian era and so have knowledge of God's will and Christ's sacrifice are really no better off than those who lived in ignorance prior to the coming of Christ. Since humans are unable by their own power to turn to God and abandon self-love, it is utterly irrelevant what the state of our knowledge is (*Letters.* 194).

If we are really to abandon self and love God purely, that cannot possibly be by our own striving. It can only be because God grants us a gift, the gift of loving God above self and of finding the fulfillment of God's will a joy and "delight" above all others.

> ...if this commandment is kept from the fear of punishment and not from the love of righteousness, it is servilely kept, not freely, and therefore it is not kept at all. For no fruit is good which does not grow from the root of love. If, however, that faith be present which worketh by love, then one begins to delight in the law of God after the inward man, and this delight is the gift of the spirit, not of the letter....(*Spirit and Letter.* XXVI)

Here let me quote again, in fuller context, the passage from *To Simplician* cited above:

> We are commanded to live righteously, and the reward is set before us that we shall merit to live happily for ever. But who can live righteously and do good works unless he has been justified by faith? We are commanded to believe that we may receive the gift of the Holy Spirit and become able to do good works by love. But who can believe unless he is reached by some calling, by some testimony borne to the truth? Who has it in his power to have such a motive present to his mind that his will shall be influenced to believe? Who can welcome in his mind something which does not give him delight? But who has it in his power to ensure that something that will delight him will turn up, or that he will take delight in what turns up? If those things delight us which

serve our advancement towards God, that is due not to our own whim or industry or meritorious works, but to the inspiration of God and to the grace which he bestows. He freely bestows upon us voluntary assent, earnest effort, and the power to perform works of fervent charity. We are bidden to ask that we may receive, to seek that we may find, and to knock that it may be opened unto us. Is not our prayer sometimes tepid or rather cold? Does it not sometimes cease altogether, so that we are not grieved to notice this condition in us. For if we are grieved that it should be so, that is already a prayer. What does this prove except that he who commands us to ask, seek and knock himself gives us the will to obey? 'It is not of him that willeth, nor of him that runneth, but of God that hath mercy' (*Romans* 9. 16). We could neither will nor run unless he stirred us and put the motive-power in us. (*To Simpl.* II. 21)[242]

We have here one of Augustine's most firmly held psychological beliefs. Largely on the basis of his own introspective experience, he is convinced that human action is *always* motivated by self-love in the final analysis. Even the most selfless acts, if they are human acts, are ones that the agent finds most gratifying. The very struggle of "good" people to overcome self-will ends only in strengthening self-will and is finally an exercise in "pride." Thus in the *City of God*, he ridicules the Stoics who pretend to be able to attain the highest good through the living of a virtuous life of self-control. The very idea that they can set themselves free by practicing the virtues reduces the virtues themselves to mere servants of human pride. Human striving ends always in pride and pretension. Happiness is a gift of God, and only by ceasing human striving and surrendering to his will can happiness be found.

The philosophers who set up virtue as the highest good for man seek to induce a sense of shame in those other philosophers who, while approving virtue, take physical pleasure as the end, and use that as the criterion of virtue; pleasure, in their view, is to be sought for its own sake, virtue as a means to that end....But in my view the picture would still fall short of the beauty we require, if it were painted with the virtues as the slaves of human glory. Glory may not be a female voluptuary, but she is puffed up with empty conceit; and it is most improper that the Virtues, with their solidity and strength, should be her servants....And yet men must not think to free themselves from this degradation by posing as despisers of glory and paying no heed to the opinions of others, while they esteem themselves as wise men and win their own approval. For their virtue, if it exists, is dependent on the praise of man in another

kind of way. For the man who wins his own approval is still a man....
This being so, we must ascribe to the true God alone the power to grant
kingdoms and empires. He it is who gives happiness in the kingdom of
heaven only to the good, but grants earthly kingdoms both to the good
and to the evil in accordance with his pleasure, which can never be
unjust. (*City.* V. 20–21)

We are commanded to love God purely and to obey God's law with no
thought of self, and yet the very striving to obey that commandment
only strengthens self-love. Only if God grants us a new love, a delight
in God's will and a new motive can we fulfill the command.

> We, however...affirm that the human will is so divinely aided in the
> pursuit of righteousness that (in addition to man's being created with a
> free-will, and in addition to the teaching by which he is instructed how
> he ought to live) he receives the Holy Ghost, by whom there is formed
> in his mind a delight in, and a love of, that supreme and unchangeable
> good which is God even now while he is still 'walking by faith' and not
> yet 'by sight;' in order that by this gift to him of the earnest, as it were,
> of the free gift, he may conceive an ardent desire to cleave to his Maker,
> and may burn to enter upon the participation in that true light, that it
> may go well with him from Him to whom he owes his existence. A
> man's free-will, indeed, avails for nothing except to sin, if he knows not
> the way of truth; and even after his duty and his proper aim shall begin
> to become known to him, unless he also take delight in and feel a love
> for it, he neither does his duty, nor sets about it, nor lives rightly. Now,
> in order that such a course may engage our affections, God's 'love is
> shed abroad in our hearts' not through the free-will which arises from
> ourselves, but 'through the Holy Ghost, which is given to us' (*Romans*
> 5. 5). (*Spirit and Letter.* V)

Perhaps we are now in a position to understand why Augustine
holds that *love* of God (i.e. wanting God's will to be done for its own
sake) is not in our power. In one sense, it *is* in our power, as he already
indicated in *On Free Choice* (I. 13. 97).[243] If we truly *want* to love God,
then we *do* love God. But it is now apparent to him that in a deeper
sense, it is not in our power. Because of the nature with which we are
born, even our wanting to love God will be motivated by a self-love
that will make the pure love of God impossible. Or to put it in other
terms, our nature is such that we always want to meet our self-needs
more than we want anything else, so that even our wanting to love God

is due to a belief that loving God will bring rewards to the self. So, in another work, he puts it poignantly:

> Whoever thinks that in this mortal life a man may so disperse the mists of bodily and carnal imaginings as to possess the unclouded light of changeless truth, and to cleave to it with the unswerving constancy of a spirit wholly estranged from the common ways of life—he understands neither what he seeks, nor who he is who seeks it. (*Harm. of Evan.* IV. x. 20)[244]

So, in summary, while it is our will that turns to God or to the flesh, that which naturally "delights" us, that which we naturally want, is the happiness and satisfaction of the self. If we are to find delight in God's will being done, that delight comes not from us, but only by the grace of God. And just why God in his mercy selects those he does to receive the saving gift remains forever a mystery, though we may be sure that God's hidden reasons are just.

> ...this will is to be ascribed to the divine gift, not merely because it arises from our free will, which was created naturally with us; but also because God acts upon us by the incentives of our perceptions, to will and to believe, either externally by evangelical exhortations...or internally, where no man has in his own control what shall enter into his thoughts, although it appertains to his own will to consent or to dissent. Since God, therefore, in such ways acts upon the reasonable soul in order that it may believe in Him (and certainly there is no ability whatever in free will to believe, unless there be persuasion or summons towards some one in whom to believe), it surely follows that it is God who both works in man the willing to believe, and in all things prevents us with His mercy. To yield our consent, indeed, to God's summons, or to withhold it, is (as I have said) the function of our own will. And this not only does not invalidate what is said, 'For what hast thou that thou didst not receive? (*I Corinthians* 4. 7) but it really confirms it. For the soul cannot receive and possess these gifts which are here referred to, except by yielding its consent. And thus whatever it possesses, and whatever it receives, is from God; and yet the act of receiving and having belongs, of course, to the receiver and possessor. Now, should any man be for constraining us to examine into this profound mystery, why this person is so persuaded as to yield, and that person is not, there are only two things occurring to me, which I should like to advance as my answer: 'O the depth of the riches!' (*Romans* 11. 33) and 'Is there unrighteousness with God?' (*Romans* 9. 14). If the man is displeased

with such an answer, he must seek more learned disputants; but let him beware lest he find presumptuous ones. (*Spirit and Letter*. LX)

We have at last completed our discussion of the doctrine of predestination. We have looked at his three ways of supporting the doctrine by scriptural authority, derivation from fundamental Christian belief and an analysis of choice. This discussion leaves us with two sets of conclusions:

First, it seems that given Augustine's understanding of voluntary action as action based on what one wants and chooses, he is able, in principle, to reconcile voluntary action with God's absolute control of creation as required by the omnipotence doctrine. And if one accepts his additional claim that voluntary action is action for which the agent is responsible, then he has also succeeded in establishing the possibility of human responsibility for sin, while maintaining God's determination of human action. That is, on his analysis, it is possible (a) that *every* action I perform is performed because it is what I want and choose to do; (b) that not only is every action in my power, but every want on which my actions are based is in my power and could be changed if I wanted and chose to do so; and (c) that even though every want is in my power, there must *in fact* be some wants which are brought about in me by God and not as a result of my own choosing. And if, as seems possible, all of my voluntary actions are rooted in basic wants that are not chosen by me (even though they are in my power), but are instilled in me by God, then it would seem that God could determine all of my actions, even as those actions remain voluntary.

Of course, one might challenge his conception of voluntary action or his view that I am responsible for every action that is voluntary by his definition, even if that action must finally rest on a want not chosen by me. But a consideration of that challenge would carry me beyond the present project, which is just to present Augustine's position as clearly and coherently as possible. I would point out only that both his analysis of choosing as based on wants and his view that not all wants can, in fact, be voluntarily chosen are plausible. And I would note once more that if acceptance of those claims undermines freedom of the will, then it does so regardless of whether the wants underlying choices are brought about by God. And if a Pelagian critic wanted really to challenge Augustine's analysis, all of these factors would need to be taken into account.

But in looking at Augustine's final doctrine of predestination, we also come to a second conclusion. It is that even though it is theoretically possible for all of my wants to be in my power, there is at least one want that is not, as a matter of empirical fact, in the power of any human. For Augustine is convinced that in our present state, our egoistic nature puts beyond our power the choice to want to love God unconditionally and to make choices based on that want. But what this means is that human beings are not, in the end, free to make that one choice that unlocks the gates of paradise. So despite his impressive effort to reconcile human freedom and divine control, Augustine himself must finally conclude that when it comes to the choice that matters most, human beings are not free. And this is indeed the conclusion he reached. In 427, near the end of his life and reviewing his earlier writings in his *Retractions*, he says of his discussion of this issue in *To Simplician*,

> In answering this question I have tried hard to maintain the free choice of the human will, but the grace of God prevailed. (*Retrac.* II. i)

This second conclusion is based, to be sure, not only on his analysis of choosing, but on a strictly empirical claim about the motives of actually existing people. The Pelagian could certainly insist that human beings are capable of utterly selfless wants, and he could insist on this possibility even if no human action to date has been based on an utterly selfless love of God. After all, what most outraged Pelagius was that human beings fail to turn to God, even though they are fully capable of doing so. But Augustine's observation of human motivation is not without plausibility, and even if it turns out to be incorrect, this does not undermine the general doctrine of predestination.

But even though Augustine does finally conclude that humans are not free to "work out their own salvation," this does not, for him, mean that they are unjustly punished for their failure. Because the very inability to love God purely that is the basis of that failure is itself the richly deserved punishment for primordial sin. What remains to be done in this part is to look at one more doctrine that is at the heart of Augustinianism, the doctrine of original sin. As we shall see, that doctrine complements the doctrine of predestination and is essential to establishing Augustinianism as a consistent system.

IV. The Doctrine of Original Sin

We have already set the stage for the doctrine of original sin, so our discussion can be more brief than might otherwise be necessary. But perhaps it will be useful to set the problem up once more.

As we have seen, Augustine holds that while it is in our power to seek God's help in behaving righteously, it is not in our power to make the choice that is really required of us, the choice to want God's will to be done for its own sake.

But obviously, this is a problem. It means that the decision who is to be saved and who damned belongs finally to God alone.

> To be sure, no one resists his will. He aids whom he will and he leaves whom he will. Both he who is aided and he who is left belong to the same mass of sin. Both deserve the punishment which is exacted from the one and remitted to the other. If you are troubled by this, 'O man, who art thou that repliest against God?' (*Romans* 9. 20). (*To Simpl.* II. 17)

Before Jacob and Esau are ever born, indeed before the very creation of the world, the eternal God has decided that to Jacob he will grant the grace to "delight" in loving him, while from Esau that grace will be withheld. But on what basis does God make this decision?

Now in one way, this is a puzzle but not a problem. One thing we may be sure of is that grace was not granted to the unborn Jacob because of any merit of his. Nor need it be. After all—and here Augustine is fond of quoting St. Paul—"If by grace, then it is no more of works, otherwise, grace is no longer grace" (*Romans* 11. 6). Grace (*gratia*) is a gift after all. And the giver of gifts may give to whom he will without needing justification. Since we know that God never acts capriciously, we know that there is *some* reason for his choice. But that reason is hidden from us, and it is not really too important, since his choice of Jacob as a recipient of his gift really requires no explanation.

> Let this truth, then, be fixed and unmoveable in a mind soberly pious and stable in faith, that there is no unrighteousness with God. Let us also believe most firmly and tenaciously that God has mercy on whom he will and that whom he will he hardeneth, that is, he has or has not mercy on whom he will. Let us believe that this belongs to a certain hidden equity that cannot be searched out by any human standard of measurement, though its effects are to be observed in human affairs and earthly arrangements. (*To Simpl.* II. 16)

But Augustine early on concluded that there is more to it than this, and that it cannot be left without further consideration. God not only "aids whom he will," he also "leaves whom he will." He not only moves the heart of Jacob, but he "hardens" the heart of Esau, just as he hardened the heart of Pharaoh when Moses called for the children of Israel to be set free (*To Simpl.* II. 15). To be sure, by this "hardening" it is not meant that God actually makes the heart impervious to his appeal, but rather only that he withholds mercy from a heart already impervious (*To Simpl.* II. 15). But still, since in deciding not to grant grace, God is also deciding that the hardened heart will be cast into everlasting torment, surely there must be *some* question of justice here. Perhaps Jacob did nothing to deserve grace, but what has Esau done to deserve the certain punishment that follows from the withholding of grace?

> Why was Esau rejected when he was not yet born and could neither believe him who called, nor despise his calling, nor do aught either good or evil? (*To Simpl.* II. 1)

Augustine could find only one answer to this question. It must be that even before their birth, both Jacob and Esau *deserved* damnation. God's merciful gift has then forgiven Jacob and granted him pardon from his deserved fate, while Esau has been left to pay his just penalty. Once again,

> Both he who is aided and he who is left belong to the same mass of sin. Both deserve the punishment which is exacted from one and remitted to the other. (*To Simpl.* II. 17)

So here we have the final component of the core of Augustinianism. We have seen that if God is indeed omnipotent and good, then not only must all events, including the fates of humans, be due to God's will, but that there is no injustice in the works of God. That means that God must determine who is to be saved and who is to be damned, but it also means that those to be damned must deserve their damnation. By an analysis of human choosing, we have confirmed that while many of the actions of humans are in their power, those actions are based on wants not all of which can be actually chosen. But then when we came to examine that crucial decision on which salvation rests—the decision whether to love God purely—we found that as a matter of psychological fact, humans are so constituted that they do not have the power to want to love God in the way required. It then appears that all humans are unable to make that choice that will bring salvation and that only by God's mercy are some few redeemed.

But this then leaves us with the conclusion that most are damned for failure to take an action that is not in their power. And that is surely unjust.

It is at this point that Augustine returns to his most basic beliefs. We know by the goodness doctrine that there is no injustice with God and so we know that no one is ever unjustly condemned. Therefore, those who are not selected for grace and so are to be damned must somehow *deserve* to be damned. And if they deserve to be damned, then they are guilty. And since the eternal God elects those who are to be saved even before they are born, it must be the case that those who are to be damned are guilty even before they are born. Therefore, there *must* be some *inherited guilt*, and this is indeed what scripture tells us when it says that "In Adam all die" (*I Corinthians*, 15. 22).

The argument is stated fairly completely and succinctly in a letter Augustine wrote in 418.

> What we seek to know is how this hardening is deserved, and we find it to be so because the whole clay of sin was damned. God does not harden by imparting malice to it, but by not imparting mercy. Those to whom he does not impart mercy are not worthy, nor do they deserve it; rather, they are worthy and do deserve that he should not impart it. But when we seek to know how mercy is deserved we find no merit because there is none, lest grace be made void if it is not freely given but awarded to merit. (*Letters*. 194)

It is no doubt difficult to explain *how* guilt may be transmitted in this way. Augustine fully recognized the difficulty, and throughout his career, he returned again and again to the question of the origin of the soul, in an effort to understand how the soul could inherit sin. Yet at every period, he freely admitted that all this remained a mystery and merely a matter of speculation.[245] Late in his life, as he came to focus more on the destructive power of sexual lust, he speculated that perhaps sin was transmitted in the semen or menstrual blood (see e.g. *City*. XIII. 14). But these speculations, which have so fascinated and preoccupied a number of commentators, were of really quite secondary importance in his own mind.

What led Augustine to his certainty regarding original sin was not a preoccupation with sexuality nor a morbid preoccupation with fleshly desire. He thought it an inescapable logical conclusion from the most fundamental Christian beliefs that each person *must* be guilty prior to any action by that person. And he believed that this conclusion is confirmed by an empirical analysis of human choosing and, in particular, of the choice that is at the heart of Christianity—the choice to love God with all one's heart, mind, soul and strength. That conclusion is the doctrine of original sin, one that he found confirmed in scripture and one on the exact form of which he speculated.

Now I very much doubt that the doctrine of original sin is intelligible. It seems to me essential to Augustine's theology to view each human soul as an independent ontological reality. To view soul in a Plotinian way, for example, as an ontological unity that only "seems" to be a plurality would make a shambles of Augustinianism. And if each soul is an autonomous reality with its own distinct will, the idea that one soul might be responsible for the choices of another or that the guilt of one might be passed on to another is probably incoherent. In fact, the implausibility of this claim is, it seems to me, the strongest argument the Pelagians had available. And as I have already pointed out, Augustine himself was very much aware of the difficulty.

The problem was, of course, that Augustine saw no way of avoiding this perplexing conclusion without denying either God's absolute control of creation, the universal sinfulness of humans or the absolute goodness and justice of God. It is easy enough to see the problems in a doctrine of inherited sin. The problem is to avoid that doctrine without sacrificing either the omnipotence doctrine, the goodness doctrine or the sin doctrine. In that sense, what Augustine's doctrine of original sin gives us is an insight into his priorities. However puzzling that doctrine might be, if the choice was between accepting it and rejecting either the power and goodness of God or the sinfulness of creatures, there really was no choice. The doctrine of original sin, however difficult, simply *must* be accepted. And for the Pelagians who scoffed at original sin, the question remained just what they were willing to give up in order to avoid it.

The doctrine of original sin leads, however, to one final problem we need to discuss to complete our account of Augustinianism. The problem is that of the fall, the primeval sin of Adam and Eve and, before them, of Satan and the angels who joined him in rebellion against God. Here was the true "original" sin, the root of all sinfulness in creation, and if Augustine was to demonstrate the compatibility of his basic beliefs, it was essential that he show both that that first sin was "in the power" of those first sinners and that it yet remains true that even that sin did not escape the will and power of the omnipotent god.

V. The Fall

It is worth noting from the outset that the particular form taken by Augustine's doctrine of the fall is grounded completely in the acceptance of Christian scripture and not at all in rational considerations. That the fall came about because some angels rebelled against God, that human sin came through some original humans called Adam and Eve or anything of the sort is based exclusively on Augustine's certainty about the existence the Christian God and the authority of his revealed scripture.

Indeed, the claim that absolutely every human is born with a nature that is inevitably egoistic is itself based largely on the authority of scripture, though it was a claim that Augustine found confirmed by his analysis of his own psychological functioning. And the claim that such a nature, even if it exists, is properly seen as "sinful" and "lost," deserving of damnation and in need of redemption, makes sense only because of his certainty that there is an imperial deity who demands complete surrender of the self. Spiritual programs of many times and places have agreed with Augustine that much human suffering is grounded in egoism, that transcendence of the egoistic self is essential to spiritual fulfillment. And many would agree that while such self-transcendence is necessary, it is also impossible to bring about by human effort and must wait upon something like a "grace" that functions inscrutably. But that this state of affairs is constituted by sinful alienation from a personal God, bringing with it both deserved damnation and the need for divine intervention for redemption, all of that flows from the imperial myth and its implications. Once more, what made all this so persuasive was the broad acceptance of that myth.

However, once the omnipotence doctrine, the goodness doctrine and the sin doctrine are accepted, something like the doctrine of the fall does seem to follow. If every human is born with a nature that guarantees sin and damnation, if that fate is deserved and can be avoided only by merciful divine intervention, if the decision as to the dispensation of grace is made before humans are ever born, then it does seem to follow that there must be sin before there is an opportunity to commit sin. And if that is true, then there must have been one or more primeval sins which are transmitted to later generations. Indeed, since all humans are born in the *same* condition, it seems at least probable that that condition is rooted in a common cause.

But even if we follow Augustine in accepting all this, there remains a considerable problem. It is simply this: if all choosing is based on wants and if, in the end, choice must be based on wants that are not in fact chosen, what is the source of the wants that led Adam and Eve and, before them, Satan and his cohorts, to reject God and plunge created souls into a state of sin? The sinfulness of present human nature may be due to an egoistic inclination inherited from our first parents, but how are we to explain the inclination that led to that original sin? Were Adam, Eve and the fallen angels created with a nature that found "delight" in loving and serving God? It seems that cannot be so, for if they did indeed most want to serve God, then they would surely have chosen to do so. Does that mean, then, that they were created with an inclination to self-love? But that also seems unacceptable, because while it does indeed explain their turning away from God, it also means that the fall was determined by God through the instilling of that inclination.

In fact, the problem can be stated even more directly from the point of view of the basic belief we have called the omnipotence doctrine. If God does indeed control all creation, if every event is due to the divine will, then that surely must apply to the fall of the angels and the first humans also. It may be that the act of rejecting God was in the power of those first sinners and was undertaken freely. It may even be that *if they had wanted to*, they could have changed their wants so that they wanted to serve God more than to serve the flesh. But everything in Augustine's analysis tells us that their choice, like that of every creature, must finally have rested on an inclination that was not chosen but was given them by God. So even if those unfortunates are rightly held responsible for doing what it was in their power not to do, surely God, as the author of their fundamental inclinations, is *also* responsible, and so a sinful creation must be taken to be directly ordained by God. And if it turns out that it was not even in their power to love and serve God purely, then it does seem that God's punishment of their failure is unjust.

Augustine struggled with this problem throughout his life. He always insisted that that primeval sin was wholly voluntary and its punishment fully deserved. And he likewise insisted that there is no incompatibility between the claim that the first sinners were wholly responsible and the claim that all things are due to the will of the omnipotent God. But here, finally, it does seem to me that he is unable to sustain the tension. And in fact, it seems to me that in his determination to maintain the absolute power of God, he is forced, in the end, into a position that entails that God is less than perfectly just.

Augustine discussed the doctrine of the fall at length and in many contexts. But I believe we can capture the heart of his reasoning by looking at a few key treatments of the problem at different stages of his career. Even this review may lead us into more detail than seems warranted by the logic of the issue. But it seems to me important to go over some of this reasoning, in order to show both Augustine's awareness of the dilemma and his determination not to draw the most obvious conclusion. Furthermore, such a review shows again just how fundamental to Augustinianism is the omnipotence doctrine. For even when faced with a problem that seems to threaten the goodness and justice of God, Augustine never gave any consideration whatever to the alternative of limiting the power or control of the imperial deity over every detail of creation.

Already in *On Free Choice*, he poses the question of what led Adam to sin.

> The following question, moreover, troubles those who consider it: 'Was it by folly that the first man departed from God, or was the first man made foolish by his departure from God?' This is troublesome, because if you answer that it was by his folly that he departed from wisdom, it appears that he was subject to folly before he departed from wisdom, so that his folly was the cause of his departure. Likewise, if you reply that he became subject to folly by departing from God, they will inquire whether it was through folly or through wisdom that he departed. (*Free Choice*. III. 24. 251)

At this point, all he is able to say is that "there must be some interme-diate state" between wisdom and folly, since Adam could have been in neither state (*Free Choice*. III. 24. 252). But this, of course, leaves open the question of what inclined Adam to the path of folly.

In the next chapter of the same work, he comes nearer the basic problem by asking what induced the first sinners to turn from God. In the case of Adam, there was at least the "suggestion of the serpent" to compete with the command of God. But in the case of the serpent's (Satan's) own sin, there was no tempter, so that his fall can only be attributed to "pride" and to "a most malevolent ill will and envy" (*Free Choice*. III. 25. 260–263). But again, this leaves us with the question as to the source of that prideful and malevolent inclination.

A few years later, in *The Literal Meaning of Genesis*, on which he worked between 401 and 415, Augustine returned to the subject of the fall and discussed it in some detail. And in that discussion, he does grant that Adam and Eve must have had an inclination to "find pleasure in what is forbidden," and that that inclination was part of the very nature given them by God. But he insists that it remained possible for them not to sin even though they had this inclination. Thus in a key passage, he writes:

> God, they say, should have made man of such a nature that he would simply not wish to sin. Now I grant that a nature that has no desire at all to sin is a better nature. But let them grant for their part that, on the one hand, a nature is not evil if it is so made that it would be able not to sin if it were unwilling, and that, on the other hand, the decree by which it has been punished is just, since it has sinned by its free will and not by compulsion. If right reason tells us that the creature is better which finds absolutely no pleasure in what is forbidden, it also tells us that that creature is good which has it in its power to control a forbidden pleasure that may arise, so that it rejoices not only in lawful and just actions but also in the control of sinful pleasure. (*Lit. Gen.* XI. 7. 9)

This tells us that while Adam and Eve (and presumably the fallen angels as well) were created with an innate inclination to sin, it was also in their power not to sin *if they were unwilling*. What it does not tell us is *why* they were in fact willing to sin and unwilling to turn to God. Everything in Augustine's analysis of choice would suggest that at the very least, it must have been the case that they were *more* inclined to sin than they were to love God. And at this point, it would seem that the next step would be to say that God is not only the source of their wanting to sin, but the source as well of their wanting that *more* than they wanted to control their lust. But this is not the step he takes, and he insists that God has no part in the fall of our first parents.

Finally, in Books XI and XII of the *City of God*, Augustine devotes considerable attention to the fall, and here we are able to see his final position more clearly. He first asks what led the fallen angels to turn from God, and he suggests that the answer may lie in a lack of knowledge. He suggests that the angels that were destined to remain loyal to God were given not only bliss, but the knowledge that their bliss would be everlasting. On the other hand, those angels who were destined to fall were also given bliss, but were not given the assurance that the bliss would be permanent. Thus he thinks that either they were given no information about their future condition, or they were given foreknowledge of their coming fall.

> In neither case could they enjoy felicity because fear would prevent it, if they knew their end, while if they did not know it, bliss would not be compatible with error. (*City*. XI. 11)

But this is, at best, only a partial explanation. Satan and his minions fell because they were a prideful and arrogant lot who took no delight in serving God. If they were, as the good angels forever are, fixed in the love of God, then even foreknowledge of impending suffering would cause no fear to those who want only the will of God to be done. But of course, if they were fixed in the love of God, there would be no fall to be foreknown. The fall of the sinful angels came not because of ignorance, but because they lacked that "delight" in the service of God that Augustine calls a "good will," while the holy angels who remain forever with God have that good will.

> The true cause therefore of the bliss of the good angels is their adherence to him who supremely is. When we ask the cause of the evil angels' misery, we find that it is the just result of their turning away from him who supremely is, and their turning towards themselves, who do not exist in the supreme degree. What other name is there for this fault than pride?...They would have existed in a higher degree, if they had adhered to him who exists in the highest degree; but in preferring themselves to him they chose a lower degree of existence. (*City*. XII. 6)

So Satan fell because he "preferred" himself to God. But now, of course, the question is: What is the source of that preference? Did

Satan also choose to prefer himself to God, or was that preference one with which he was created? And if he did *choose* to prefer himself to God, why did he make that choice? Can there be an answer to that other than that he *wanted* to choose that preference *more* than he wanted to choose to prefer God? And if that is the answer, we are back once again asking as to the source of that more basic want.

Now Augustine clearly sees that he has a problem here, because he immediately launches into a major discussion of the question: What is the *cause* of the evil will of the fallen angels? And he insists that the only possible answer to that question is that an evil will has *no* cause whatever.

The argument that an evil will has no cause is one he had used as early as the work *On Free Choice*, and it is based on the Plotinian identification of being with goodness and of evil with nothingness.

The Plotinian view of reality sees all being as hierarchically ordered. In order for something to be or to have any property, it must have received form from the intellectual-principle, which is the source of all form. And in the Christianized version of the myth, this becomes the claim that all things that exist do so because they receive their form from God. Furthermore, the myth identifies "goodness" (in a "metaphysical" sense) with form, asserting that to be good is to have form and that to lack form is also to lack goodness.[246] Thus both being and goodness are identified with possession of form, while lack of form is identified with lack of being and with lack of goodness. So that which is fully "formed" also fully "is" and is fully "good," while that which lacks form is, to that extent, also lacking in being and goodness. And lastly, "evil" is just another name for the relative lack of goodness that is also a lack of being and form.[247]

This identification of form with being and goodness and of lack of form with non-being and evil gives rise to two sorts of hierarchies of being. One of these is a hierarchy of *kinds* of beings and is apparently based, at least in part, on the *number* of forms possessed by different things. Thus, for example, brute animals are said to be "superior" to inanimate objects because they possess forms which give them life and sensation, in addition to that form which gives them mere being, while humans are "superior" to brutes because they possess all the forms possessed by brutes plus the form which makes them capable of reason (*Free Choice*. II. 3. 20–24). Now from this point of view, those things which possess fewer forms are "lower" in the scale of being than those which possess more forms, but since the forms those beings lack are not ones they are designed to have, this kind of lack of form Augustine seems not to identify with "evil."

The second sort of hierarchy is generated by the fact that beings may fail to realize fully the forms that they *are* designed to have. Thus, to come right to the point, a being that is supposed to be rational but that fails to be fully rational is one that fails to realize fully the form of rationality and so is inferior to a rational being that does fully realize that form. Failure to realize one's *proper* form in this way makes a being "defective," and it is this defective lack of form that is identified with "evil" (*Free Choice*. III. 13. 126–133). One reason Augustine had trouble abandoning the Manichaean myth was that he thought that evil obviously exists and so must have a cause. But surely God, who is perfectly good, could not be the cause of evil. So, he thought, the Manichaeans must be right in thinking that there is an evil cosmic power which is the source of evil being (*Conf.* V. 10). The Plotinian identification of being, form and goodness rescued him from this perception by suggesting that whatever is is good, that evil is just a lack of form or being and so nothing whatever (*Conf.* VII. 12–13).

Augustine falls back on this Plotinian view in his attempt to evade the problem of how sin first came into the world. Both in *On Free Choice* and in the *City of God*, he argues that God could not be the cause of sin, and in both cases he gives as a reason that an evil will has no cause.

One argument he uses is that since an evil will is "defective," it is really nothing at all. And since such a "defect" could be caused only by something that was itself evil, that means that the cause of an evil will must itself be nothing at all (*Free Choice*. II. 20. 204).[248]

But can the Augustine of the imperial myth still make any sense of such an argument? In particular, what does it mean to say that either an evil will or its cause is nothing at all? Does it mean that there are no beings who make choices that violate the commands of God? Clearly not. Does it mean that no choices contrary to divine edicts ever occur? Clearly not. Not only are there sinful creatures, but *all* rational creatures except the holy angels are sinful. And not only do sinful choices occur, but they occur inevitably unless God intervenes. And we have already seen that Augustine is at great pains to insist not only that God is the cause of every being that exists, but also that no choices occur that are not willed by God. Therefore, for Augustine, the Plotinian claim that the evil will has no cause because it is "nothing" seems to be just false. Since both sinners and sinful choices clearly occur, to claim that they are not caused by God is to claim that there are either beings or events in the universe that do not occur by the will of God. And that seems obviously inconsistent with Augustine's most fundamental beliefs.

Both in *On Free Choice* and in the *City of God*, he gives a second and rather complicated argument for the view that an evil will can have no cause.[249] First, he argues that a good will (such as the will of God) cannot be the cause of an evil will, because what causes an evil will must itself be evil, so that a good will causing an evil will would not, after all, be a good will, which is a contradiction.[250]

Second, he argues that an evil will cannot be caused by another evil will. For suppose that it were. Then we must ask as to the cause of that prior evil will. If it also had yet another evil will as its cause, we must ask as to the cause of that will until we arrive at an evil will that had no cause. The only other alternative is to say that the cause of the evil will did not itself have a cause. Therefore, in either case, we must admit the existence of an evil will which has no cause and has always existed. But what we call evil comes about only because a good nature is corrupted and made defective, so that there cannot be a nature which has forever existed as evil.

Third, he argues that the only other possibility is to claim that an evil will is caused by something that itself had no will. But a being without will falls lower in the scale of being than one with will, and a lower being cannot be the cause of a defect in a higher being.

I shall leave it to the reader to reach a judgment about this argument. On the face of it, it certainly seems unpersuasive. While it does seem plausible to claim that a good will cannot be the cause of an evil will, all that follows from that is that *either* God is not the cause of an evil will *or* that God is not perfectly good. And as for the idea that an evil will cannot exist forever, but can only come about by the corruption of a previously good nature, that would, to say the least, require considerable justification. And clearly, both of the arguments he develops depend on his being able to establish the intelligibility of the Plotinian view of reality, a project that he never really undertook.

For the moment, I shall just note that these are the arguments that he does, in fact, use—both early and late in his career—to conclude that there is no cause of an evil will, and that

> it is the will itself, because it is created, that desires the inferor thing in a perverted and inordinate manner. (*City.* XII, 6)

Thus, apparently, the answer to the question why the first created wills chose to turn to sin is that that is just what they did and that there was no cause of their turning.

But regardless of how we view the intelligibility of the Plotinian myth and so of these arguments, we can ask whether this conclusion is one that Augustine can possibly hold without contradicting the most fundamental propositions of his theology. Whatever may be meant by claiming that Satan's turn to sin had no "cause," can he mean to suggest that this event occurred against the will of almighty God or even that it occurred other than by the very will of that God? Does he mean to assert that Satan (and, after him, Adam and Eve) brought about events that God did not will to be brought about? Is it possible that the God who arranges every being and event according to his purpose did not, after all, control those events that most crucially affected the course of created history?

When he is forced to look at these questions, Augustine himself seems to recognize that only one answer is possible. In Chapter 9 of Book XII of the *City of God*, he is indeed forced to that point when he comes to consider the good will of the holy angels. Having argued that the evil will of Satan had no cause, he now must decide whether that means that the good will of the holy angels likewise had no cause. Did those blessed angels, in turning to a pure love of God, do so completely on their own or was their turning due to the agency of God?

Once again, there are two possibilities. One is that God created the holy angels with a will that was already fixed on God, so that "as soon as they were created they adhered to their Creator with that love with which they were created." On this account, the evil angels fell away from this blissful state "by an act of will which was evil in the very fact that they fell away from that good will." He can offer no reason why the evil angels might have done such a thing, though he is sure that "they would not have fallen away, had they not willed to do so."

The unanswered question is, of course, whether they would have done so if *God* had not willed it so.

The other possibility is that the good angels were not created with their hearts already fixed on God, but that they produced that perfectly good will by turning to God themselves. And when he puts it this way, he is quick to insist that the holy angels could not have made themselves better than God originally made them, so that their good will could not be due to themselves, but must have been created in them by God.

> But if they could not by themselves have improved upon the work of the best possible Creator, then clearly they could only have gained possession of a good will, by which they would be improved, by the assistance of the Creator's activity. And the effect of their good will was to turn them not to themselves who were inferior in being, but to him who supremely exists, so that by adhering to him they might advance in being and live in wisdom and felicity by participation in him. And so they demonstrate just this: that any good will would have been impoverished, remaining in the state of longing, had it not been that he who made, out of nothing, a nature that was good and capable of enjoying him, made it better by fulfilling that desire, first having excited it to greater eagerness for that fulfillment. (*City*. XII. 9)

The good will of the holy angels, unless it is created by God with the angels themselves, can only be like the good will which saves Jacob from the fate of Esau. That is, it can only be a gift of God:

> If the angels themselves created this good will in themselves, did they do this by some act of will? If there was no act of will, they could not have created it. That needs no saying. Then, if there was some act of will, was it a bad or a good act of will? If the former, how could a bad will produce a good? If the latter, then they had a good will already. And who had produced that will but the one who created them with a good will, that is with pure love, the love with which they could adhere to him, the one who showered grace on them at the same time as he formed their nature? Hence we must believe that the holy angels were never without good will, never that is, without the love of God. (*City*. XII. 9)

But now if the holy angels were never "without the love of God," what must we say about the fallen angels who did *not* turn to God?

Augustine does indeed address this question. First, he repeats his claim that they "were created good but have become evil by their own bad will." But now he recognizes that he must answer the question why they chose as they did. And his reply is:

> Either they received less grace of the divine love than did the others, who continued in that grace; or, if both were created equally good, the one sort fell through their evil will, while the others had greater help to enable them to attain to the fullness of bliss with the complete assurance that they will never fall away....(*City.* XII. 9)

So now we are back on familiar ground, with the claim that *any* created will will surely be lost unless it receives the wholly undeserved grace of God that renders it able to turn to God in pure love or (if it is created already good) to persevere in that love.

In light of this full discussion, we can now re-examine Augustine's claim that the evil will of the fallen angels (and so, presumably, of Adam and Eve) has no "cause." This is true in the sense that the bad choices of those angels (and our first parents) were brought about not by any external being, but only by their own "perverse love" which "turned to themselves," rather than to God.

> We must believe that the difference had its origin in their wills and desires, the one sort persisting resolutely in that Good which is common to all—which for them is God himself—and in his eternity, truth, and love, while the others were delighted rather with their own power, as though they themselves were their own Good. (*City.* XII. 1)

But this very thing can be said of *all* sinners, and as regards the predestination of the angels (and the first humans), the obvious conclusion is that their destinies are as fixed by the divine will as those of any member of the fallen human race.

It seems that the position Augustine must finally take is that while all the angels were created "good" and so "capable of enjoying him," only some were given the gift of "delight" and "eagerness for fulfillment" that results in a choice to love and serve God purely. With that gift, it is absolutely certain that the holy angels will adhere to God forever. And without that gift, it is equally certain that those unfortunates will "turn to themselves" and remain in a "state of longing." By giving or withholding the gift of "delight," God predestines the angels and the first humans just as completely and certainly as he does fallen humankind.

In insisting that there is no "cause" of an evil will, Augustine seems to be trying to stress that God himself never *makes* any evil choices, that those choices are made by the created will itself. But however we take the word "cause," it remains true that God's granting of the gift of "delight" is a condition both necessary and sufficient to bring it about that the created will chooses to serve God purely. And furthermore, the withholding of that gift is a condition sufficient to insure that the will remains lost in self-love and longing.

The omnipotence doctrine is the heart of Augustine's imperial myth, and when "push comes to shove," it is the doctrine that cannot be compromised. God is the absolute ruler of the universe whose will directs every event in creation. That fundamental certainty cannot be qualified in any way, regardless of any consequences it may have.

But what consequences does it have? In particular, does the fact that God is responsible for evil choices of creatures entail that God himself is less than perfectly good? That is, can Augustine preserve the omnipotence doctrine only by qualifying the goodness doctrine?

There may be one sense of "good" in which God's total control does not qualify his goodness. We have already seen above that Augustine holds that the evil choices of creatures not only do not compromise the perfection of God's order, but actually add to that perfection.[251] Since God uses every event to complete the "goodness" of his order, it must certainly be true that the sins of the angels and the first humans were also used in that way. The choices are evil because they violate the command of God that every creature should love him purely, but as events in the created order, those choices help complete the perfection of that order and so are "good." Thus, when "good" is used in this sense, there seems to be no contradiction in holding both that God brings about evil choices and that, in doing so, God is making a good choice.

Now I must admit that I find all this very problematical, principally because it is not clear to me what "good" means in this context. When it is said that God's created order is maximally good, does that mean that there is some objective standard of "goodness" to which the order conforms, or does it mean that the order is the one God chooses and that "good" means precisely "that which God wills"?

If the order is good because it conforms to some objective standard, then there seem to be two obvious questions. First, there is the question of what sort of standard this could possibly be, so that, once again, it is unclear what "good" means. And second, there is the question how it is possible to regard God as absolutely omnipotent if his nature makes it necessary for him to conform to a standard independent of him.

On the other hand, if the order is said to be good just because it conforms to the will of God, then it follows that *whatever* God might will would be good, even if it violated every standard of justice, mercy, love, etc. And leaving aside all other considerations, it seems to me that this is just not consistent with the way Augustine wishes to speak of God throughout his writing. When he says that God is good, he seems always to mean at least that God is always just, merciful, loving, etc.

And when "good" is used in this sense, it seems to me that in the end, consistency would force Augustine to abandon the goodness doctrine in his determination to preserve the omnipotence doctrine. If God is to be in absolute control of creation, then it does seem finally to follow that God must be the source of that "delight" which is the necessary and sufficient condition of the goodness of the holy angels and the withholding of which is the sufficient condition of the corruption of Satan and his fellows. And while we may think that God is merciful in granting that "delight" to the holy angels, I do not see how (looking back to parallel reasoning in the case of Esau) we can think that God is just in condemning those angels who fell because of a lack over which they had no control. So it seems to me that in the final analysis, Augustine is not able to sustain the perfect goodness of the god of the imperial myth. And I think it was clearly his unbending determination not to qualify the absolute control of that god over creation that left him in this radically uncomfortable position.

Summary

This concludes our discussion of the core ideas of Augustinianism as derived from a few basic beliefs that Augustine took to be fundamental to Christianity. While there are many philosophical and theological issues that have not been considered, the discussion has still been rather detailed and tedious. But I think that if we are to understand the power of Augustinianism as an ideology, it is important to see not only that it rested on broadly shared beliefs, but that it was by far the most complete, consistent and coherent attempt to develop the implications of those beliefs.

In summary, from the belief that the world is created and directed by an absolutely omnipotent and omniscient god, Augustine infers that every event, including every human action, must be due to the will of that god. From the belief that every human being is a sinner in need of redemption, he infers that humans are free agents responsible for their actions. And from the belief that the omnipotent god is also perfectly good, he infers that divine punishment of sinners is just. Combining these conclusions, he then finally comes to the view that every human action and the fate of every soul is not only known but unalterably determined by God from creation, that humans are nonetheless fully responsible for their sins and that since persons are born with their fate determined, they must be born already in a state of sin and guilt. Thus does Augustine arrive at the doctrines of predestination and original sin that are at the heart of his thought. And the truth of these doctrines he takes to be further confirmed not only by scriptural authority, but by an analysis of human choosing as well.

However, I have suggested that in trying to explain why the fallen angels and the first humans sinned in the first place, he is finally forced to an inconsistency that he cannot resolve. Augustine could preserve his conception of an imperial deity in absolute control of the universe only by sacrificing the justice of that deity, and the most marked incoherence in his thought comes from his inability to face that conclusion. That the incoherence went unchallenged by the Pelagians and others is due to the fact that no one was willing to assert that one must sacrifice either God's perfect goodness or the absolute efficacy of his will. So powerful was the imperial myth.

Concluding Remarks

Augustine's influence has been and remains enormous. It is probably not too much to say that he is unmatched as an ideological force in western civilization. While his ideas have roots in his predecessors, they are, in their final forms, distinctively his own and constitute a fundamental reorientation of thought concerning the structure and process of reality. Perhaps more importantly, he developed and combined those ideas into a coherent and comprehensive world-view that has proved to be astonishingly resilient and adaptable to evolving material conditions. While his ideas were very much a product of his milieu, often clearly provincial and time-bound, and while some of them often seem quaint and primitive to modern readers, they have been able to serve material interests and meet felt needs in historical conditions vastly different from those in which they were born. It has been more than five hundred years since major thinkers were apt to regard themselves as "Augustinians," but when students today encounter the Augustinian system, there is almost always the shock of recognition that they are here dealing with ideas that remain fundamental to the way we think about ourselves and our relations with the rest of reality.

Augustinian ideology has at its heart two fundamental ideas—the idea of God and the idea of the human soul. Neither of those ideas belongs wholly to Augustine, and aspects of both have roots in many of his predecessors. But taken in their entirety, both ideas are unique to him. Furthermore, he combined those ideas and others into a systematic conception of the nature of the universe, its history and its destiny, that can only be regarded as revolutionary. From the outlook of his provincial boyhood and, later, the intuitions of his adopted class, he built an ideological superstructure that has proved adaptable, in whole or in part, to the needs of dominant classes in conditions that he could not have imagined.

For Augustine himself, it was the idea of God that pervaded his consciousness. At a time when virtually everyone, whether Christian, pagan or Jew, focused on relations with the gods and with eternal reality, he defined the nature of deity in a way that was both intensely personal and universally persuasive.

His god is not one of a host of willful and arbitrary deities to be propitiated in the hope of winning favor and escaping wrath. But God differs from the pagan gods not because he is less demanding, but because he is the implacable ruler who demands *exclusive* cult and absolute submission.

On the other hand, if Augustine's god had offered his devotees the well-being in this world that was the chief aim of pagan cult, the promise would have run head-on into the acute awareness of the misery and seeming capriciousness of existence that was so much a part of consciousness for the vast majority. In that case, God would have seemed just another deity too impotent or too fickle to warrant exclusive devotion. But Augustine was able to undermine such misgivings. For those who might doubt God's power, he was able to offer the spectacle of the imperial deity destroying the temples and shrines of his competitors and establishing his church throughout the empire, a deity obviously in charge of every event in creation, however obscure might be his purposes in many cases. And for those who might puzzle at the lack of correlation between devotion to God and earthly happiness, he was able to portray this world as a way-station and testing ground in which good or ill fortune was of no account whatever and in which the only happiness lay in the hope of eternity.

Nor did Augustine's portrayal of his god neglect the sensibilities of that tiny but crucial elite who looked to link their souls to an eternal reality that they felt was their proper abode. To retain a hold on that consciousness (which was, in many respects, his own consciousness) he always retained the paradoxical view that God is not only active in the world, but timeless and utterly unchanging, that God is not only the creator of the world by his active will, but also the seat of the eternal exemplars of which all earthly things are participations. What he could not accept was the arrogance which saw the "noble" soul as itself somehow divine or which pretended to an ability to rise up to eternity by the power of unaided human reason. But for those willing to substitute faith for dialectic, he was able to offer assurance that eternity is indeed our home and that the divine Word of God (echoing the Plotinian *Nous*) links us with that eternity and calls us home.

The paradox in Augustine's conception of God is a reflection of the division in his own religious consciousness between the sensibilities into which he was socialized in childhood and those that he acquired as he sought entry into aristocratic circles in Rome and Milan. But once he had made his commitment as priest and bishop, once he was on the front lines in the battle against paganism, Donatism and Pelagianism, much of that paradox dropped away. Platonist language still crops up from time to time, and the Plotinian myth still appears sometimes when he encounters intractable inconsistencies such as that between God's goodness and power. But in most cases and where it is most crucial to his theology, Augustine's mature conception of God is clear and unambiguous.

That Augustinian god is the absolutely omnipotent creator and sustainer of the universe, the source of every being who directs every event by his irresistible will. By a completely free act, God has created this world for his own purposes, and every creature belongs wholly to him and exists and acts wholly to realize his perfect if inscrutable aims. As part of that creation, human beings also are instruments of God's will, and their every action is a fulfillment of divine purpose. But as the only rational creatures on earth, humans not only do act at God's will, but they are commanded to do so *willingly*. And what is demanded of them is clear, though it is also certain that they will fail to meet the demand unless they receive divine aid. They are to act always and only from a love of God, to turn away from all self-love and egoistic desire. And that means, among other things, that they are to accept whatever social position they find themselves in and to obey both earthly rulers and the holy church that God has established as his instrument. So long as they are not required to act against the will of God, all persons are to carry out whatever roles and tasks are assigned on this earthly pilgrimage and to wait in hope for eternity.

Augustine's god was, in short, a support for a hierarchical social order not only in the context of the later empire, but in any social order ruled by Christian priests and Christian kings. And it was able to serve this purpose at least in large part because it was a god which satisfied the intuitions and needs of most people, including those of Augustine himself.

Augustine's conception of the human soul or human being is no less distinctive. To begin with, there is almost no hint of the conception of human beings as social or "political" animals that had been so much a part of ancient thought. He has no idea of society as prior to or constitutive of human beings. Nor does he see humans as perfectible by living in a "good" state or by receiving a proper education. Certainly, he does not think of humans, as did Plato and Plotinus, as sharing in eternal reality or even as capable of grasping eternity by reason.

The unit of human reality for Augustine is the single individual. He does share with many spiritual traditions an emphasis on the need to transcend egoism, but not because he thinks that the ego is in any sense illusory or that individual ego is an aspect of some transcendent reality. While we get hints of such a view during his Manichaean and Platonist flirtations, it is quite absent from his mature thought. In fact, it is a measure of the power of Augustinian ideology that while such a view of human spirituality was enormously influential prior to Augustine, it largely disappeared from western thought after him. And when it occasionally resurfaced, as in the mystical philosophy of John Scotus Eriugena in the ninth century, it had no chance of gaining a foothold.

For Augustine, human reality *is* egoistic reality. Each soul is created whole and entire, a finished product with its own desires and drives, its own sins and its own unique and pre-determined destiny. What awaits such souls is not a merging into a common ground of being, but an eternity living in heaven or hell as just those individuals they have always been (suitably transformed, of course, in the case of those fortunates who win heaven).

While it is certainly the duty of parents, teachers and all Christians to make every effort to develop piety and faith in such souls, there should be no illusion about the power of instruction or exhortation to shape and mold them. Each soul stands before God with a terrible and lonely responsibility, and each makes a solitary decision that seals its future.

Another insight that Augustine shares with other spiritual traditions is that while each soul may strive to forget itself and to transcend self-centeredness, the effort is inevitably futile, and egoistic striving to overcome egoism only reinforces the strength of self-consciousness and self-will. But unlike some other traditions, the "grace" that makes that impossible task possible does not lead to a transcendence of individual existence, but rather makes it possible for the atomistic individual to turn its full attention from itself to another and quite separate individual, the one called God. The city of God, no less than the earthly city, is a collection of citizens, each of whom directs her or his individual will by the will of the god who remains absolutely distinct as the object of worship.

These two ideas, that of deity as the imperial god and of humanity as a collection of atomistic souls, have had very great staying power. In Christian theology, this is especially clear. There the central problem, almost to the present day, has been that of reconciling the conception of the omnipotent and perfectly good deity with two other apparently incompatible conceptions: (1) that of the seemingly obvious existence of evil in a world supposedly ruled by a benevolent imperial god; and (2) that of the freedom of will and responsibility of human souls created and ruled by that god. Without even beginning to review the host of arguments advanced on these issues, what can be said is that the problems disappear as soon as one is willing either to accept limitations on the power of God or to modify the conception of human beings as distinct, autonomous souls. In that sense, the very persistence of these problems is a testament to the power of Augustinian ideology. But the staying power of these ideas and the reluctance to abandon either the notion of absolute deity or that of atomistic humanity has been grounded as well in material conditions which, while constantly evolving, have continued to find support in such an ideology.

For many centuries, the identification of western civilization with the notion of "Christendom" meant that the imperial god remained the centerpiece of dominant ideology. God himself appeared less and less as time went by, but his church remained both as a material force in its own right and as an instrument of Christian princes. Indeed that conception of deity remains much alive today. Those, for example, who struggle to develop an alternative Christian theology that can serve the oppressed poor in Latin America, Africa and Asia are very much aware that the imperial god still stands as the bulwark of conservative ideology.

But while Augustine's God has continued to play an ideological role, it is the other actor in Augustine's cosmic drama, the atomistic human individual, who has captured center stage in the modern period. Luther's "Christian man" who is his own priest and stands before God without sanction or protection of sacrament was already a reassertion of Augustinian individualism. And as new economic forms emerged and the feudal nobility, both secular and sacred, gave way to new interests and new elites, the individual soul gradually separated itself from absolute dependence on God and asserted its autonomy. And that atomic individual remains the core concept of dominant ideology today. However alien or fantastic Augustine's world may seem in many respects, this fundamental idea remains, that human reality is just what he said it was, a collection of self-interested atoms, each born with its own already complete and individual personhood, possessed of its own individual will and reason and driven by its own imperatives to seek its personal and private satisfactions. It is a conception that gives support to claims of inalienable individual rights, the sanctity of individual conscience and the dignity of each person as what Kant called a "legislator in a realm of ends." It is also a conception that supports a glorification of self-interest and unlimited acquisitiveness. It helps support the illusion that an "invisible hand" will direct private greed to public good. And perhaps most importantly, it persuades us that a more rationally cooperative and less competitive economic system is impossible, since it would presuppose human motivations other than narrow private interest and so would fly in the face of "human nature."

While these remarks are intended to suggest something of the importance of Augustine in the history of western thought, they are, of course, great over-simplifications and over-generalizations. An account of the myriad ways in which ideology has developed in response to changing conditions would be an undertaking certainly beyond the scope of this discussion. But I do think that it was Augustine who gave distinctive formulation to these seminal ideas and placed them in a systematic context that could be adapted to future needs. It is a long way from the myth of the citizen of the city of God who remains an obedient subject of earthly rulers while pursuing individual salvation to the myth of the citizen of the democratic republic who obeys his elected representatives while pursuing maximization of profit. And while each of these concepts may serve simultaneously to support and to mask a reality oppressive in many ways, the realities they serve are vastly different. Still, there are foundational ideas here that did not spring full-blown from the brow of Locke or Rousseau and that gained their first clear formulation in the mind of a melancholy African saint.

Notes

Notes for Part One

1. Possidius, *The Life of Saint Augustine*, tr. by M. O'Connell. Villanova, PA, 1988, Ch. XXXI. Possidius was bishop of Calama and a disciple and close friend and ally of Augustine almost from the time he returned to Africa from Italy.
2. R. Lane Fox, *Pagans and Christians*. New York, 1987, p. 137. Cf. P. Brown, *Augustine of Hippo*. Berkeley, CA, 1967, pp. 50-51.
3. Lane Fox, *Op. Cit.*, p. 38.
4. For example, G.E.M. de Ste. Croix, "Why Were the Early Christians Persecuted?" *Past and Present*, 26 (1963), pp. 6-38.
5. Lane Fox, *Op. cit.*, p. 425.
6. *Ibid.*, pp. 102-123.
7. *Ibid.*, p. 121.
8. *Ibid.*, pp. 168-200.
9. A.H.M. Jones, *The Later Roman Empire*. Norman, OK, 1964, pp. 957-964.
10. R. MacMullen, *Christianizing the Roman Empire*. New Haven, CN, 1984, pp. 62-63.
11. Cf. Lane Fox, *Op. cit.*, p. 330.
12. *Ibid.*, p. 165.
13. *Ibid.*, p. 170.
14. Epicurus, *Letter to Menoeceus*, 123-124 and *Leading Doctrines* 1, in *The Philosophy of Epicurus*, tr. by G.M. Strodach. Evanston, IL, 1963. Cf. Lucretius, *On Nature*, tr. by R.M. Geer. Indianapolis, 1965, Bk. I, 44-49 and Bk. II, 1093-1095.
15. P. Brown, *The World of Late Antiquity*. New York, 1971, p. 12.
16. *Ibid.*, p. 13.
17. Lane Fox, *Op. cit.*, pp. 38-40.

18. A.H.M. Jones, "The Social Background of the Struggle between Paganism and Christianity," in *The Conflict between Paganism and Christinaity in the Fourth Century*, ed. by A. Momigliano. Oxford, 1963, pp. 17-37 (on this particular point, see pp. 23-26). Cf. Lane Fox, *Op. cit.*, p. 304.

19. See K. Hopkins, "On the Probable Age Structure of the Roman Population," *Population Stuidies*, 20 (1966), pp. 245-264. Cf. Lane Fox, *Op. cit.*, p. 46.

20. Jones, *Later Roman Empire*, p. 1045.

21. K. Marx, *Grundrisse*, tr. by M. Nicolaus. New York, 1973, p. 156.

22. G.E.M. de Ste. Croix, *The Class Struggle in the Ancient Greek World*. Ithaca. NY, 1981, p. 209.

23. *Ibid.*, p. 54.

24. Ste. Croix, for example (*Ibid.*, pp. 423-425), makes quite a point of this.

25. Lane Fox, *Op. cit.*, pp. 295-299.

26. Ste. Croix, *Class Struggle*, p. 143.

27. Lane Fox, *Op. cit.*, p. 59.

28. Ste. Croix, *Class Struggle*, p. 57.

29. Brown, *World of Late Antiquity*, p. 12.

30. Ste. Croix, *Class Struggle*, p. 204.

31. E.M. Wood, "Oligarchic Democracy," *Monthly Review*, July/August, 1989, pp. 42-51. The quotation is on p. 42.

32. Ste. Croix, *Class Struggle*, p. 371.

33. Brown, *World of Late Antiquity*, pp. 36-45.

34. Ste. Croix, *Class Struggle*, p. 241.

35. *Ibid.*, p. 210.

36. Cf. Ste. Croix, *Class Struggle*, pp. 409-416.

37. *Ibid.*, pp. 454-461.

38. Jones, *Later Roman Empire*, pp. 1045-1049.

39. Brown, *World of Late Antiquity*, p. 12.

40. Ste. Croix, *Class Struggle*, pp. 219-221.

41. *Ibid.*, p. 207.

42. *Ibid.*, p. 372.

43. Lane Fox, *Op. cit.*, p. 580.

44. *Ibid.*, p. 59.

45. Ste. Croix, *Class Struggle*, pp. 249-255.

46. Jones, *Later Roman Empire*, pp. 1040-1045.

47. *Ibid.*, pp. 1039-1040.
48. *Ibid.*, pp. 1040-1045.
49. *Ibid.*
50. *Ibid.*, pp. 1050-1053.
51. Lane Fox, *Op.cit.*, 53-57.
52. Ste. Croix, *Class Struggle*, pp. 405-407.
53. Brown, *World of Late Antiquity*, pp. 34-36.
54. Ste. Croix, *Class Struggle*, pp. 373-399.
55. Lane Fox, *Op. cit.*, p. 580.
56. Jones, *Later Roman Empire*, pp. 1058-1064.
57. Ste. Croix, *Class Struggle*, p. 465.
58. Brown, *World of Late Antiquity*, pp. 22-28.
59. *Ibid.*, pp. 26-27.
60. *Ibid.*, pp. 28-31.
61. Jones, *Later Roman Empire*, pp. 1053-1058.
62. Brown, *World of Late Antiquity*, 36-45.
63. *Ibid.*, p. 115; cf Jones, "Social Background," pp. 26-29.
64. Ste. Croix, *Class Struggle*, pp. 488-493.
65. Brown, *World of Late Antiquity*, pp. 28-31.
66. *Ibid.*, p. 61.
67. See, for example, T.D. Barnes, *Constantine and Eusebius.* Cambridge, 1981, p. 191.
68. Lane Fox, *Op. cit.*, pp. 317 and 592.
69. Jones, "Social Background," p. 18.
70. See Lane Fox, *Op. cit.*, pp. 444 and 597-598.
71. *Ibid.*, pp. 268-293.
72. H. Bloch, "The Pagan Revival at the End of the Fourth Century," in Momigliano (ed.), *Op. cit.*, pp. 193-218. The reference is to p. 194.
73. Brown, *World of Late Antiquity*, pp. 104-112.
74. Bloch, *Op. cit.*, p. 198.
75. Jones, "Social Background," pp. 33-36.
76. Lane Fox, *Op. cit.*, pp. 609-627.
77. Jones, *Later Roman Empire*, pp. 895-896.
78. Ste. Croix, *Class Struggle*, pp. 495-497.
79. Jones, *Later Roman Empire*, pp. 933-934.
80. Lane Fox, *Op. cit.*, pp. 609-627.
81. Brown, *World of Late Antiquity*, p. 126.

82. MacMullen, *Op. cit.*, p. 54.

83. Jones, *Later Roman Empire*, pp. 938-943.

84. MacMullen, *Op. cit.*, p. 101.

85. Brown, *World of Late Antiquity*, p. 104.

86. MacMullen, *Op. cit.*, p. 95.

87. Brown, *World of Late Antiquity*, p. 104.

88. Jones, *Later Roman Empire*, pp. 938-943.

89. See P. Courcelle, "Anti-Christian Arguments and Christian Platonism: from Arnobius to St. Ambrose," in Momigliano (ed.), *Op. cit.*, pp. 151-192. Cf. Brown, *World of Late Antiquity*, pp. 70-81.

90. MacMullen, *Op. cit.*, p. 119.

91. Jones, "Social Background," p. 18.

92. W. H. C. Frend, "The Gnostic-Manichaean Tradition in Roman North Africa," *Journal of Ecclesiastical History*, IV (1953), pp. 13-26.

93. Ste. Croix, *Class Struggle*, p. 343; cf. Lane Fox, *Op. cit.*, pp. 312-335.

94. Jones, "Social Background," pp. 19-21.

95. *Ibid.*, pp. 26-32.

96. *Ibid,.* pp. 32-33; cf. Courcelle, *Op. cit.*, passim.

97. *Ibid.*, pp. 31-32.

98. MacMullen, *Op. cit.*, p. 65.

99. Lane Fox, *Op. cit.*, p. 296.

100. *Ibid.*

101. *Ibid.*, pp. 293-299.

102. *Ibid.*, pp. 321-322.

103. MacMullen, *Op. cit.*, p. 39.

104. *Ibid.*, p. 55.

105. Lane Fox, *Op. cit.*, p. 291.

106. *Ibid.*, p. 21.

107. *Ibid.*, pp. 321-323.

108. Brown, *World of Late Antiquity*, p. 61.

109. Lane Fox, *Op. cit.*, pp. 299-301.

110. Brown, *World of Late Antiquity*, p. 68.

111. Lane Fox, *Op. cit.*, pp. 308-311.

112. *Ibid.*, p. 613.

113. J. Vogt, "Pagans and Christians in the Family of Constantine the

Great," in Momigliano, *Op. cit.*, pp. 38-55. Cf. Lane Fox, *Op. cit.*, pp. 615-617.

114. *Ibid.*, p. 618.
115. *Ibid.*, pp. 627-662.
116. *Ibid.*, p. 672.
117. Brown, *World of Late Antiquity*, p. 115.

Notes for Part Two

118. See, for example, E. R. Dodds, *Pagan and Christian in an Age of Anxiety*. Cambridge, 1965; or the classic work of Gilbert Murray, *Five Stages of Greek Religion*. London, 1925.
119. He states this explicitly several times. See, for example, *Cath. & Man.* I. 6. 10: "As for those who may deny that God exists, I cannot concern myself with arguments by which to persuade them, for I am not sure that we ought to enter into discussion with them at all."
120. H. M. Gwatkin, *Studies of Arianism*. Cambridge, 1900.
121. W. H. C. Frend, *The Donatist Church: A Movement of Protest in Roman North Africa*. Oxford, 1952, p. 49; see also A. H. M. Jones, *Later Roman Empire*, pp. 950–956.
122. W. H. C. Frend, "Religion and Social Change in the Late Roman Empire," *The Cambridge Journal*, II (1949), pp. 487–496.
123. Peter Brown, *Augustine of Hippo*, p. 25.
124. *Ibid.*, pp. 20–21.
125. Frend, *Donatist Church*, pp. 230–233.
126. Brown, *Augustine of Hippo*, p. 32.
127. Frend, *Donatist Church*, pp. 79–81.
128. *Ibid.*, p. 66; cf. John J. O'Meara, *The Young Augustine*. London, 1954, pp. 24–25.
129. Brown, *Augustine of Hippo*, p. 20.
130. *Ibid.*, p. 25.
131. Cf. Brown, *Augustine of Hippo*, p. 21.
132. Frend, *Donatist Church*, pp. 234–235; cf. Brown, *Augustine of Hippo*, p. 24.
133. Brown, *Augustine of Hippo*, p. 22.
134. Frend, *Donatist Church*, 230–233.
135. Cf. Frend, *The Donatist Church*, pp. 230–233.

136. See, for example, two accounts of pagan rituals in *City*. II. 4, and II. 26.
137. See *Conf.* III. 6. 11, where he treats the myth of Medea as fanciful. As just one example of his seeing the gods as demons, see the remarks about pagan festivals mentioned in the previous note from *City*. II. 4: "Who could fail to realize what kind of spirits they are which could enjoy such obscenities? Only a man who refused to recognize even the existence of any unclean spirits who deceive men under the title of gods, or one whose life was such that he hoped for the favour and feared the anger of such gods, rather than that of the true God."
138. O'Meara, *The Young Augustine*, p. 30.
139. Cf. *Conf.* VI. 5.
140. Yearning for heaven is put into the mouth of Monica at *Conf.* IX. 10.
141. In Augustine's report, it is not perfectly clear whether Monica took the shining young man of her dream to be God himself or another heavenly being acting as representative.
142. For Augustine's own remarks on his early education, see *Conf.* I. 9–17.
143. Brown, *Augustine of Hippo*, p. 36.
144. *Ibid.*, p. 37.
145. An excellent example of this can be found in Augustine's *Contra Fortunatum*, in which the Manichee Fortunatus depends almost wholly on citations of Pauline epistles to support his position against the Catholic Augustine. See also *Rep. to Faustus*. I. 2, where Faustus is depicted as calling the Catholics "semi-Christians" and seeing the Manichees as the true Christians. See also P. J. Menasce, "Augustin Manicheen," in *Freundesgabe fur Ernst Robert Curtius zum 14. April 1956*. Bern, 1956, p. 87. The best treatment of Manichaeism as a cult of redemption is still the excellent study of H. C. Puech, "Der Begriff der Erlosung im Manichaismus," in *Eranos-Jahrbuch*, 1936, pp. 183–286.
146. G. Widengren, *Mani and Manichaeism*, tr. by C. Kessler. London, 1961, p. 117; cf. Brown, *Augustine of Hippo*, p. 46, and also Augustine's *Cath. & Man.* II. 19. 69.
147. A good overview of this is in W. H. C. Frend, "The Gnostic-

Manichaean Tradition in Roman North Africa," *Journal of Ecclesiastical History*, IV (1953), pp. 13–26.

148. See W. H. C. Frend, "Manichaeism in the Struggle between St. Augustine and Petilian of Constantine," *Augustinus Magister*, II (1954), pp. 859–866.

149. Cf. *Rep. to Faustus*. III. 1.

150. The same point is made many times. See for example, *Ag. Ep. Fund*. XXXVII. 42. And for a very clear statement, see *Rep. t o Faustus*. XXV. 1: "But to determine whether the one true God is infinite or not, we need only refer to the opposition between good and evil. If evil does not exist, then certainly God is infinite; otherwise He must be finite. Evil, however, undoubtedly exists; therefore God is not infinite. It is where good stops that evil begins."

151. Cf. *De Duabus Animabus Contra Manichaeos*. I. See also *True Rel*. IX. 16.

152. The following presentation of the myth is taken from H. C. Puech, *Op. cit.*, pp. 213–246. It is essentially the same as the version presented and interpreted by G. Widengren in *Mani and Manichaeism*, pp. 43–73.

153. Brown, *Augustine of Hippo*, pp. 54–55.

154. On his acceptance of the myth as literal truth, see *Conf*. III. 6; IV. 16.

155. This is discussed in some detail by Frend, "The Gnostic-Manichaean Tradition in Roman North Africa."

156. *A Manichaean Psalm-Book* (Part II), ed. C. R. C. Allberry. Stuttgart, 1938, Hymn CCXXIII.

157. *Ibid.*, Hymn CCXXXIX.

158. Widengren, *Op. cit.*, p. 123.

159. *A Manichaean Psalm-Book*, Hymn CCXLVI.

160. *Ibid.*

161. Puech, *Op. cit.*, p. 251; see also *Contra Fortunatum*. II. 20, where Fortunatus argues that we sin because we take "delight" in sinning and that this "delight" is a part of our very nature.

162. *A Manichaean Psalm-Book*, Hymn CCLXIV.

163. Jones, "The Social Background of the Struggle Between Paganism and Christianity," pp. 33–37; Jones, *The Later Roman Empire*, II, p. 909. While it does seem likely that Augustine, filled

as he was with guilt at what he saw as his own profligacy, did hold the ascetic Elect in the highest esteem, his recollections of his devotion to them are filled with the contempt of the Catholic convert. See, for example, *Conf.* III. 10.

164. He also found in Cicero discussions of eclipses that treated them as a "result of the invariable laws of the sun's course"—*City.* III. 15.

165. See, for example, Nebridius' objection to the Manichaean myth mentioned at *Conf.* VII. 2.

166. Brown, *Augustine of Hippo*, p. 66.

167. John Ferguson, *Pelagius: A Historical and Theological Study.* Cambridge, 1956, p. 11.

168. Brown, *Augustine of Hippo*, p. 90.

169. Cf. *Div. Prov.* 2. 5.

170. See the two letters written by Ambrose to Valentinian II in 384: *Letters*, tr. by M. M. Beyenka (Fathers of the Church, Vol. 26). Washington, 1954, Letters 7 and 8 (17 and 18 in the Benedictine text used by Migne). See also Augustine's account of one aspect of this struggle in *Conf.* IX. 7.

171. Ambrose, *Op. cit.*, 3 (51).

172. *Ibid.*, 11 (57).

173. Simplician, the teacher of Ambrose, told Augustine the story of one such person, Victorinus, the translator of Plato, Aristotle and Plotinus, who professed Christianity secretly long before he was prepared to make a public commitment. See *Conf.* VIII. 2.

174. The particular context of this remark is his hearing a story of others who had turned to God. But Books VI, VII and VIII of the *Confessions* are filled with his account of his torment while trying to bring himself to commit his life to the Catholic god.

175. Brown, *Augustine of Hippo*, p. 91. The remark about Plato living again in Plotinus is from Augustine's *Ans. to Skep.* III. 18. 41.

176. For a summary of evidence that Plotinus was Augustine's main source, see Brown, *Augustine of Hippo*, p. 94.

177. For classical statements of this view, see Plato, *Republic*, VII. 514a–520d; also Aristotle, *Nichomachean Ethics*, X. 1178b and *Politics*, VII. 1323a–1325b.

178. Most of our information about the life of Plotinus is based on the biography which his pupil Porphyry wrote as an introduction to

The Enneads. It is included in *The Enneads*, tr. by S. McKenna. London, 1969.

179. Porphyry, *Op. cit.*, p. 12.
180. Plotinus, *The Enneads*, I. 6. 2.
181. *Ibid.*, VI. 7. 38.
182. *Ibid.*, VI. 9. 5.
183. *Ibid.*, VI. 8. 13.
184. *Ibid.*, VI. 7. 39.
185. *Ibid.*
186. *Ibid.*, V. 4. 1.
187. *Ibid.*, V. 4. 1.
188. *Ibid.*, V. 9. 6.
189. *Ibid.*, VI. 7. 12.
190. For example, *Ibid.*, V. 1. 6.
191. *Ibid.*, IV. 1. 1.
192. *Ibid.*, II. 9. 3.
193. *Ibid.*, I. 5. 7.
194. *Ibid.*, II. 9. 8.
195. *Ibid.*
196. *Ibid.*, II. 9. 9.
197. *Ibid.*
198. *Ibid.*, VI. 8. 13.
199. *Ibid.*, IV. 8. 4.
200. *Ibid.*, II. 9. 9.
201. *Ibid.*, V. 5. 12.
202. *Ibid.*, IV. 8. 5.
203. *Ibid.*, I. 1. 12.
204. *Ibid.*, I. 3. 4.
205. *Ibid.*, I. 6. 8.
206. *Ibid.*, I. 6. 9.
207. *Ibid.*, VI. 9. 11
208. *Ibid.* IV. 8. 1.
209. *Ibid.*, VI. 9. 10.
210. Brown, *Augustine of Hippo*, p. 98.
211. Plotinus, *Op. Cit.*, II. 9. 8.
212. See Plato, *Phaedo*, 63d–77a. An example of this reasoning in Plotinus is in *Op. cit.*, I. 6. 2.
213. The more extended form of the reasoning is in *Free Choice*. II.

6–15 and 54–155. See also *Conf.* VII. 12. The characterization of the reasoning as the "exceptionally well-known argument" is in *Letters*. 4, written from Cassiciacum to Nebridius in 387.

214. The other works written during this period are *Div. Prov.*, *Ans to Skep.* and *Sol.*

215. This passage is sometimes taken to be an account of a mystical experience or "vision," but while there may have been some sort of "spiritual awareness" involved, it seems clear that the vision described is something yearned for, not something attained.

216. Brown, *Augustine of Hippo*, p. 95, comments that Ambrose "patently ransacked" the writings of Plotinus and included "literal borrowings" from Plotinus in his sermons. However, Ambrose was not a systematic theologian, and Brown is right in suggesting (p. 86) that it is impossible to determine just what Augustine took from Ambrose beyond a sense that the "best" men, such as Ambrose, had found a profound truth in the Catholic scriptures that he was not able to grasp. Cf. *Conf.* V. 14 and VI. 3.

217. Justin Martyr, *Dialogue with Trypho*, tr. (with other works) by T. B. Falls. Washington, 1948, Chs. 1–8. See also Origen, *Contra Celsum*, tr. by H. Chadwick. Cambridge, 1980. And from scripture, see *John* 1. 1–14; *Colossians* 1. 16; I *Corinthians*. 1. 24 and 2. 10–11.

218. The main pagan objection to Christianity had always been that its exclusive worship of a single God invited the wrath of offended deities and so undermined the security of the community. The view of God as the triumphant ruler of the universe undermined those objections. See G. E. M. de Ste Croix, "Why Were the Early Christians Persecuted?" *Past and Present*, 26 (1963), reprinted in M. I. Finley (ed.), *Studies in Ancient Society*. London, 1974, p. 238.

219. The closest Augustine comes to confronting this paradox is in Book XI of the *Confessions*, where he puzzles over the nature of time in light of the fact that creation is by the "Word...which is spoken eternally, and in which all things are spoken eternally" (*Conf.* XI. 7). There he seems, in the end, to flirt with the idea that perhaps time is merely "subjective" and that it appears to exist only because of human memory and expectation. But throughout most of his work, he gives no hint of thinking that time is unreal,

and he talks comfortably both of God's eternity and of God's acting in creation at different times. For just one of many examples,
see *City*. XI. 21: "Things which happen under the condition of
time are in the future, yet not yet in being, or in the present,
already existing, or in the past, no longer in being. But God com-
prehends all these in a stable and eternal present....He knows
events in time without any temporal acts of knowledge, just as he
moves events in time, without any temporal motions in himself."

220. For an interesting commentary on this basic difference between
Plotinus and Augustine, see A. H. Armstrong, "Salvation,
Plotinian and Christian," *The Downside Review*, 75 (1957), pp.
126-139 (esp. pp. 134–135).

221. Cf. the lengthy passage at *Conf*. VII. 9, where he tells how he
learned from the Platonists that the Word was from the beginning
one with God, but did not learn that the Word "was made flesh"
or that those who "believe in his name" receive "the power to be
made sons of God."

222. See Brown, *Augustine of Hippo*, pp. 132–137.

223. These words are put into the mouth of Evodius in the dialogue,
but it is clear that he is expressing Augustine's own position.

224. By the way, this passage offers a good example of the way in
which Augustine takes it as obvious that the "best" men of the
Old Testament must have seen reality through the same Platonist
eyes as the "best" men of Rome.

225. Cf. *Free Choice*. II. 12. 130–136.

226. Again, this point is put into the mouth of Evodius. See also *Free
Choice*. I. 4. 30, where "lust" is defined as "the love of those
things which a man can lose against his will," i.e. temporal things.

227. The fallen angels were, of course, Lucifer and his minions, who
rebelled against God and were cast out of heaven.

Notes for Part Three

228. See, for example, *Letters*. 215 and 225.

229. See *Gift of Persev*. 22. 58-62, where he says of the doctrine of
predestination that "although these things are true, yet they must
not be said to a large congregation in a way that the sermon
appears to be addressed precisely to them...." He then goes on to

discuss ways in which the doctrine may be presented so that it does not appear to be "a curse or a kind of prophecy of evil."

230. Brown, *Augustine of Hippo*, p. 36.

231. A good deal more will be said about this in the next section on the analysis of willing and in the later section on original sin. For present purposes, the reader may set this aside.

232. While this is true, it is also true that I may perform an action that is in my power and fail to attain the intended end because it is not in my power. That is, I may *believe* that a certain action will bring about the end I want when, in fact, that end is not in my power at all. On this point, see below, p. 188.

233. One implication of this is relevant to the discussion of voluntariness above. Since I may be more or less ignorant of the consequences of my action (and so make choices on the basis of false beliefs), it is possible for an action to be voluntary and yet for the end of the action to be brought about involuntarily. Augustine is very much aware of this problem, and he always insists that, despite our ignorance we have *enough* knowledge for God to hold us responsible. That is, at least where we are concerned with those choices that affect salvation and demnation, we have enough knowledge of the consequences of available actions to warrant the claim that bringing about certain consequences (and failure to bring about others) is voluntary. But as we shall see below (p. 206), he also concludes ultimately that where the very most crucial choice is concerned (that bearing on eternal life), it is *irrelevant* whether we are ignorant of the consequences. On all this, see for example, *Free Choice*. III. 22. 216-220 and *Letters*. 140 and 194.

234. See, for example the long passage quoted on pp. 189-190 below. See also the passage quoted on p. 160 above.

235. See *De duabus animabus*.

236. Early in his career, Augustine believed that once the searching soul has turned to God and found grace, it can then live sinlessly. But within a few years, he became convinced that grace is required not only for turning to God, but for persevering in loving service. The most poignant discussion of this is in *Conf.* X. 30–35, where he laments his inability, even after conversion, to keep his mind focused exclusively on God and to act wholly out of the love of God, condemning himself for such seemingly harm-

less deviations as allowing himself to be distracted by seeing a dog chasing a rabbit. The clearest contrast between his earlier and later positions can be found by comparing *Prop. on Rom.* 35, with *Gift of Persev.* 23. 65.

237. See above, pp. 190–192.

238. See below, p. 214.

239. See above, p. 178.

240. See above, p. 179.

241. This is, by the way, Augustine's must fundamental criticism of the Pelagians. By insisting on the power of the human will to turn to God, they undermine that *surrender* of the will that is the most fundamental demand of God.

242. See above, p. 203.

243. See above, pp. 161–162.

244. Quoted in Brown, *Augustine of Hippo*, p. 147.

245. For example, in *Free Choice.* III. 19-21. 180-215, he offers a number of theories of the origin of the soul and how it inherits Adam's sin, but he endorses none of them. Some years later, in correspondence with Jerome (see *Letters.* 165 and 166), he again presents several possibilities as to the origin of the soul, but still insists that it would be rash to endorse any one of them. And in a late letter to Optatus, bishop of Tingitana, written in 420 (*Letters.* 202A), he again affirms his ignorance as to the origin of the soul and the transmission of sin.

246. See below note 250.

247. Augustine develops all of this at length in *Free Choice.* II. 15–17. 153–177.

248. Cf. *City.* XII. 7.

249. This is developed in *City.* XII. 6, and in *Free Choice.* I. 1. 1–2 and I. 10. 71–73.

250. It is characteristic of Plotinian metaphysics to conflate what seem to be two senses of the word "good." It may be taken in the metaphysical sense described above, where it is synonymous with "being." But it may also be taken in something like a moral sense, as it is in this portion of the argument. And in the Plotinian myth, those senses are hardly ever distinguished. As problematic as all this is, an analysis of it would go beyond the present project, so that I shall simply present it as Augustine does.

251. See above, pp. 174–175.

Index

251

DATE DUE

DEC 1 0 2001			
NOV 2 7			
MAR 1 8			